11/30/13
$26.95
R↓+
AS

Killing Machine

Also by Lloyd C. Gardner

The Road to Tahrir Square: Egypt and the United States from the Rise of Nasser to the Fall of Mubarak

Three Kings: The Rise of an Empire in the Middle East After World War II

The Long Road to Baghdad: A History of U.S. Foreign Policy from the 1970s to the Present

Economic Aspects of New Deal Diplomacy

Architects of Illusion: Men and Ideas in Foreign Affairs, 1941–1949

The Creation of the American Empire: U.S. Diplomatic History (with Walter LaFeber and Thomas McCormick)

American Foreign Policy, Present to Past

Looking Backward: A Reintroduction to American History (with William O'Neill)

Imperial America: American Foreign Policy, 1898–1976

A Covenant with Power: America and World Order from Wilson to Reagan

Safe for Democracy: The Anglo-American Response to Revolution, 1913–1923

Approaching Vietnam: From World War II to Dienbienphu

Spheres of Influence: The Great Powers Partition in Europe, from Munich to Yalta

Pay Any Price: Lyndon Johnson and the Wars for Vietnam

The Case That Never Dies: The Lindbergh Kidnapping

Edited by Lloyd C. Gardner

The Great Nixon Turnaround: America's New Foreign Policy in the Post-Liberal Era

America in Vietnam: A Documentary History (with Walter LaFeber, Thomas McCormick, and William Appleman Williams)

Redefining the Past: Essays in Honor of William Appleman Williams

On the Edge: The Early Decisions in the Vietnam War (with Ted Gittinger)

International Perspectives on Vietnam (with Ted Gittinger)

Vietnam: The Search for Peace (with Ted Gittinger)

The New American Empire: A 21st Century Teach-In on U.S. Foreign Policy (with Marilyn B. Young)

Iraq and the Lessons of Vietnam: Or, How Not to Learn from the Past (with Marilyn B. Young)

Killing Machine

*The American Presidency in the
Age of Drone Warfare*

LLOYD C. GARDNER

THE NEW PRESS

NEW YORK
LONDON

Requests for permission to reproduce selections from this book
should be mailed to: Permissions Department,
The New Press, 38 Greene Street, New York, NY 10013.

Published in the United States by The New Press, New York, 2013
Distributed by Perseus Distribution

LIBRARY OF CONGRESS CATALOGING-IN-PUBLICATION DATA

Gardner, Lloyd C., 1934–
Killing machine : the American presidency in the age of drone
warfare / Lloyd C. Gardner.
pages cm
Includes bibliographical references and index.
ISBN 978-1-59558-918-7 (hardback) — ISBN 978-1-59558-943-9 (pbk.)
1. Executive power—United States.   2. War and emergency powers—
United States.   3. Drone aircraft—Government policy—
United States.   4. Targeted killing—Government policy—United
States.   5. United States—Military policy—Moral and ethical aspects.
6. Obama, Barack.   7. United States—Politics and government—2009–
8. Afghan War, 2001—Aerial operations.   9. Iraq War,
2003–2011—Aerial operations.   I. Title.
JK558.G37 2013
352.23'5—dc23   2013022628

The New Press publishes books that promote and enrich public discussion
and understanding of the issues vital to our democracy and to a more
equitable world. These books are made possible by the enthusiasm of
our readers; the support of a committed group of donors, large and
small; the collaboration of our many partners in the independent
media and the not-for-profit sector; booksellers, who often hand-sell
New Press books; librarians; and above all by our authors.

www.thenewpress.com

Composition by Westchester Book Composition
This book was set in Goudy

Printed in the United States of America

2   4   6   8   10   9   7   5   3   1

CONTENTS

INTRODUCTION

I did not intend to write a book about drones. I planned to write a chapter on counterinsurgency in Iraq and Afghanistan as part of another work. But then counterinsurgency doctrine disappeared in the Hindu Kush, and drones soared upward out of the confusion, becoming the weapons of choice against would-be evildoers everywhere. It all happened so fast that the usual chronological organization historians rely upon will hardly do. I have written this book, therefore, as an observer of when public attention became focused on a particular question in the headlines and commentary of the day. The narrative begins with an Illinois state representative challenging the Bush White House's determination to go to war with Iraq in 2002, but a history of unmanned aerial vehicle (UAV) attacks on al Qaeda targets going back to the 1990s does not come until chapter 5. Even though there were critics who wrote early on about the blowback danger involved with the use of drones, few people paid much attention to drone warfare before 2010, when the number of attacks on Pakistani borderlands increased dramatically, as did the crucial role of the Central Intelligence Agency.

Partly this is because, as President Obama's first press secretary, Robert Gibbs, confirmed in an interview recently, "one of the first things they told me was, you're not even to acknowledge the drone program. You're not even to discuss that it exists." Gibbs knew it was "crazy," because everyone out there asking questions knew it existed, and they were being told to "pay no attention to the man behind the curtain." This mandate not to acknowledge the existence of the program, Gibbs believes—as do most other observers we will encounter in the chapters that follow—"undermines people's confidence overall in the decisions that their government makes."[1]

Along with the Gibbs revelations have come other disclosures about Obama's foreign policy, such as information that the United

States has quietly resumed sales of arms to countries that use children in their armies—effectively circumventing a ban enacted in the George W. Bush years.

> Penalties were put in place by Congress to prevent U.S. arms sales to countries determined by the State Department to be the worst abusers of child soldiers in their militaries, but the Obama administration has waived almost all of them each year, arguing that continued arms sales to abuser countries are needed either to bolster those countries' fragile security or to support cooperation with the U.S. military in areas such as counterterrorism.[2]

"Through all this," writes Peter Beinart, "mainstream liberal Democrats have mostly yawned." They are not thrilled about drone warfare, but they trust the president more than they did George W. Bush, and they do not question the wisdom of breaking the ban on arms sales to such "allies." The president's lack of availability to the press—which ABC White House reporter Ann Compton has called "a disgrace"[3]—means that Gibbs and later his successor as press secretary, Jay Carney, have seemed to be defending the president's policies from a defensive crouch.

There are no archival sources available for a book about recent events such as these, and there probably will not be for a long time. The ability of governments to keep embarrassing—or at least controversial—decisions secret, on the other hand, has crumbled under the pressure of reporters and other commentators reluctant to accept government's assertions of "trust me." The classifier's TOP SECRET stamp has been overwritten not simply by WikiLeaks but by the plethora of information made available from legions of government insiders who talk anonymously to investigative reporters. Drone warfare is a very special case, however, for government officials—pleading different reasons at different times—have refused in public speeches and in responses to lawsuits to acknowledge ownership of attacks on certain targets, especially those outside recognized war zones. I hope this book will provide some insight into the reasons for this. Particularly controversial in this regard is the Obama administration's refusal thus far to declassify a fifty-five-page memorandum prepared over a six-month period in the Office of Legal Counsel that lays out the legal basis for lethal attacks on American citizens living in foreign countries without regard for Fifth Amendment protections calling for due process under the normal procedures of a court trial. There are also indications that more than one memorandum on the subject exists, and that a reason for keeping them all secret is that the authors apply different standards depending on what particular events seem to require.

Ever since John Yoo of the White House Office of Legal Counsel (OLC) authored the infamous 2002 memoranda on torture, the OLC has put itself in a position not unlike that of farmers who force-feed grain to captive geese in order to produce the abnormally distended livers eaten as the delicacy foie gras. The OLC's memos distort the Constitution to provide presidents with the swollen powers they desire. Perhaps the most revealing aspect of this behavior pattern became public in the aftermath of President Obama's reelection, when newspaper articles carried stories about his desire to write a "rule book" for drone warfare. The administration was said to be concerned about a Republican victory bringing Mitt Romney into the Oval Office. Hence the need for rules in place by the time of the inauguration—the assumption being that Romney and his people would be less careful about paying attention to American responsibilities under international law.

It was hard to say what was more disturbing about this revelation: the implicit belief that Obama was more trustworthy than any of his successors would be, or the explicit assertion that the White House enjoyed the sole right to develop regulations governing this new form of warfare. It was said that the administration felt its responsibilities so keenly because the nation—and the world—was entering upon new territory, just as we had at the beginning of the atomic age. The ability of each successive president to write his or her own rule book governing the use of drones certainly raised questions about the responsibility being left to the executive branch.

When Barack Obama ran for president in 2008, he talked about the Iraq War as not just an aberration of American foreign policy but the culmination of trends and impulses of a long-standing nature. Here is what he said in one of his campaign appearances: "I don't want to just end the war, but I want to end the mind-set that got us into war in the first place." After that declaration, however, he added, "We need to have a strike force that can take out potential terrorist bases that get set up in Iraq." The one thing to avoid, he said, was "mission creep," which would have the United States keep a large number of troops on the ground in a Middle Eastern country. Was this statement an early indication of how Obama would seize upon drone warfare as the ultimate escape from past mistakes?

As in so many cases, how one parsed presidential language supplied answers—if not always the right ones—to such questions. Many of Obama's listeners, it seemed, wanted to pay attention only to his statements about winding down the Iraq War. Obama's views were never so uncomplicated, however: he was not a "McGovernite," as some in the Democratic Party hoped and many others feared. The "mind-set that got us into war" was really a description of the neocon obsession with Saddam Hussein, not a more general commitment to peaceful diplomacy over the use of force. The broader quest, in Obama's vision, was for "a strike force that can take out potential terrorist bases." And within that sentence, the key word would turn out to be "potential," for there is where the drone debate eventually led—whether the threats to be addressed by the use of drone attacks were "potential" or "imminent," and whether they were the same thing.

It could be argued that Barack Obama was trapped or fell into the embrace of Reaper and Predator drones by circumstances beyond his control. He had not been the first to use UAVs. Counterinsurgency strategies clearly were not working, and the ambiguous attitudes of government leaders in Afghanistan's neighboring countries only exacerbated its failure. Moreover, the Great Recession put limits on future military budgets in a global theater of war in which the enemy wore no uniforms and box cutters could be deadly weapons.

That there is terrific pressure on federal budgets is absolutely the case, so much so that Republicans have so far not flinched in a showdown with the president over "sequestration," the implementation of automatic budget cuts that would scale back the Department of Defense's procurement of new weapons. Rep. Tom Cole, a Republican from Oklahoma, told the *New York Times*: "Fiscal questions trump defense in a way they never would have after 9/11. But the war in Iraq is over. Troops are coming home from Afghanistan, and we want to secure the cuts." Falling for drone warfare as a substitute for manpower-heavy defense appears to some to be the best way to "Lean Forward."

Polls showed that Americans overwhelmingly favored the use of drones, even if they had some doubts about things such as "signature" strikes, where Hellfire missiles were launched at gatherings of supposed plotters, and follow-up attacks against those who came to the scene in the aftermath of a strike—and even if they felt especially uneasy about the possibility that drones could be used inside the United States, either by a foreign country or by American officials at different levels of government. In an article in the *Washington Post*, "Who Signed Anwar al-Awlaki's Death Warrant?" the noted columnist Richard Cohen pondered the meaning of the drone attacks on Awlaki, an American citizen living in Yemen. Cohen was not sorry he was dead: "A little 'yippee' emitted from me when I heard the news. Awlaki was a traitor to his country and its values." But there was a nagging sense that somehow, somewhere, the administration knew it had crossed a line in a secret memo, on the sneak.

> We live in a soft police state. It's not a film-noir one, based on ideology and punctuated by the crunch of hobnailed boots, but one created in response to terrorism and crime. Cameras follow us. Our travels, our purchases, are recorded. Our computers and cellphones snitch on us. There's no Orwellian Big Brother, just countless little ones, all of them righteously on the lookout for the bad guys. It's necessary, I suppose. It will be abused, I don't suppose.[4]

There were those, on the other hand, who had *absolutely* no doubts about the drone policy: it was the only "realistic" way to deal with jihadist death threats emanating from seven thousand miles away that could be handled by guys hunched over before bright computer screens inside trailers. The counterterrorism adviser to George W. Bush and Barack Obama, Richard Clarke, wanted to claim paternity for the drones. He had opposed the war on Iraq and claimed that 9/11 might have been prevented if Bush had listened to him: "We found him [Osama bin Laden] in October 2000 using a Predator. There was, however, no such thing then as an armed Predator, so we saw him but could not kill him." After that experience, Clarke avers, President Bill Clinton gave orders to create an armed drone force. But when George Bush came into office, "the CIA and DOD refused to fly the armed Predator to get Bin Laden in Afghanistan, including balking at a cabinet level meeting *on Sept. 4, 2001*."[5]

So one week before the tragedy, George W. Bush had an opportunity to take out the author of the worst attack on America since Pearl Harbor—and he refused. This is close to calling out the president for dereliction of duty. Then there is Senator Lindsey Graham, a former U.S. Air Force judge advocate general officer, who claimed in a speech in his home state, South Carolina, that drones have killed 4,700 people: "We've killed 4,700. Sometimes you hit innocent people, and I hate that, but we're at war, and we've taken out some very senior members of Al-Qaeda." Graham put no numbers on "innocent people" versus "senior members of Al-Qaeda." Graham's figures were close to the highest estimates by various groups that opposed the use of drones, and far and away above any figures the administration admitted to. One study concluded, "The number of 'high-level' targets killed as a percentage of total casualties is extremely low—estimated at just 2%."[6]

The chapters that follow wrestle with these issues without hiding my view that the United States has already flown drones across constitutional boundaries and has them headed dead on for the foundations of the Republic. This book is dedicated to all those writers who have given us the information—if we will only use it—to halt the flight before the drone hits its target.

Acknowledgments

My greatest debt for encouraging me all along the way is to Marc Favreau. No author could have a better editor and friend than Marc. He knows when I go overboard and gets me back to the heart of the matter. The book reflects his good sense of what is important and what is not. My old friends and colleagues are the usual suspects who turn up in all my books: Marilyn Young, who showers me with crucial information on a daily basis, and Walter LaFeber and Tom McCormick, who are still always ready to offer their best opinions—after nearly fifty-seven years of a never-ending conversation on American foreign policy. Warren Kimball, a colleague from the Rutgers days and a friend forever, never lets me get too sure of my opinions. Then there is a wise old colonel, Paul Miles of West Point and Princeton, with whom lunch has become a seminar on U.S. military policy and the state of diplomatic history. What I have learned about counterinsurgency owes much to the work of Gian Gentile and Greg Daddis. Copy editor Sue Warga and Sarah Fan of The New Press are superb editors, with a keen eye for the right word in the proper place whenever I bog down in the midst of a sentence. Thanks also to the history department of Wofford College, which provided me with a temporary home in the fall of 2012 as visiting occupant of the Jones Chair in History. I will always feel honored that Rutgers graduate John Adams has created a seminar in my name for undergraduates to prepare themselves for careers in public service, and it is to those students present and future as well that this book is dedicated.

So thanks to all these people but, of course, especially to Nancy for hearing me out on all these questions—and for being there always.

Newtown, Pennsylvania
February 24, 2013

1

THE DREAM CANDIDATE

And then, on September 11, the world fractured. It's beyond my skill as a writer to capture that day and the days that would follow—the planes, like specters, vanishing into steel and glass; the slow-motion cascade of the towers crumbling into themselves; the ash-covered figures wandering the streets; the anguish and the fear. Nor do I pretend to understand the stark nihilism that drove the terrorists that day and that drives their brethren still. My powers of empathy, my ability to reach into another's heart, cannot penetrate the blank stares of those who would murder innocents with abstract, serene satisfaction.

—Barack Obama, *Dreams from My Father:*
A Story of Race and Inheritance

The meteoric rise of Barack Obama began with a speech to a Chicago antiwar rally in October 2002. Three days after the 9/11 attacks, Congress had voted on a resolution authorizing the president to use all "necessary and appropriate force" against those whom he determined "planned, authorized, committed or aided" the September 11 attacks, or who harbored said persons or groups. The Authorization for Use of Military Force (AUMF) passed with only one nay vote and was signed by President George W. Bush on September 18, 2001. Now, a year later, most Democrats were unwilling to take on the White House when the president asked Congress for a blank-check resolution to deal with Iraq's supposed weapons of mass destruction, one he could interpret as empowering him to act as he saw fit, including going to war.

Obama, an Illinois state legislator, took up the challenge. "What I am opposed to is a dumb war," he declared. "What I am opposed to is a rash war. What I am opposed to is the cynical attempt by

1

Richard Perle and Paul Wolfowitz and other armchair, weekend warriors in this administration to shove their own ideological agendas down our throats, irrespective of the costs in lives lost and in hardships borne."[1]

He did not stop with neocon presidential advisers. Obama went after the man in the Oval Office. "You want a fight, President Bush? Let's finish the fight with Bin Laden and al-Qaeda, through effective, coordinated intelligence, and a shutting down of the financial networks that support terrorism, and a homeland security program that involves more than color-coded warnings." However hateful Saddam Hussein was, he posed "no imminent and direct threat to the United States, or to his neighbors." That phrase sounded very much like an opening call for a foreign policy debate on national security policy beyond the rhetoric of American exceptionalism and Cold War triumphalism—somewhere that maybe 80 to 90 percent of the members of his own party feared to tread. And there was more yet. The Iraqi economy was in shambles, he said, and the dictator's military was but a fraction of its former strength: "In concert with the international community he can be contained until, in the way of all petty dictators, he falls away into the dustbin of history."

The speech was a stunner, and obviously very risky. Two weeks later Congress passed the Iraq War Resolution—the vote was lopsided but not unanimous, for doubts had begun to creep into the minds of some legislators. In the House a majority of Democrats voted no, but in the Senate twenty-one Democrats voted no while twenty-nine said yes, including Hillary Clinton—already looking ahead to 2008—and a wavering John Kerry, whose ambitions were focused on 2004. Six months later the United States was at war, with its "coalition of the willing" contributing a few non-U.S. soldiers and a thin international cover for Washington's determination to bring down Saddam Hussein. Only Great Britain from what Secretary of Defense Donald Rumsfeld dismissed as "old Europe" showed interest in sending troops, while there were nearly six thousand from former Soviet satellites.

Had the war gone as the White House predicted it would—a quick march to Baghdad with Iraqis cheering their "liberators" all along the way—Obama's rhetoric would have landed him in obscurity, alongside a deflated peace wing of the Democratic Party. But the war did not go well, and Obama became a Kennedyesque profile in courage for speaking out while others cowered and sought political safety in Bush's assurances that Hussein's weapons of mass destruction really did exist someplace besides Vice President Dick Cheney's version of Grimms' fairy tales.

The opening salvo of the war was a series of decapitating air strikes to kill the tyrant. They failed. Next there was "shock and awe" and the march on Baghdad. But once the coalition of the willing got there and Saddam Hussein's statue was pulled down, there came conditions that looked more like chaos and incipient civil war than World War II liberation. And there was still no sign of those weapons of mass destruction the White House had warned the nation could show up as mushroom clouds over American cities; finally it came time to admit that they simply did not exist. That being the case, the administration turned to historical analogies to find the justification for war and the need to spend billions upon billions of dollars in new weaponry not only to destroy Saddam Hussein's army but to spread truth, justice, and the American way to the whole Middle East.

Thus national security adviser Condoleezza Rice in a June 2003 speech to the International Institute for Strategic Studies in London spoke of World War II: "No less than Pearl Harbor, September 11 forever changed the lives of every American and the strategic perspective of the United States. . . . [W]e resolved that the only true defense against a threat of this kind is to root it out at its source and address it at its fundamental and ideological core." Not just the United States, she intoned, but "all civilized nations" were called upon to fulfill this duty, one that presented both "unparalleled opportunities" and "unprecedented challenges." Magnifying Saddam Hussein's army to the status of America's World War II enemies or the Cold War military challenge was, of course, nonsense, but she had in mind the need to link Osama bin Laden and the "al Qaeda network" to the "fundamental and ideological core" of a global conspiracy. The task for "all civilized nations" was, therefore, an ongoing struggle on many fronts, even though she said half the al Qaeda leadership had already been captured or killed and "the rest is on the run—permanently."

If al Qaeda had lost half its leadership, had been deprived of its sanctuary in Afghanistan, and was on the run—"permanently"— what was left of this "unprecedented" challenge? She had no good answer even as events in Iraq constantly called into question the decision to invade. As General Omar Bradley had once said about Korea, Iraq was the wrong war against the wrong enemy.

To reclaim the world's respect, George Bush also used a London audience to sell the war as but a prelude to the great things that would materialize in the near future. Noting the protesters on the streets outside Whitehall Palace, he began his speech with a clever reference to the Anglo-American tradition of free speech. The protesters were exercising that right "with enthusiasm," he said, and, after being interrupted by laughter, he suddenly switched to Iraq, noting that now Iraqis "have that right in Baghdad as well."

There was his theme. Baghdad was only the beginning, despite all the "stuff" that was happening there, as Rumsfeld had described the looting and fighting that seemed to grow worse by the day. The president then proceeded to describe what made up the American character and determined its sense of mission to the world.

> We're sometimes faulted for a naive faith that liberty can change the world. If that's an error, it began with reading too much John Locke and Adam Smith.
>
> Americans have on occasion been called moralists, who often speak in terms of right and wrong. That zeal has been inspired by examples on this island, by the tireless compassion of Lord Shaftesbury, the righteous courage of Wilberforce and the firm determination of the Royal Navy over the decades to fight and end the trade in slaves.
>
> It's rightly said that Americans are a religious people. That's in part because of the good news that was translated by Tyndale, preached by Wesley, lived out in the example of William Booth.

At times Americans are even said to have a Puritan streak. And where might that have come from?

The quip brought more laughter. Turning to the immediate situation in November 2003, Bush blamed the troubles in Iraq on the neglect of the very Anglo-American traditions he described and the failure to fulfill the principles championed by those ancestors he had invoked.

> We must shake off decades of failed policy in the Middle East. Your nation and mine in the past have been willing to make a bargain to tolerate oppression for the sake of stability. Longstanding ties often led us to overlook the faults of local elites.
>
> Yet this bargain did not bring stability or make us safe. It merely bought time while problems festered and ideologies of violence took hold.

In their own way, Bush's remarks were as radical—if not actually more so—than Obama's antiwar speech seemed to be. Did he really mean to cast off policies that went back to the end of World War I, when the British and French took over the Ottoman Empire and carved out new nations to suit the geopolitical and economic interests of the victors? Here was the president of the United States seemingly criticizing as well America's post–World War II policies in the Middle East, including interventions in Iran and Iraq, to overthrow regimes that threatened American "interests" in controlling cheap oil supplies for the West, and building military alliances with other regimes that had little interest in free speech.

As he spoke about the dangers of overlooking the faults of "local elites," however, the CIA was sending suspected terrorists to some of those countries, including Syria and Egypt, where they could be "interrogated" using practices that went beyond "enhanced interrogation" methods like waterboarding. At the same time, American military police were assisting CIA interrogators in softening up detainees at the Abu Ghraib prison in Baghdad, a situation that began to come to light in April 2004. When pictures of what was happening appeared on the web, the Pentagon sent Major General Antonio M. Taguba, the first Philippine American to reach that rank, to conduct an investigation. Among the abuses he found:

> Breaking chemical lights and pouring the phosphoric liquid on detainees; pouring cold water on naked detainees; beating detainees with a broom handle and a chair; threatening male detainees with rape; allowing a military police guard to stitch the wound of a detainee who was injured after being slammed against the wall in his cell; sodomizing a detainee with a chemical light and perhaps a broom stick, and using military working dogs to frighten and intimidate detainees with threats of attack, and in one instance actually biting a detainee.[2]

The story of how America's mission in Iraq fit into the grand narrative Bush outlined had been interrupted—and in the most damning way imaginable.

The 2004 Convention

When Democratic Party leaders looked around for someone to keynote their 2004 convention, there was Obama, now a candidate for the U.S. Senate. It could be assumed that had he already been in the Senate he would have voted no on the key resolution that turned the question of war or peace over to the White House. He was a creditable if untested new figure. The speech he gave at the convention scored well again with peace Democrats and with all those looking for a new face for the party. Richard Lowry, editor of the conservative *National Review*, reported in his column that he received a "rapturous" outburst from the convention. But Lowry was impressed with several things Obama said about "faith" and community that seemed to him out of the ordinary for a Democrat to say in such a setting. Lowry asserted the speech was actually not a dove's cri de coeur but a critique of how an inept White House had mishandled the way America went to war. "He made this week's best, most trenchant criticism of the Iraq war, saying we should 'never ever go to war without enough troops to win the war, secure the peace, and earn the respect the world.' The criticism reflects a hawkish attitude: We need more troops. It invokes the opinion of the world but also with a hawkish tinge: The world should respect us, because when we confront an enemy we do it right." Lowry went on, "By the end, when Obama said 'the people will rise up in November,' and 'this country will reclaim its promise, and out of this long political darkness a brighter day will come,' it seemed more than garden-variety political rhetoric. Because it was."[3]

Perhaps such comments merely reflected conservative disillusion with George Bush's failure to plan a war of liberation beyond a staged landing on an aircraft carrier, the USS *Abraham Lincoln*, the first president to jump out of a fighter jet in a flight suit to proclaim "mission accomplished."[4] Certainly listeners heard in Obama's speech what they wanted to hear, not least because the prospect of Obama as a possible future presidential candidate represented a dramatic breakthrough. Above all the cheering for a rousing speech, however, many Democrats feared a rerun of the McGovern debacle in 1972, when during another war their candidate called out, "Come home, America," yet voters instead went to the polls to reelect Richard Nixon. The only way for John Kerry to win, Democratic regulars thought, was to turn the tables on the White House and portray Iraq as an obstacle to a successful war on terrorism. With the outrages of the Abu Ghraib scandal and the misuse of the detention facility at Guantánamo Bay on the front pages, it should have been easy for the Kerry campaign to argue that the Bush administration had accomplished the unimaginable in just one year of the Iraq War: it had forfeited moral leadership abroad and at home. Stuck with the feckless "mission accomplished" boast President Bush had made as he posed next to the fighter jet, moreover, the administration could not deal with Osama bin Laden's taunts from his hideout in the mountains between Afghanistan and Pakistan.

Obama had obviously designed the speech to show the nation that neither the Democrats nor he personally was a proponent of a

weak America. But that task proved not easy at all. The classic
dilemma facing both members of Congress and presidential candidates came down to the problem of opposing a war without being
blamed for failing to support American soldiers on the front—the
White House's ultimate weapon. Presidential candidate John Kerry
got caught up in this dilemma. Famous as a U.S. Navy veteran who
came to oppose the Vietnam War, as a senator from Massachusetts
Kerry had a difficult time with the Iraq issue. In October 2003, a year
after voting to support the use of force in Iraq, Kerry voted against
an $87 billion supplemental funding bill for U.S. troops in Iraq and
Afghanistan. He did support an alternative bill that funded the $87
billion by eliminating some of the 2001 Bush tax cuts, but when
that failed he voted against the appropriation. Kerry complicated
matters beyond repair by saying, "I actually did vote for the $87 bil-
lion before I voted against it"—an explanation that he eventually
characterized as "one of those inarticulate moments."

Maybe it was this lapse that doomed Kerry's presidential hopes—
or maybe not. On November 1, the Al Jazeera network released a
"message" from Osama bin Laden to the United States that accused
Bush of lying about the reasons for the 9/11 attack: "Despite entering
the fourth year after September 11, Bush is still deceiving you and
hiding the truth from you and therefore the reasons are still there
to repeat what happened." There were speculations about bin Laden's
motives—perhaps he just enjoyed pulling Uncle Sam's beard—but
it did seem to be the sort of insult designed to rally people around
the president. Whatever the reasons (there were also charges of ir-
regularities at the polls), Kerry narrowly lost the election, amid much
controversy.

Bush's second inaugural address promised recommitment to the
Wilsonian themes he had sounded in London.

> We are led, by events and common sense, to one conclusion: The
> survival of liberty in our land increasingly depends on the success
> of liberty in other lands. The best hope for peace in our world is
> the expansion of freedom in all the world.

America's vital interests and our deepest beliefs are now one. From the day of our Founding, we have proclaimed that every man and woman on this earth has rights, and dignity, and matchless value, because they bear the image of the Maker of Heaven and earth. Across the generations we have proclaimed the imperative of self-government, because no one is fit to be a master, and no one deserves to be a slave. Advancing these ideals is the mission that created our Nation. It is the honorable achievement of our fathers. Now it is the urgent requirement of our nation's security, and the calling of our time.

So it is the policy of the United States to seek and support the growth of democratic movements and institutions in every nation and culture, with the ultimate goal of ending tyranny in our world.

From its outset, however, the second Bush administration struggled with questions and deepening anxiety about Iraq. And so long as Osama bin Laden remained hidden somewhere, moreover, the administration could make no claim to have set al Qaeda permanently on the run.

Here I Come, Ready or Not

The Democrats regained control of both houses of Congress in the 2006 elections, and it appeared the Republican grip on national security issues in the post-Vietnam era had at last loosened up. The Bush administration confronted a desperate situation in Iraq in which civil war loomed on the horizon, and it had to deal with a Democratic Congress apparently elected to end the war. Appearances were deceiving, however, as the Democrats had as yet no real sense of their next steps. In this vacuum Bush acted, in February 2007 promising a new way forward with a "surge" of additional troops and naming General David Petraeus to take command in Iraq.

At approximately the same time, Barack Obama, a first-term Democratic senator from Illinois, declared he would run for president in 2008. It was an equally audacious move, given the expectation that Senator Hillary Clinton would sweep the primaries. Her problem was Iraq. Like Kerry, she had some explaining to do about her votes, but she had lots of support in the party and was also a pathbreaker as the first serious female contender.

National discontent over the Iraq War had not quite reached its highest point. Congress confirmed the Petraeus appointment, but the public did not welcome the idea of sending more troops to a war that many now considered a terrible blunder. By June only 10 percent of those answering an opinion poll thought the situation had been made better by the surge, while 54 percent thought the situation had gotten worse. And as for what to do next, the public opinion poll gave an unequivocal answer: "Despite four months of a military surge in Iraq, 68 percent of the public either want to withdraw right away (25 percent) or begin bringing troops home within the next year (43 percent). Just 26 percent want to keep troops in Iraq 'for as long as it takes to win the war.'"[5]

Since Iraq absorbed the public's attention, the "other war" in Afghanistan was not the subject of many polls in 2007. Senator Obama's qualifications centered on his supporters' faith that he would end the Iraq War if elected. Moreover, several important Republican senators held similar views about the war. Richard Lugar of Indiana, George Voinovich of Ohio, and John Warner of Virginia expressed skepticism about the administration's plans. "Lugar said the military escalation, the so-called surge that began in the spring, has 'very limited' prospects for success and called for troop reduction, a statement praised by Warner. And Voinovich called for 'a comprehensive plan for our country's gradual military disengagement' from Iraq."[6]

In a major speech on August 1, 2007, Obama promised to do just that, and even asserted that President George W. Bush, "by refusing to end the war in Iraq, . . . is giving the terrorists what they really want, and what the Congress voted to give them in 2002: a U.S. occupation of undetermined length, at undetermined cost, with underestimated consequences."[7] These were bold accusations. They confirmed a belief that Obama would challenge not only the White

House but also the Clinton-centrist dominance of the Democratic Party. Before Obama started stealing headlines from her, Senator Clinton had been the odds-on favorite for the nomination. But, again, she was vulnerable on Iraq, having cast a vote in 2002 in favor of the president's request for open-ended support in the run-up to the war.

The president, meanwhile, gave a speech to the Veterans of Foreign Wars in an attempt to shore up public opinion by urging the nation not to lose its will to win the fight, as had happened in Vietnam. Essential to the rationale for the surge, of course, was this rewriting of the narrative of the Vietnam War, with its new emphasis on how successful the military counterinsurgency strategy had been after General William Westmoreland had been removed from Saigon and sent back to the Pentagon. To make his point, Bush did something unusual, including in the speech a long section on the disastrous impact of British novelist Graham Greene's *The Quiet American*, recently remade as a movie, on opinions about the American effort in Vietnam.

At key moments since World War II, the president began, critics and doubters had dismissed American policy in Asia as "hopeless and naive." These feelings surfaced most dramatically during the Vietnam War, leading to a tragedy for the Vietnamese people when Saigon fell to the Communists. "In 1955, long before the United States entered the war, Graham Greene wrote a novel called, 'The Quiet American.' It was set in Saigon, and the main character was a young government agent named Alden Pyle. He was a symbol of American purpose and patriotism—and dangerous naivete. Another character describes Alden this way: 'I never knew a man who had better motives for all the trouble he caused.'"[8]

As American involvement deepened with no resolution in sight, Bush went on, "the Graham Greene argument gathered some steam." War critics insisted there would be no consequences for the Vietnamese if we pulled out. They were wrong. "Three decades later, there is a legitimate debate about how we got into the Vietnam War and how we left." But the price of America's withdrawal could not be ignored: it "was paid by millions of innocent citizens whose agonies would add to our vocabulary new terms like 'boat people,' 're-education camps,' and 'killing fields.' "

In other words, maybe there weren't any WMDs in Iraq after all, but the Iraq War was still justified given Saddam Hussein's loathsome regime, which had inflicted such terrible suffering on the Iraqi people. If America bailed out, Iraq could face even worse troubles, chaos being only one possibility—al Qaeda would still have a platform from which to both pursue its political goals and launch terrorist attacks on the West, or the Iranians might come in to take control. There had been only two democracies in the Far East before World War II, he said, Australia and New Zealand. "Today most of the nations in Asia are free, and its democracies reflect the diversity of the region." The lesson for America in Iraq was obvious.

Obama, on the other hand, had yet to convince party leaders and the rank and file he could go beyond opposition to the Iraq War with a counternarrative to the Bush arguments, however skeptical Americans were about the current president's message. Campaigning in New Hampshire in July 2007, Obama assailed Bush's new surge strategy. It would only make things worse, he insisted. "Here's what we know. The surge has not worked. And they [the Bush administration] said today, 'Well, even in September, we're going to need more time.' So we're going to kick this can all the way down to the next president, under the president's plan."[9] The only way to protect national security, said Obama, was to "hunt down and take out" terrorists worldwide. He even pegged their number at twenty thousand worldwide.

Ten days after his attack on the surge in New Hampshire, Obama delivered a long speech on foreign policy at the Wilson Center in Washington, D.C., designed to show he was a creative thinker on national security issues. He began by invoking his personal memory of 9/11. "It seemed all of the misery and all of the evil in the world were in that rolling black cloud, blocking out the September sun." That morning of the black cloud we saw we were "no longer protected by our own power." In years past, America had always turned tragedy into triumph. "An attack on Pearl Harbor led to a wave of freedom rolling across the Atlantic and Pacific." And so it would have been this time, too, but instead of finishing the job against al Qaeda in Afghanistan or launching "a comprehensive strategy to dry up the terrorists' base of support," the Bush administration insisted "the 21st century's stateless terrorism could be defeated through the invasion and occupation of a state." The White House had pursued a "deliberate strategy to misrepresent 9/11 to sell a war against a country that had nothing to do with 9/11."[10]

The problem, therefore, was not a lack of will to finish the job, but the need to pick the right enemy and the right way to go after them. So Obama felt he had to explain once more what he had meant at the 2002 Chicago rally in opposing the administration's determination to go to war against Saddam Hussein. "I did not oppose all wars, I said. I was a strong supporter of the war in Afghanistan." The war against Iraq should never have been waged; it only added to anti-Americanism throughout the Muslim world. "We are now less safe than we were before 9/11." However well he succeeded in dispelling lingering notions that he was a "peacenik," he still had to go beyond critiques of a failed strategy. In doing so, however, Obama's argument foreshortened history to the post–9/11 years, so that everything turned on how mishandling the attacks on the World Trade Center and the Pentagon had brought about such a sorry state of affairs. In effect, he was playing on Bush's home ground, quarreling only about the play calling for the American team. Pakistan's ambiguous role in Afghanistan, the supposed Iranian quest for atomic weapons, the threats to Israel's existence—all these and more, he argued, were the result of a misguided decision to invade Iraq.

Bush had actually created new threats to the United States by invading Iraq, Obama asserted, yet he all but adopted the White House view that terrorists were at war with the United States—and everyone else—because they hated American freedoms. "They kill man, woman and child; Christian and Hindu; Jew and Muslim. They seek to create a repressive caliphate." The Bush administration had used similar language to explain what Saddam Hussein intended to do with the phantom WMDs. "This caliphate," Bush had averred, "would be a totalitarian Islamic empire encompassing all current and former Muslim lands, stretching from Europe to North Africa, the Middle East and Southeast Asia."[11] Apparently there was there nothing wrong with Bush's assessment of the threat, then, only that he had gone to war against the wrong country. Beyond that difference, however, Obama had accepted the basic Cold War formulation that America faced an implacable ideological threat. Instead of international Communism, however, now it emanated from extremist elements led by al Qaeda and the Taliban.

They operated out of "tribal regions" in northwest Pakistan, the place where the 9/11 attacks had been imagined and ordered. It was difficult terrain for Westerners seeking to find and defeat an enemy.

> This is the wild frontier of our globalized world. There are wind-swept deserts, and cave-dotted mountains. There are tribes that see borders as nothing more than lines on a map, and governments as forces that come and go. There are blood ties deeper than alliances of convenience, and pockets of extremism that follow religion to violence. It's a tough place.[12]

How did this description of the problem confronting the United States differ from neoconservative theories? One might say it updated them by positing an even more encompassing global ambition to meet the challenge of places left behind in the West's attempts at a postimperial organization of the world political economy. Obama's speech showed familiarity with the basics of the new counterinsurgency strategy and implied that he knew how to do it. Force, Obama argued, was only part of the solution. Success would require extending economic aid to "fund projects at the local level to impact ordinary Afghans," and "better performance from the Afghan government" on all levels. Defeating extremism required "increased international support to develop the rule of law across the country." Listed here were almost all elements of nation building, precisely the sort of open-ended commitment that he had criticized the Bush administration for undertaking in Iraq—by all accounts a much more modernized nation than Afghanistan.[13]

He promised to send a clear message the United States would not turn its back on Afghanistan a third time, as it had twice before—first when it abandoned the country after the Soviet Union withdrew, and then again when it drove the Taliban from Kabul, leaving the country to civil war and anarchy. Those accusations were true enough, of course: in both cases Washington had lost interest in Afghanistan when the immediate objective had been achieved. "It is time to turn the page," said Obama. "When I am President, we will wage the war that has to be won with a comprehensive strategy with five elements: getting out of Iraq and on to the right battlefield in Afghanistan and Pakistan; developing the capabilities and partnerships we need to take out the terrorists and the world's most deadly weapons; engaging the world to dry up support for terror and extremism; restoring our values; and securing a more resilient homeland."[14]

It was a far more ambitious—and specific—foreign policy agenda than any candidate had put forth in the recent past. George W. Bush in 2000 had eschewed any desire for "nation building," it should be remembered, and backed into it out of desperation in Iraq when the supposed weapons of mass destruction never turned up in order to justify his war. Obama here embraced nation building with enthusiasm as the right way to eliminate terrorism, while passing over the objection that neither Afghanistan nor Pakistan had ever had control in those regions he identified as the source of the threat, the area the British once called the Northwest Frontier.

While the first step had to be getting out of Iraq, he said, referring to a resolution submitted to the Senate calling for withdrawal of "all combat brigades by March 31, 2008," as president he would deploy "at least" two additional brigades to reinforce counterterrorism operations and support NATO's efforts against the Taliban in Afghanistan.

I will not hesitate to use military force to take out terrorists who pose a direct threat to America. This requires a broader set of capabilities, as outlined in the Army and Marine Corps's new counter-insurgency manual. I will ensure that our military becomes more stealth[y], agile, and lethal in its ability to capture or kill terrorists. We need to recruit, train, and equip our armed forces to better target terrorists, and to help foreign militaries to do the same. This must include a program to bolster our ability to speak different languages, understand different cultures, and coordinate complex missions with our civilian agencies.[15]

Lest there be any doubt he had become familiar with the recommendations of the counterinsurgency manual he referred to (Field Manual 3-24), Obama added: "I will increase both the numbers and capabilities of our diplomats, development experts, and other civilians who can work alongside our military. We can't just say there is no military solution to these problems. We need to integrate all aspects of American might."

Obama and the Surge

On September 10, 2007, a day before congressional testimony on the effects of the surge was to begin, the progressive lobbying organization MoveOn ran a full-page ad in the *New York Times* accusing Petraeus of "cooking the books for the White House" in his report to Congress on the progress made since the troop increase began. The ad asked: "General Petraeus or General Betray Us?"

Republican presidential candidates jumped all over the ad. Arizona senator John McCain called it a "McCarthyite attack on an American patriot. . . . No matter where you stand on the war, we should all agree on the character and decency of this exceptional American." Former senator Fred Thompson, a long shot for the nomination, called the ad "outrageous" and said, "MoveOn.org has today, in effect, said that the General leading our brave troops in Iraq is betraying his country. This is the group that funds the Democratic Party. I call upon the Democratic Party and all of the Democratic candidates for President to repudiate the libel of this patriotic American."[16]

Democrats protested the characterization and criticized Republicans for trying to divert attention from the substance of Petraeus's testimony, legitimate matters for debate. "Sen. Obama's question is not about General Petraeus's patriotism," said a spokesman for the putative candidate. "It's about his logic. There's no evidence that this surge is producing the political progress needed to resolve the civil war in Iraq, or that it will be accomplished through more of the same."[17]

The next day Petraeus and Ambassador Ryan Crocker testified before the Senate Foreign Relations Committee, with the nation watching how Senator Obama would deal with the situation. Instead of asking brief questions to allow the two witnesses to expand on their written statements, Obama used his time to stake out a position that praised the general and American soldiers for their performance in Iraq, while still raising his main complaint that the mission could not be accomplished. He began, however, with a comment about the timing of the hearing. Holding it on the sixth anniversary of the 9/11 attacks confused the issues, he argued, and symbolically tied the war in Iraq to a response to the attacks. Beyond the argument over whether regime change had been a good idea—the case Condoleezza Rice, now secretary of state, was making in the court of elite opinion—stirring up emotions through such symbols served no good purpose in gauging what the next steps should be. Interestingly, Obama argued that the surge confused tactics with strategy. Yes, violence had been reduced some, but where was it all going? Obama cited the written statements offered by the witnesses to make a point about the improving situation in Anbar, where a shift had already begun by the time Petraeus arrived in Iraq (ultimately Petraeus wound up paying Sunni sheikhs and their followers millions of dollars to serve as neighborhood guards; the cash surge proved to be more useful there than the increased number of troops). Toward the end of his allotted time, Obama did ask a direct question: were there no criteria at all for deciding that it was time to leave Iraq?[18]

Like all other challenges to the policy, the question received no clear answer from Ambassador Crocker, while Petraeus continued to make notes on a yellow pad. According to a writer who interviewed the general, Obama's questions gnawed at him as he left the hearing room because they centered on the question of what was minimally acceptable to the United States in the Iraqi endgame? He could not answer with specifics in the fall of 2007, he told Steve Coll, out of fear that it would only increase violence again.[19]

Because of their different roles, therefore, the differences between the two men looked broader and deeper than they actually were. In a January 31, 2008, debate with his strongest rival in the Democratic Party, Senator Hillary Clinton, Obama argued that setting a specific time for American troop withdrawal from Iraq would force the contending groups to come together and focus on a national solution. "It can't be muddy, it can't be fuzzy. They've got to know that we are serious about this process." As the only prospective nominee who opposed the war from the beginning, he was, he said, in a perfect position to pressure Iraqi factions to cooperate, because they could be sure he meant what he said. His opposition to the war also made him the best candidate to go up against Senator John McCain, because it drew a clear line beneath all previous arguments over the best way to exit the war. "I will offer a clear contrast as somebody who never supported this war, thought it was a bad idea." And then he delivered the most dramatic statement of his political career that sent hopes soaring among critics—not just of the war but the assumptions behind American policy: "I don't want to just end the war, but I want to end the mind-set that got us into war in the first place."

Just prior to that rousing finale, however, Obama had made a more ambiguous statement about the future of American military bases in Iraq. Referring to Clinton's position, he said, "We have both said that we need to have a strike force that can take out potential terrorist bases that get set up in Iraq. But the one thing that I think is very important is that we not get mission creep, and we not start suggesting that we should have troops in Iraq to blunt Iranian influence." Senator McCain seized on this statement to point out contradictions inherent in Obama's position. It was a strategy based on a decision to accept defeat disguised as a timetable, McCain argued, with the prospect of restarting the war under worse circumstances. Troop withdrawals, unless Petraeus approved them, would be waving the "white flag." "And my friends, if we left, they [al-Qaeda] wouldn't be establishing a base," McCain said. "They'd be taking a country, and I'm not going to allow that to happen, my friends. I will not surrender. I will not surrender to al-Qaeda."[20]

With Obama aides suggesting that their candidate might leave thirty thousand to fifty thousand soldiers behind to deal with any contingency, McCain's criticism touched on a soft spot in Obama's pledge to change the mind-set that led to war. Throughout the 2008 campaign, however, Obama had it both ways: he continued to criticize the surge while promising that he would take the war to al Qaeda in the borderlands between Pakistan and Afghanistan, prompting a frustrated John McCain to say that his opponent's proposals unwisely disregarded Theodore Roosevelt's counsel to speak softly and carry a big stick.

Obama whipsawed his opponent by opposing a narrow surge as an inadequate strategy and all but embracing the main elements of counterinsurgency as the alternative. Yet it appeared to voters, nevertheless, that Obama intended to follow a narrow counterterrorism strategy, not an ambitious scheme that involved nation building in Afghanistan. McCain's *Dirty Harry*–esque threat that Osama bin Laden "will be the last to know" about plans to root him out of hiding certainly made him the campaign's prototypical exponent of "shoot first, ask questions later." By contrast, Obama's cool assertions about finding the right way to defeat terrorist plots against America using all of the nation's "might" did not produce skepticism in liberal circles. Because of McCain's bluster, hardly anyone took notice, for example, when Obama referred to the new army counterinsurgency manual in his speeches laying out detailed strategies for dealing with America's present and future wars. His supporters preferred the 2002 Obama and saw little in his speeches that touched on matters of national security policy other than their own projections. Anything else they dismissed as standard political deflectors put on to protect against right-wing attacks—such as his decision to wear an American flag in his lapel for the rest of the primaries after someone questioned its absence during a debate with Hillary Clinton and Joe Biden.

The surge had been in effect for a few months before there was a decline in casualties. But back in the United States, where the main concern was to find a way out of Iraq, Petraeus became known as something of a miracle worker. Suddenly Obama faced a new challenge in the heroic general who had emerged from what had been called perhaps America's greatest foreign policy and military blunder ever. A sharp-eyed reporter for the New York *Daily News* noted that Obama's campaign site had removed references to the troop surge as being part of "the problem." An Obama spokeswoman said it was just part of an "update" to "reflect changes in current events." The update included a new section on the rise of al Qaeda violence in Afghanistan, the subject of both an op-ed piece Obama wrote and another major speech on foreign policy.[21]

In that op-ed, "My Plan for Iraq," written for the *New York Times*, the Democratic candidate wrote that in the eighteen months since President Bush had announced his plan, American troops "have performed heroically in bringing down the level of violence." In a somewhat oblique fashion, he agreed that the credit would have to go to Petraeus for reshaping the battle lines. "New tactics have protected the Iraqi population, and the Sunni tribes have rejected Al Qaeda—greatly weakening its effectiveness." But the factors that had led him to oppose the surge still held true: the costs to the military and the added financial burden it had imposed on Americans, already over $200 billion, could have been avoided. Meanwhile, Iraq's leaders had failed to invest tens of billions of dollars of their oil revenues in rebuilding the nation's economy, and had failed to reach "the political accommodation that was the stated purpose of the surge."[22]

Despite this failing—and what it indicated about future Iraqi stability—Obama then cited those same leaders, principally Prime Minister Maliki, as desiring to set a timetable for "the removal of American troops." "Meanwhile, Lt. Gen. James Dubik, the American officer in charge of training Iraq's security forces, estimates that the Iraqi Army and police will be ready to assume responsibility for security in 2009." Instead of seizing this moment, Obama wrote, President Bush and Senator McCain "are refusing to embrace this transition—despite their previous commitments to respect the will of Iraq's sovereign government." Getting out of Iraq by the summer of 2010 (except for residual forces to "perform limited missions") was not a precipitous withdrawal, he insisted, and was the only way to secure the resources needed to finish the job in Afghanistan. Iraq was not the central front "in the war on terrorism" and never had been, despite President Bush's insistence that it was. Therefore, as president, Obama would send at least two additional combat brigades to Afghanistan, as well as more helicopters, better intelligence-gathering support, and nonmilitary assistance. "I would not hold our military, our resources and our foreign policy hostage to a misguided desire to maintain permanent bases in Iraq."[23]

There had been too much talk, he concluded, about flip-flopping and surrender in American politics in the past several years. "It's not going to work this time. It's time to end this war." Once again, as had been the case with his major 2007 speech, Obama's final words resonated with supporters far more than his accompanying discussion of what yet had to be done in Afghanistan. In a speech that served as a companion piece to the op-ed, the presumptive Democratic nominee ticked off the list of things that could have been done in the wake of 9/11 to make the nation safer. It began, "We could have deployed the full force of American power to hunt down and destroy Osama bin Laden, al Qaeda, the Taliban, and all the terrorists responsible for 9/11, while supporting real security in Afghanistan." The list went on to include Kennedy-esque steps that individuals in "a new generation" could have taken, such as joining the Peace Corps, while the nation could have acted to rebuild roads and bridges, construct new rail and broadband and electricity systems, and make college affordable for every American.[24]

Listeners heard echoes of the "New Frontier" and the "Great Society" before Vietnam devoured everything. It was an ambitious list—but the point Obama hoped to make was that the cost of the Iraq War had prevented the nation from doing any of these things.

He repeated what he had been saying about getting American combat troops out of Iraq within sixteen to eighteen months of his taking office. Both McCain and President Bush attempted to use that
"commitment" (or any timetable) to accuse Obama of not being
willing to listen to the commander in the field, General Petraeus,
before making or even considering such an important decision.

Obama left on a battlefield tour a week after his op-ed piece and
speech, beginning, however, with Afghanistan, which reemphasized
what he had been saying for months: Iraq was the wrong war. Accompanied by media news "stars" from all three TV networks, he told
CBS in Kabul, "For at least a year now, I have called for two additional brigades, perhaps three. I think it's very important that we
unify command more effectively to coordinate our military activities.
But military alone is not going to be enough." Two other senators,
Republican Chuck Hagel and Democrat Joe Reed, accompanied
Obama on this fact-finding mission. They issued a joint statement:

> We need a sense of urgency and determination. We need urgency
> because the threat from the Taliban and al Qaeda is growing and
> we must act; we need determination because it will take time to
> prevail. But with the right strategy and the resources to back it
> up, we will get the job done.

McCain was left in the unhappy position of denying the importance of the Afghan front—in large part, ironically, because Petraeus had not as yet issued any call for a surge there. It was Obama
who was doing all the talking about sending almost the same number of troops as Bush had sent to Iraq to prop up (and shape up)
Hamid Karzai in Kabul. The Afghan president's office described the
senator's discussion with Karzai, which included the problem of corruption and the illegal drug trade, "pleasant," and even reassuring
about American commitments.[25]

When the trio arrived in Baghdad, however, discussions with
Petraeus were much less than pleasant, at least according to several
accounts that apparently emanated from someone in the senators'
entourage. "Petraeus laid on one of his epic PowerPoint slide presen-

tations, which annoyed members of the group. It was propaganda, assuming we didn't know anything," one of those present told a columnist. "We wanted to ask questions, and when we did, Petraeus treated us badly, interrupting Obama continually, taking a very hard stand." The meeting dissolved into a heated exchange between Obama and Petraeus over Obama's stated intention to withdraw all U.S. combat troops from Iraq by 2010.[26]

"You know, if I were in your shoes, I would be making the exact same argument," Obama began. "Your job is to succeed in Iraq on as favorable terms as we can get. But my job as a potential Commander in Chief is to view your counsel and interests through the prism of our overall national security." Obama then shifted to talk "about the deteriorating situation in Afghanistan, the financial costs of the occupation of Iraq, the stress it was putting on the military."[27]

Returning home, Obama was again challenged to admit that he had been wrong in criticizing the Iraq surge before it had had an opportunity to work. Pressed by right-wing TV host Bill O'Reilly, he maneuvered to have it both ways. It was true, he said, that the surge had succeeded beyond its sponsors' wildest dreams.

OBAMA: There is no doubt that the violence is down and that is a testament to the troops that were sent and General Petraeus and Ambassador Crocker. I think that the surge has succeeded in ways that nobody anticipated, by the way, including President Bush and the other supporters. . . .

O'REILLY: But if it had been up to you there would not have been a surge. You and Joe Biden, no surge.

OBAMA: Hold on, if you look at the debate that was taking place. We had gone through five years of mismanagement of this war, which I thought was disastrous, and the president wanted to double down and continue and open-ended policy that did not create the kind of pressure on the Iraqis to take responsibility and reconcile.

O'REILLY: But it worked, come on.

OBAMA: Bill, look—I already said it succeeded beyond our wildest dreams.[28]

Petraeus had another visitor that summer: Steve Coll, a seasoned observer of American policy in Afghanistan from the time of the Soviet occupation in 1979, author of the most important book on that era, *Ghost Wars* (2004), and now a writer for the *New Yorker*. Coll had a conversation with Petraeus about the basics of the counterinsurgency strategy that Obama had not raised.

> I tried to summarize a recent essay by Zbigniew Brzezinski, the national-security adviser to President Jimmy Carter. Brzezinski had seemed to suggest that a problem with America's counterinsurgency strategy in countries like Iraq lay in its proximity to European colonial policies; we send out expeditionary armies and civilian administrators whose missions look uncomfortably like those of imperial subdistrict officers of old. Brzezinski, I said, seemed to argue that the United States had yet to come to terms with the strategic requirements of a post-colonial era.
>
> "It's a wonderful debate to have," Petraeus answered. "But we are where we are." The United States had two counter-insurgency wars on its hands, in Iraq and in Afghanistan. My question reminded him, he continued, of a conversation he had joined a couple of nights before, in Amman, at a dinner party attended by Jordanian intellectuals. . . . "At a certain point," he remarked, "you have to say, with respect, 'Let's take the rearview mirrors off this bus.'"[29]

When the election finally rolled around, Obama received more than twice as many electoral votes as McCain, 365 to 173, and won the popular vote by eight million votes. On election night he addressed a crowd estimated at 250,000 in Chicago's Grant Park. He began his speech to supporters by saying it was a "defining moment" in American history.

> If there is anyone out there who still doubts that America is a place where all things are possible; who still wonders if the dream of our founders is alive in our time; who still questions the power of our democracy, tonight is your answer.[30]

One has to wonder whether many of those who came out that night expected what would happen in the next few weeks as the president-elect assembled his team.

The New Team

Petraeus's answer to Steve Coll seemed in conflict with the heavy emphasis in the new army manual on learning from the past. But not really. What sometimes goes unnoticed is that in general-speak, there is a world of difference between saying one should learn from the past and urging one to learn from past mistakes. When Petraeus spoke, as he often did, about taking the rearview mirrors off the bus, he was actually referring directly to that difference. The lessons the manual recommended learning came from the French experience in Algeria and the successful British efforts against a Communist insurgency in Malaya. One of the manual's authors, John Nagl, wrote that no book was as important to the preparation of the manual as David Galula's *Counterinsurgency Warfare: Theory and Practice* (2006). Galula, a French army officer in Algeria, summed up what had gone wrong: "If the individual members of the organizations were of the same mind, if every organization worked according to a standard pattern, the problem would be solved. Is this not precisely what a coherent, well-understood, and accepted doctrine would tend to achieve?" In other words, the answer was really very simple: everyone had to be on the same page. "Precisely," wrote Nagl.[31]

Obama's relationship with the history of America's engagement in the Middle East was equally ambivalent and equally narrowly focused on a useful past. During the campaign he had asserted that he wanted not only to end the Iraq War but to change the mind-set that had led to the war. Yet none of his speeches reflected such a broad purpose. Instead, all of his speeches, beginning even with the 2002 Chicago peace rally speech, read forward from 9/11—and were limited to the mistake of going to war with the wrong country. He should not have played the role of history professor in the campaign, obviously, but his possible advisers on foreign policy—later set aside in favor of an entire crew from the Center for New American

Security—exhibited very different outlooks on America's challenges in the post–9/11 world, and a willingness to rethink the mind-set much more than the candidate who had expressed the desire to look at fundamentals.

Despite the hard edge to their primary campaign debates over foreign policy, and despite what his supporters might have hoped, Obama asked Clinton to be his secretary of state. Perhaps the most telling decision Obama took before inaugural day, however, was retaining Robert Gates as secretary of defense. The president-elect met with Gates not in the Oval Office or in the Pentagon, but in the fire station at Reagan National Airport. "They pulled the trucks out so that our cars could go in," said Gates, describing what had happened. He also announced that after this Deep Throat–style get-together he found Obama's plan for removing combat troops from Iraq within a sixteen-month period, an "agreeable approach." That was somewhat short of a full endorsement of the president-elect's plan, but Obama himself was now emphasizing the need to be as responsible about getting out of Iraq as we had been irresponsible about getting into it. He still held to his timetable—but now it appeared more as an aspiration than a settled question. He also said that he would listen to the views of the Joint Chiefs and the commanders in Iraq about the "transition."[32]

Moreover, it now appeared that there would be 50,000 troops remaining for some time—"remissioned" as advisers, who would nonetheless shoot at people on certain occasions. Gates and Petraeus, along with the commander in Iraq, General Ray Odierno, had come up with "remissioning" as a formula that would allow Obama to keep his pledge to Democrats without entering into a confrontation with the Pentagon. Like all other members of the Bush team, the secretary of defense had opposed all timetables until the Iraqis themselves pushed Washington into accepting one that would have most American forces out by 2012. "The question is, How do we do this in a responsible way? . . . I think the president-elect framed it just right yesterday."

Gates also told reporters that he had no intention of being a caretaker secretary of defense, a comment that indicated he expected to play a key role in policy decisions. Bob Gates had a long record in national security affairs—much of it filled with controversy. During the 1980s he was a leading hawk in the Reagan administration, convinced even that Mikhail Gorbachev represented nothing more than a Soviet schemer who had pulled the wool over his admirers' eyes and was actually as dedicated to nefarious Communist ambitions as any predecessor in the Kremlin had ever been. In the Reagan administration, and then in the George H.W. Bush follow-up, Gates managed to alienate two secretaries of state, George Shultz and James Baker, by his attempts as deputy national security adviser and CIA director to shape policy toward Russia.

Somehow he had shed that ideological persona by the time he, as a member of the Iraq Study Group that recommended an alternative plan for ending the war, expressed skepticism about staying the course or escalating the number of troops in Iraq. Bush ignored the study group's recommendations when he sent 30,000 troops and Petraeus back to Iraq. But he replaced Don Rumsfeld with Gates, now praised as a realist—and identified as such when Obama announced his decision. "He restored accountability," the president-elect said. "He won the confidence of military commanders, and the trust of our brave men and women in uniform, as well as their families. He earned the respect of members of Congress on both sides of the aisle for his pragmatism and competence. He knows that we need a sustainable national security strategy, and that includes a bipartisan consensus at home."[33]

Taken together, Obama's comments certified Bob Gates as a wise man who, when the president's hand had been forced, accepted the call of duty to get rid of the zealots and bring back "accountability . . . pragmatism and confidence." What he did not talk about was Gates's enthusiasm for counterinsurgency theory, which was sweeping through the Pentagon and which, it will be remembered, Obama had picked up on in his 2007 speech at the Wilson Center. Gates expanded on the emerging American strategy for maintaining its world position in a lengthy speech at Kansas State University after a year as the Pentagon's new leader. He began by recalling anxious times in the past, beginning with how Sputnik in 1957 had brought fear of being left behind in the missile race, continuing with the shock of the Tet offensive, and then moving into the 1970s, "when it seemed that everything that could go wrong for America did." What was not apparent at these times, however, were the long-term effects of key presidential decisions from the time of Harry Truman and "the doctrine of containment" through the "muscular words" of Ronald Reagan and the "masterful endgame diplomacy of George H.W. Bush."

The new challenge that began with 9/11 "may be unprecedented in complexity and scope." In many respects, he said, all the challenges of the twentieth century had their beginnings in ancient hatreds and conflicts, buried alive during and after World War I. "But, like monsters in science fiction, they are returned from the grave to threaten peace and stability around the world." Echoes of the long years of religious warfare in Europe were present "in the growing Sunni versus Shia contest for Islamic hearts and minds in the Middle East." And in our own country, between Lincoln and Kennedy, two presidents and one presidential candidate "were assassinated or attacked by terrorists—as were various tsars, empresses, princes, and, on a fateful day in June 1914, an archduke."

We needed also to remember, he went on, that four times in the past century the United States had come to the end of a war convinced that "the nature of man and the world had changed for the better," and, turning inward, had unilaterally disarmed, "in the process giving ourselves a so-called 'peace' dividend. Four times we chose to forget history." Holding a doctorate in history, Gates rejected neocon theories about the "end of history" and the global triumph of liberal capitalism. That separated him from the Bush true believers, yet also from those realists who criticized the invasion of Iraq. It may have been undertaken in the mistaken notion that Saddam Hussein had an active WMD program, but he held it was justified on other grounds. Still, his message in the lecture at Kansas State University was not about the defense budget or military power as such, he said, but about the need to integrate all elements of national power to meet the challenges. "I am here to make the case for strengthening our capacity to use 'soft' power and for better integrating it with 'hard' power."

Almost paraphrasing the new counterinsurgency manual and the writings of Petraeus advisers David Kilcullen and John Nagl, the secretary of defense predicted that "asymmetric warfare will be the mainstay of the contemporary battlefield for some time. . . . Success will be less a matter of imposing one's will and more a function of shaping behavior—of friends, adversaries, and most importantly, the people in between." That was what we finally did in Vietnam, he said, however uncomfortable it might be to bring up that war, under General Creighton Abrams, who brought all the multiple agencies involved into alignment, "all of *us* on one side and the enemy on the other." By the time American troops "were pulled out," Abrams had "helped pacify most of the hamlets in South Vietnam."

He had reversed the fortunes of war and the mistakes of his predecessor, General William Westmoreland, and Westmoreland's losing strategy of "search and destroy," and provided the intellectual platform for a counterinsurgency plan. Nowhere had a top leader before Gates explained it in such detail. The argument was readily accepted by an unusual "coalition" of neocons and "liberals" who peopled the Washington think tanks and moved back and forth between downtown D.C. and across the river at the Pentagon. Gates saw himself as both a witness to and presiding over this developing strategy.

In Afghanistan the military has recently brought in professional anthropologists as advisors. The *New York Times* reported on the work of one of them, who said, "I'm frequently accused of militarizing anthropology. But we're really anthropologizing the military."

And it is having a very real impact. The same story told of a village that had just been cleared of the Taliban. The anthropologist pointed out to the military officers that there were more widows than usual, and that the sons would feel compelled to

take care of them—possibly by joining the insurgency, where
many of the fighters are paid. So American officers began a job
training program for the widows.[34]

The dream candidate was about to become the counterinsurgent
president who depended more on Bob Gates than any other foreign
policy adviser. But the decision to surge in Afghanistan had already
been foretold—if anyone had been listening carefully. The shift to
a counterinsurgency strategy by George Bush—a choice forced, of
course, by the debacle Iraq had turned into—had become the guiding star. Secretary of State Condoleezza Rice explained all this to
the policy-making readers of *Foreign Affairs*. "In these pages in
2000," she wrote, "I decried the role of the United States, in particular the U.S. military, in nation building. In 2008, it is absolutely
clear that we will be involved in nation building for years to come.
But it should not be the U.S. military that has to do it. Nor should
it be a mission that we take up only after states fail."[35]

The real reason why the United States had to take up this burden, it turns out, was the unstoppable progress of globalization. "As
globalization strengthens some states," explained Rice, "it exposes
and exacerbates the failings of many others—those too weak or
poorly governed to address challenges within their borders and
prevent them from spilling out and destabilizing the international
order. In this strategic environment, it is vital to our national security that states be willing and able to meet the full range of their
sovereign responsibilities, both beyond their borders and within
them."[36]

When Barack Obama became president, his liberal critics
complained that he had abandoned his original positions and adopted most of Bush's foreign policy positions. His outlook fitted
Rice's analysis, albeit without her rearguard defense of the Iraq War.
As she put it: "This story is still being written, and will be for many
years to come. Sanctions and weapons inspections, prewar intelligence and diplomacy, troop levels and postwar planning—these are
all important issues that historians will analyze for decades. But
the fundamental question that we can ask and debate now is, Was

removing Saddam from power the right decision? I continue to believe that it was."[37]

What, then, was the primary lesson of the war for Obama? That the United States had to be prepared for an age of nation building, and that simply breaking up a dangerous conspiracy or axis of evil was not enough. For Obama, as he moved from war protester to presidential candidate to White House occupant, the problem became how to get beyond his role as Iraq dissenter and stay on track with Bob Gates and the new icon of counterinsurgency General David Petraeus—a very different direction than most of his supporters had ever imagined. It proved a complicated business.

2

AFGHANISTAN SHORTCHANGED

Now let me be clear. None of this will be easy. The struggle against violent extremism will not be finished quickly, and it extends well beyond Afghanistan and Pakistan. It will be an enduring test of our free society, and out leadership in the world. And unlike the great power conflicts and clear lines of division that defined the twentieth century, our effort will involve disorderly regions, failed states, diffuse enemies.
—President Barack Obama, "The Way Forward in Afghanistan and Pakistan," speech at West Point, December 1, 2009

To all appearances, the new president seemed headed on a course toward nation building in Afghanistan. The reappointment of Bob Gates was seen as a follow-up to Obama's preelection pledge to send three brigades to shore up American forces there. These developments had been greeted with something less than enthusiasm by the supporters of his 2002 speech, but they "had no place else to go," as the pundits put it. Yet this commitment—outlined in his West Point speech near the end of 2009—was not rock solid, but in fact a temporizing balancing act to test how well Hamid Karzai's government could hold up its end of the arrangement. Looking back, it almost seems COIN's rise and fall passed in a display that lasted less than a Fourth of July fireworks show.

The president's speech to West Point cadets deserved, and received, a lot of press scrutiny nevertheless, for it was thought to be the culmination of a debate that had gone on for months, ever since General Stanley McChrystal's review of the Afghan situation "leaked" to the *Washington Post* in September. But the debates continued and, as they did, more questions were raised than answered. Before the speech there were rumors that Gates and Petraeus were ready to resign if the president turned down his field commander's request for large numbers of new troops to implement a counterinsurgency strategy. Afterward there were questions about sending more troops but putting a time limit on the Afghan surge, as he had said the troops would start coming home after eighteen months.

Other presidents had often used uncertainty to their advantage, but Obama had come into office carrying on his back a heavy load of specific promises, and that made things much more difficult for him. He had promised to shut down CIA "black sites" where suspected terrorists were held. He kept that promise. But he had also pledged to shut down Guantánamo, which, along with Abu Ghraib's history of abuses, was characterized in the media as a prime indicator of whether Obama would make a clean break with the Bush policies pursued under the cover of the 2001 Authorization to use Military Force and the subsequent rulings out of the Justice Department's Office of Legal Counsel in 2002 authored by John Yoo, whose interpretation of the president's power to deal with prisoners taken in the global war on terror (as it was being called) clashed with common understandings of the Geneva Conventions on treatment of POWs.

Obama issued an executive order two days after delivering his inaugural address that called for Guantánamo to be shut down within a year, beginning with speedy reviews of the 241 detainees then being held there. But Republicans who had been open to arguments in favor of the closing—even George Bush had talked about closing down the facility—turned away and made the issue a loser for the administration. The worst moment came when the White House sought to arrange for a secret transfer and integration of seventeen Uighurs of Chinese extraction into a northern Virginia community of Uighurs—a plan that had been approved at the end of the Bush administration. The *Washington Post* reported on what happened next: "Before the plane could leave Cuba, word leaked to Rep. Frank R. Wolf that Guantanamo detainees were on their way to his district in Northern Virginia. Wolf, a Republican, had not been briefed on the matter by the White House, despite his history of defending the Uighur community in his district, and was infuriated by the move." He faxed a letter to the White House and released it to the news media, declaring that the "American people cannot afford to simply take your word that these detainees, who were captured training in terrorist camps, are not a threat if released into our communities."[1]

It was a taste of things to come. From that moment on, the administration backed off, citing the pressing need to enact health legislation. But the *Post*'s investigation revealed that the real problem was a lack of coordination and an unwillingness to challenge congressional opposition, which after the Uighur debacle included many Democrats as well. It was perhaps not surprising, then, that the West Point speech encountered similar criticisms as the sort of mishmash that could be expected from an administration unable to make up its mind about what it really wanted to accomplish in Afghanistan.

The Early Decisions

Obama had pledged during the campaign to send more troops to Afghanistan. But had he really given thought to what a counterinsurgency strategy would entail? After a meeting in Canada with other defense ministers with troops in Afghanistan—including the defense minister of Estonia, which had sent 150 troops—Secretary Gates said that Afghanistan needed a surge. The purpose of sending additional forces, however, would be to shield the Afghan elections scheduled for August against efforts to disrupt the process. "The notion that things are out of control in Afghanistan or that we're sliding toward a disaster, I think, is far too pessimistic," Gates said. The Canadian defense minister wondered why Obama wasn't knocking on the door of other NATO countries not present at the meeting. Gates reiterated that the American mission was to protect a "freely elected" government against the threat to elections. "This isn't our war, necessarily."[2]

It was a somewhat ambivalent answer, to say the least. Had Gates gone back on his own commitment to a counterinsurgency strategy? Close observers were puzzled. In congressional testimony before the election he questioned the Afghan commander's call for additional troops: "Are we better off channeling resources into building and expanding the size of the Afghan national army as quickly as possible as opposed to a much larger western footprint in a country that has never been hospitable to foreigners, regardless of why they are there."[3] Gates even expressed doubts about the long-term outcome in Iraq, and warned that the greatest threat to American security "was in western Pakistan," where al Qaeda and Taliban fighters plotted attacks against Afghanistan and "against the United States and other western countries." And after Obama took office, Gates said he would be "deeply skeptical" of any further troop increases, again repeating his warning that unless the Afghan police and national army took the lead, there were greater problems ahead. "My worry is that the Afghans come to see us as part of their problem rather than part of their solution, then we are lost." The idea of exporting democracy to Afghanistan he dismissed as a perfectionist illusion.

> This is going to be a long slog, and frankly, my view is that we need to be very careful about the nature of the goals we set for ourselves in Afghanistan. If we set ourselves the objective of creating some sort of central Asian Valhalla over there, we will lose, because nobody in the world has that kind of time, patience and money.[4]

Gates almost seemed, in these comments, to be abandoning much of the rationale for counterinsurgency, which he had embraced in other statements. There were several possible reasons for the apparent contradiction. Perhaps he had looked down the road a second time, saw disaster ahead, and thought he had been too ready to credit Pentagon optimists who said a "clear, hold, and build" strategy—one in which the enemy threat is cleared, the area is held free of enemies, and local democratic institutions are built—could be achieved in Afghanistan with a lot more troops and a little more patience. Whatever the reason, Gates had moved to the "show me" position, willing to consider all options.

But there were those on the COIN side who stood ready with backbone implants for waverers harboring the slightest doubts about the American capacity to succeed—and the supposed disasters that loomed ahead for the faint of heart. Not surprisingly, as he did at the outset of every administration, former secretary of state Henry Kissinger stepped forward to offer his take, projecting a dark vision reminiscent of the "domino thesis" that once held policy makers mesmerized for almost a generation in Vietnam. "Victory for the Taliban in Afghanistan would give a tremendous shot in the arm to jihadism globally—threatening Pakistan with jihadist takeover and possibly intensifying terrorism in India. . . . Russia, China and Indonesia, which have all been targets of jihadist Islam, could also be at risk."[5]

At risk for what, exactly? Kissinger did not talk about specific dangers if this or that was not done, nor did he argue for a nationwide cleansing operation that some counterinsurgency advocates believed was the only meaningful way to eliminate a terrorist threat like another 9/11. "Gen. David Petraeus has argued that, reinforced by the number of American forces he has recommended, he should be able to control the 10 percent of Afghan territory, where, in his words, 80 percent of the military threat originates. This is the region where the 'clear, hold and build' strategy that had success in Iraq is particularly applicable."[6]

Leave 90 percent of Afghanistan alone for al Qaeda to roam at will? Where did that get anyone? Doomsday statements to boost sagging support for the war inside the government and among opinion makers were no help at all. How would it be possible to eliminate the terrorist threat unless all Afghan territory was under tight control by the friendly government the United States had set up in Kabul? Obama must already have been thinking of an alternative to taking on such a burden. Finding it difficult to articulate a doable strategic vision, policy makers drifted from rostrum to rostrum, seeking to satisfy all audiences that there actually were "metrics" being developed to measure "progress." More and more the new president's 2007 promise to eliminate al Qaeda strongholds in the "wild frontier of our globalized world" challenged his advisers (and his critics) to show how counterinsurgency provided answers to any of the questions that most concerned the nation.

There was Richard Holbrooke's view that the answer was not military—or at least not solely military. Within days of taking office, Obama appointed Holbrooke, a diplomatic veteran with counterinsurgency credentials that went back to Vietnam, and more recently an architect of peace accords in the Balkans, as his special representative to oversee the implementation of a new Afghan policy. Queried at a press conference about how to tell when victory in Afghanistan had been achieved, Holbrooke said that victory in the purely military sense had never been in the cards. Surrounded by ten newly appointed aides he had brought along to demonstrate interagency cooperation in the new Afghan project, Obama's special representative declared that, ultimately, success would reveal itself as in a Supreme Court justice's comment about pornography: "We'll know it when we see it."[7]

The more statements there were about the stakes in Afghanistan and the likely outcome, the greater the confusion. A year later Holbrooke seconded an offer Afghan president Hamid Karzai made to insurgent groups to sever ties to al Qaeda, forswear violence, and accept the Afghan constitution in exchange for an opportunity to play a role in the country's future. "If they are willing to accept the red lines and come in from the cold, there has to be a place for them," the special representative told reporters at a press briefing.[8] This was identical to the offer Lyndon Johnson's national security adviser Walt W. Rostow had once made to Vietnam insurgents, to quiet growing rumbles of dissent at home when prospects for "victory" vanished from sight under the jungle canopy beyond the rice paddies. And it had about the same chance of success.

Then there was Bruce Riedel's vision. For the moment, he seemed to have the president's ear more often than Holbrooke, who became (and wanted to become) the voice of "Vietnam past" in the Oval Office meetings. A long-term CIA expert who had advised the White House for several years on Middle East issues, Riedel had recently written a book, *The Search for Al Qaeda*. Obama asked Riedel to come up with a new plan for the region. If he looked closely at Riedel's book, however, he would see that it argued against itself at points. On one hand, Riedel wrote, al Qaeda constituted a serious threat to Pakistan and its nuclear arsenal, as well as a dangerous presence in countries around the world; on the other hand, he said, only a small splinter faction enjoyed support among Muslims.

To defeat al Qaeda would require a complete change of mission in Afghanistan, Riedel argued, involving military, political, and especially economic aid, something on the order of the Marshall Plan for Europe after World War II. And yet success was not really so far away, Riedel insisted, despite those who worried it would take decades. Not so, unless the United States pursued policies like those it had in Iraq: "More blunders like Iraq and more prison camps like Abu Ghraib and Guantanamo Bay can only help al Qaeda." "At the end of the day, al Qaeda is not Nazi Germany," said Riedel, "Imperial Japan, or the Soviet Union. It is a relatively small organization that can be defeated by wise and smart policy. Though it is responsible for the worst day save one in U.S. history, its demise should not take decades to achieve."[9]

His confidence persuaded Obama to put Afghanistan on a fast track to stability with its assurance that getting at al Qaeda's top leadership was the key, even though the Marshall Plan stuff might take a little longer. Riedel presented his new strategy paper to President Obama on board Air Force One flying to California. Counterinsurgency talked about eliminating breeding grounds for insurrection, often referred to as "draining the swamp," but that was an inappropriate image for Afghanistan's mountains and arid terrain. Riedel's version skipped that step and talked about the need for holding on to Kabul. Afghanistan was a symbol, said Riedel in an interview on PBS NewsHour. "If they can defeat us in Afghanistan, they will trumpet that this is the second superpower that they have defeated in the same place. It will have enormous resonance throughout the Islamic world."[10]

Riedel's emphasis on global implications, Kissinger style, of the struggle turned local conditions into a side issue of the clash of civilizations. Yet Riedel pooh-poohed Afghanistan's reputation as a graveyard of empires. It was a myth that Alexander the Great had failed there; he had established Kandahar (ironically now a strong-hold of the Taliban/Pashtun insurgency). Neither had the British failed. It was only the Russians who had failed. Riedel saw no option for the president except a "bold gamble" to rescue the war from eight years of neglect by George Bush.

> If the situation a year from now is not moving in the right direction, then Obama will face the same tough options he has looked at since his inauguration. He knows he can't cut and run. That would give al-Qaeda a world-changing victory, threaten the stability of both Afghanistan and Pakistan as well as India and vastly increase the threat to the American homeland from a larger terrorist base. The future of NATO itself will be in doubt.[11]

Despite its almost blithe assurances that Afghanistan was no Herculean task, Riedel's white paper for Obama on U.S. policy toward Afghanistan and Pakistan, made public on March 27, 2009, was loaded with these dire predictions. A clue to the confusion it harbored could be found in its introduction, where Riedel inverted the usual priority accorded to America's enemies, placing "the Taliban and related organizations" ahead of al Qaeda, now downgraded to a related organization. But why the change? The Taliban had not launched the 9/11 attacks on the World Trade Center and the Pentagon, yet here it became the first objective of the war, even though the "core goal" still must be to "disrupt, dismantle, and defeat al Qaeda and its safe havens in Pakistan, and to prevent their return to Pakistan or Afghanistan."[12]

What stands out about Riedel's efforts to clarify the issues in the Afghan War—after all the toing and froing—was that the war still lacked a clear strategic vision, resting on a cloudy set of contradictory assertions. The paper's recommendations could be read either as support for a counterterrorist effort to prevent al Qaeda's "return" or as a counterinsurgency strategy for securing Kabul's total victory over the Taliban and extending its rule across the land from East to West. Reconciling these divergent attack plans proved a daunting challenge.

As these gaps in logic opened a vast and yawning gulf, Obama turned more and more to CIA veteran John Brennan for answers. Brennan offered a different plan, one involving drone attacks, but the counterinsurgency advocates were far from finished and resisted drone attacks as unproductive and, worse, a leading cause of surging anti-Americanism. For a time (quite a while) the debate was a stand-off, with each side getting some—but not all—of what it wanted.

President Obama liked the idea of drones and hankered for some clear indication of the direction he should go. Classified briefings he received within days of his election from Brennan and Vice Admiral Mike McConnell revealed to him the "deepest secrets" of the intelligence community—the inner workings of the covert drone program. McConnell stressed the duplicity of the Pakistani intelligence service, the ISI, in aiding the Taliban as a supposed counterweight to Indian or Iranian influence in Afghanistan. But Brennan and Obama took to each other instantly: Obama had found his sounding board for quiet philosophical discussions about taking responsibility for life-and-death decisions. Terrorism dominated their first conversation, with Brennan speaking plainly of his unsentimental view about using hard power against terrorists when appropriate. They agreed, however, that the mow-them-down approach was useless and counterproductive in the situation confronting the United States in the present and in the likely future of American warfare.[13]

Obama was so impressed with Brennan's perspicuity that he wanted him for his CIA director, but, writes Daniel Klaidman, as soon as his name surfaced, "left-wing bloggers railed against him for his supposed associations with the Bush administration's enhanced interrogation program," and the nomination was dropped. The way Klaidman puts it, "the left-wing bloggers" were the source of trouble, not really anything in Brennan's record. However that may be, even though there was disagreement about drones within Obama's inner circle of advisers, the president kept him close by inside the White House as special adviser on counterterrorism, where he "would come to have unrivaled influence with the president on matters of national security."[14]

In some ways this episode prefigured Obama's entire first term. He listened to Bruce Riedel, communed with John Brennan, and delivered contradictory policy statements. Rather than work from his base, as Republicans did with theirs, moreover, the Obama White House complained of unreasonable "left-wing" demands, thereby stigmatizing a large body of supporters, and supplying ammunition to Obama's critics that would—whether the White House realized it or not—come back to haunt him on a whole range of domestic issues as well. Obama made his commitment to Brennan as his chief terrorism adviser knowing he was a drone advocate even before he had had an opportunity to review with other advisers the legal, moral, and practical questions that accompanied such a decision. What the president-elect took away from those first conversations with Brennan and McConnell were only the advantages of drones: fewer casualties, less need for more troops to dig out an enemy fighter, and—the strongest selling point of all—a way to strike at the Taliban and al Qaeda leadership inside the frontiers of an ambiguous ally, Pakistan, and eventually even to chase down presumed terrorist inspirers in Yemen and other places. Without an open discussion of drones, however, Obama and Brennan fostered a deceptive aspect to the new administration's approach that did not provide space for serious discussions on the core issues of national security, including the problem of blowback.

The first instance of serious disagreement about the wisdom of using drones surfaced quickly inside the circle of Petraeus advisers in an op-ed article by David Kilcullen and Andrew McDonald Exum, "Death from Above, Outrage Down Below." Drone missions had steadily grown in the early months of the new administration, they wrote. From September 2008 to March 2009 alone, "C.I.A. operatives launched more than three dozen strikes."[15]

The direct pinpointing of CIA responsibility was part of Kilcullen and Exum's argument that the American mission was being undercut from within the White House. They argued that while it was easier to kill some enemy leaders using the drones, and certainly less costly in terms of American casualties, the tactic was sure to backfire and very likely increase the number of insurgents, plus spread the infection to other countries.

> First, the drone war has created a siege mentality among Pakistani civilians. This is similar to what happened in Somalia in 2005 and 2006, when similar strikes were employed against the forces of the Union of Islamic Courts. While the strikes did kill individual militants who were the targets, public anger over the American show of force solidified the power of extremists. The Islamists' popularity rose and the group became more extreme, leading eventually to a messy Ethiopian military intervention, the rise of a new regional insurgency and an increase in offshore piracy.
>
> While violent extremists may be unpopular, for a frightened population they seem less ominous than a faceless enemy that wages war from afar and often kills more civilians than militants.[16]

What was remarkable here, although largely unnoticed in media commentary after the article appeared, is that the authors had written a piece that broke completely with the self-justifying explanation of the need for a war on terror—"they hate us for our freedoms"—to discuss what we might be doing to incur such anger. That had been forbidden territory after 9/11. Here as well was a sharp-edged controversy wrapped inside the larger controversy, for using the CIA to manage and direct the attacks was questionable under the international rules of warfare. The debate grew more confusing as it went on, as the defeated Republican candidate John McCain used his first speech on foreign policy since the election to decry counterterrorism advocates for giving up on nation building: "Some suggest it is time to scale back our ambitions in Afghanistan—to give up on nation-building and instead focus narrowly on our counterterrorism objectives, by simply mounting operations aimed at killing or capturing terrorist leaders and destroying their networks."[17]

New CIA director Leon Panetta went after Kilcullen and Exum as well as McCain. There was really no alternative to drones, he said, in his first speech after being confirmed by the Senate. "Very frankly, it's the only game in town in terms of confronting and trying to disrupt the Al Qaeda leadership," especially compared to other American military operations such as the "attacks from F-16s and others that go into these areas which do involve a tremendous amount of collateral damage."[18]

Counterinsurgency Wins the First Toss

In March 2009, when he approved the Riedel white paper's recommendations and ordered seventeen thousand additional troops to Afghanistan, Obama told the nation his goal was to disrupt the al Qaeda leadership. Afghanistan faced an "increasingly perilous" situation, the president said. After so many years of being misled about the war there, the American people deserved a "straightforward answer" to the question of why our men and women "still fight and die there." The al Qaeda terrorists who planned the 9/11 attacks were now in Pakistan as well as Afghanistan. If Kabul fell to the Taliban—or if the Afghan government "allows al Qaeda to go unchallenged—that country will again be a base for terrorists who want to kill as many of our people as they possibly can."[19] He did not mention drone warfare.

Despite Obama's promise of a "straightforward answer," the constant interweaving of the Taliban and al Qaeda in policy statements did little to clarify what the war was about. There was Obama's assertion that it was about keeping al Qaeda from enjoying a base inside Afghanistan. For others, the war was a crusade to prevent the Taliban from coming to power and setting back Afghan women's rights. For still others, it was about the very survival of NATO as an effective instrument for combating threats to the international order. And then there was the underlying fear that an Afghanistan under Taliban rule would unsettle Pakistan to the extent that the latter's government might fall, increasing the danger that Pakistan's nuclear weapons could fall into the hands of terrorists.[20]

Theoretically (or even practically), therefore, it was perfectly possible, given Obama's description of the "border region" between

Afghanistan and Pakistan as "the most dangerous place in the world," to defeat the Afghan Taliban completely without eliminating the terrorist threat. Besides that border region, moreover, there were many other places where al Qaeda could set up camp, such as Yemen—where months later Washington would send more drones to attack supposed terrorist strongholds. The neglect of those possibilities would prove to be a major issue in coming years.

We were not in Afghanistan to dictate that country's future, the president insisted in the spring of 2009, though he could not help mentioning the fate of women and girls if the Taliban won. What was still unclear was what would happen if al Qaeda was totally destroyed. Would the United States continue to fight until the Taliban had no chance of imposing its extremist views on issues of women's rights? Leaving that unanswered, Obama turned to Pakistan, announcing a new aid package for Islamabad. It would not be a blank check: "Pakistan must demonstrate its commitment to rooting out al Qaeda and the violent extremists within its borders." If necessary, the United States would take unilateral action. "And we will insist that action be taken—one way or another—when we have intelligence about high-level terrorist targets."

He knew, he said, that the campaign would not succeed with bullets and bombs alone. While al Qaeda offered the people of Pakistan "nothing but destruction," "we stand for something different." In addition to a foreign aid program that included funds for roads and schools and hospitals, plus the seventeen thousand additional troops, the American emphasis would be on training security forces. The Iraq War's need for funds had prevented this action from being taken earlier. "We will accelerate our efforts to build an Afghan Army of 134,000 and a police force of 82,000 . . . and increases in Afghan forces may very well be needed as our plans to turn over security responsibility to the Afghans go forward." This was all part of a program to advance security, opportunity, and justice not just in Kabul but "from the bottom up in the provinces."

For the time being, at least, counterinsurgency had been given its opportunity. Again using a reference to current counterinsurgency theories, essentially those pushed hard by David Kilcullen, the president said there was an "uncompromising core of the Taliban" that must be met with force and defeated. But there were also those who had "taken up arms because of coercion, or simply for a price," and who must be given an option to choose a different, better course. That was why it was necessary to work with leaders in every province. As their ranks dwindled, an enemy that had nothing to offer but terror and repression would be further isolated. "And we will continue to support the basic human rights of all Afghans—including women and girls." Then, in a vague final gesture toward skeptics, especially so-called realists, the president promised that, "going forward, we will not blindly stay the course." Instead, the United States would set clear metrics to measure progress and hold itself accountable.

> We'll consistently assess our efforts to train Afghan Security Forces, and our progress in combating insurgents. We will measure the growth of Afghanistan's economy, and its illicit narcotics production. And we will review whether we are using the right tools and tactics to make progress towards accomplishing our goals.[21]

Strikingly absent was any significant reference to what role the Karzai government—or a potential successor regime—would have in these assessments. The United States might claim not to be interested in dictating the future of the country, but Obama's list of American initiatives left very little to Afghan self-determination in the present—and for some time to come. The review the president promised to undertake in the next few months was only about the "right tools and tactics to make progress towards accomplishing our goals." Despite the counterinsurgency rhetoric employed here, Obama had left his military options open, and was cautiously preparing the way for greater use of, and justification for, drones inside Pakistan and other countries. Foreign policy in the new administration seemed to be determined to cover all bets, in the hope that one or more would pay off big.

A Brief Season of Optimism

On March 29, 2009, Secretary of Defense Gates went on the Sunday morning news show hosted by Fox News' Chris Wallace. Although this was enemy territory for Obama administration figures, Wallace had also asked difficult questions of Bush's vice president, Dick Cheney, and his insights were often like pointed daggers. This time he began with a question about the differences between Bush's policy and the new Obama policy. After all was said and done, were there any real differences about the expected outcome in Afghanistan? Had Obama narrowed the mission or not? Gates stumbled a bit at the outset: "I think the—the near-term objectives have been narrowed. I think our long-term objective still would be to see a flourishing democracy in Afghanistan." But for the immediate future the focus was making headway against the Taliban, reversing its momentum, really going after al Qaeda.[22]

Would seventeen thousand additional troops really be enough, Wallace asked, to mount an effective counterinsurgency strategy? Gates's response was a study in ambiguity.

> We have fulfilled all of the requirements that General McKiernan has put down for 2009, and my view is there's no need to ask for more troops, ask the president to approve more troops, until we see how the troops we—he already has approved are in there, how they are doing, what the Europeans have done. And we will be reviewing that come the end of the year . . . About a year from now we need to reevaluate this strategy and see if we're making progress.

Wallace zeroed in on the ambiguity in the message Obama had delivered two days earlier and in what Gates was now saying.

> WALLACE: The commitment to defeat the Taliban and al Qaeda—
>   is that subject to review?
> GATES: I don't think so.
> WALLACE: That is the commitment.

GATES: Certainly, to defeat al Qaeda and—and make sure that
  Afghanistan and western Pakistan are not safe havens for them.

Wallace zeroed in on another crucial matter: what about reports
that Pakistani intelligence had provided the Taliban and other extremists with money, supplies, and even tips on what the coalition
planned to do next? Gates did not deny the accusation, and indeed
elaborated on his personal contact with Pakistani agents who had
had contacts with "these groups" during the Soviet occupation of
Afghanistan. His mission then had been to see that weapons got
sent to the right people to use against the Russians, he told Wallace. Pakistani eagerness to cooperate always had much to do with
the long-term question of which country would have a dominant
influence in Afghanistan: Pakistan or India, or possibly Iran. So
Pakistani behavior was partly a hedge against what would happen if
the Americans walked away. The United States needed to convince Islamabad that it would be there as a steadfast ally and "that
they don't need the hedge."
  Were America's allies willing to support all these goals? Obama
had alluded to the sacrifices the allies were making, but he could
not hide the truth that the "coalition," as it was called, was largely
an Anglo-American affair, with token contributions from others—
just enough to portray such support on Capitol Hill as an international consensus for the war. But Wallace was not having any of
that feel-good stuff: "Have we given up on the idea of getting our
allies to send more combat troops to fight alongside the U.S. in
Afghanistan?"
  "No, we haven't," Gates protested. "I think some of our allies will
send additional forces there to provide security before the August
elections in Afghanistan." He realized, of course, that such an answer was unlikely to impress Wallace or any of his viewers, and
added, "I think what we're really interested in for the longer term
from our partners and the allies is helping us with this civilian surge
in terms of experts in agriculture, and finance, and governance and
so on to help us improve the situation inside Afghanistan, give a
sense of forward progress on the part of the Afghan people."

If there was one word American policy makers could never stop repeating, it was "progress." Just like their predecessors in the Bush administration, Obama administration officials constantly talked about "progress," or used the phrase "metrics of progress." After the Wallace interview with Gates, there was the equally important session *Philadelphia Inquirer* columnist and foreign policy expert Trudy Rubin had with General David Petraeus, then head of Central Command, whose oversight stretches from Lebanon to Pakistan's border with India. She began with a tough question about the new policy: why should Americans support it? It had to do with al Qaeda, the general replied, which had established itself in the border areas between Pakistan and Afghanistan. Al Qaeda and its extremist Islamist allies, including the Taliban, posed "an ever-more-serious threat to Pakistan's very existence." What stands out in the general's answers is the indeterminate nature of the enemy.[23]

Sending seventeen thousand troops, said Rubin, did not constitute a surge. Replied Petraeus, "You don't have a raging insurgency in every part of Afghanistan. Seventy percent of the violence is in 10 percent of the districts." Hence it was not necessary to have the ratio of troops to population called for by counterinsurgency rules of thumb. But, insisted Rubin, hadn't the commander in Afghanistan, General David McKiernan, asked for ten thousand more troops over and above the seventeen thousand? Petraeus asserted that more were not needed, adding that there should be assessments made over time. "What struck me most about my conversation with Petraeus," commented Rubin, "was the complexity of the AfPak project he described."

Petraeus's prediction about troop needs could have proven embarrassing, though few would recall his words later, when Obama called for an additional thirty thousand soldiers to complete the job. What did arise, again, was the troubling matter of defining the enemy. The issue was neatly framed during a question-and-answer session with Secretary Gates some weeks afterward, where the first question was about the new president's first hundred days, the Franklin D. Roosevelt New Deal standard by which all later presidents were judged by the press. "I think he's doing very well" given all the challenges that he faced when he took the oath of office, Gates replied. The subject quickly turned to Afghanistan and rumors about possible negotiations with Taliban leaders. A reporter noted that Gates had said that "perhaps even the majority of people fighting, though not the leadership, might be reconcilable." There were also stories of American military officers making such approaches. Was there an effort being made to draw away parts of the Taliban from the central leadership? Gates replied, "Based on the information available to us, some considerable proportion of the Taliban essentially do this as a job. They get paid for it. And if alternative means of employment can be found, they probably could be fairly easily drawn away. And there is really no political agenda associated with it at all."[24]

Within a few weeks the American commander in Afghanistan, General David McKiernan, was out—a change that Petraeus wanted—and had been replaced by Petraeus's candidate, General Stanley McChrystal, who was given a fourth star and put in charge of turning things around. This was definitely not an Obama "take-charge" moment, in which the president showed the Pentagon who was boss. It had been rumored for some time that McKiernan would be replaced, as observers noted that Gates had little tolerance for what he considered inadequate performance by subordinates. When Gates traveled to Kabul to tell McKiernan the bad news personally, the secretary said to reporters without further elaboration, "It's time for new leadership and fresh eyes." Behind the scenes, however, Pentagon officials talked about how McKiernan had gotten stuck in old thinking as the military moved to the new counterinsurgency paradigm.

One of the marks against McKiernan was that he had asked for more troops than the seventeen thousand Obama approved upon announcing the new policy. Apparently it was what McKiernan might do with those troops that mattered, not the request itself. He was accused of not paying enough attention to training an Afghan army—presumably the backbone of the new Afghanistan state to be built to counterinsurgency specifications. In another sign of the times, a principal backer of McChrystal was retired general Jack

Keane—sometimes called the godfather of the Iraq surge. Keane had gotten to know Secretary of State Hillary Clinton during her Senate years, and they got along famously. Meeting her early in the Obama administration, Keane bear-hugged his friend and then got straight to the point. Clinton had been saying that there was no use trying to build up a first-class army, but Keane frowned on such talk: "Don't let people tell you we can't do this." And as for whom he had in mind for such a task? McChrystal, who was, "without a doubt, the best candidate."[25]

McChrystal's reputation was built as a commander of the special forces team in Iraq, which used interrogations of prisoners to hunt down and kill al Qaeda leaders such as Abu Musab al-Zarqawi in 2006. Zarqawi was killed by a five-hundred-pound bomb in an air attack after McChrystal's unit discovered his hiding place. Defense secretary Donald Rumsfeld, joined by others such as British prime minister Tony Blair, had exulted in this achievement. The killing of Zarqawi, said Rumsfeld, eliminated "the leading terrorist in Iraq and one of the three senior al-Qaeda leaders worldwide." In a news conference after a NATO meeting, he said, "I think arguably over the last several years, no single person on this planet has had the blood of more innocent men, women and children on his hands than Zarqawi." For once, however, President Bush did not rush in with a "mission accomplished" moment, but greeted the news with a somber mien. "We can expect the terrorists and insurgents to carry on without him," Bush said in a Rose Garden statement, with several top aides standing by, including Vice President Cheney, national security adviser Stephen Hadley, and deputy chief of staff Karl Rove. "Yet the ideology of terror has lost one of its most visible and aggressive leaders."[26]

Bush's comment raised, however indirectly, the question of why McChrystal, "a renowned manhunter," was put "in charge of a population-centric counterinsurgency strategy."[27] For security reasons, little was known of McChrystal's previous history as commander of special operations in charge of units from all the services. That history was filled with shadowy doings, including black ops connected with a notorious interrogation center in Iraq known as Camp

Nama, where the military held suspected terrorists and refused to allow the Red Cross access. His most criticized action, however, resulted from the case of Corporal Pat Tillman. He was accused of abetting a cover-up of Tillman's death from "friendly fire" in order to create a heroic legend around the feel-good story of a National Football League player who volunteered in the aftermath of 9/11. Through perseverance the Tillman family ultimately discovered the truth, and McChrystal was reprimanded for his part in the deception. But getting Zarqawi was more important to the war effort, it was clear, and the general got his fourth star and sailed through congressional hearings on the Afghan command.[28]

According to one analysis of the firing of McKiernan and McChrystal's appointment, there were two main reasons—beyond the personal intervention of his sponsor, Petraeus—this was so easily accomplished. The first was his reputation for getting things done with the resources at hand. A retired Army officer and military commentator, Ralph Peters, said, "McChrystal will ask for more authority, not more troops." The second reason was that the Joint Chiefs of Staff expected McChrystal to take a firm stand with Afghan president Hamid Karzai about drug-running operations that funded the Taliban and about the thick atmosphere of corruption that hung over Kabul. Gates's press secretary, Geoff Morrell, enthused in an interview that McChrystal and his deputy commander were "champing at the bit" to get back on the front lines. "They're rested and raring to go," he said. "They understand the strategy. They're determined to win. They will do what is necessary to win."[29]

Gates had declared in an interview that the pace of the war had to change; now it would for certain. After Iraq, nobody was prepared for a long slog, "where it is not apparent we are making headway." "The troops are tired; the American people are pretty tired." Americans would have the patience to continue only if the new military approach began to move the conflict out of deadlock. "If we can show progress, and we are headed in the right direction, and we are not in a stalemate where we are taking significant casualties, then you can put more time on the Washington clock."[30]

Within a short time, however, the clock hands moved in the wrong direction. The seventeen thousand troops Obama sent were supposed to guarantee that the upcoming election in Afghanistan was held under circumstances ensuring not only that the Taliban would not intimidate voters but that Karzai would keep to his promise that the election would be fair and free. Instead, the presidential election in Afghanistan reeked of fraud, threatening stability within Afghanistan and worrying American policy makers. Even with his attempt to rig the results, Karzai still did not gain a majority, and there was a need for a run-off. At first Karzai, who had expected full backing from the United States and resented its neutral stance, refused to participate, declaring he had won. Obama had to send out a special emissary, Senator John Kerry, to persuade him otherwise. As matters turned out, however, there was no run-off, because the opposing candidate, Abdullah Abdullah, pulled out, declaring there could be no honest result under the prevailing conditions.

It was the fist bitter disappointment of the war for Obama. The administration's sense of the situation, commented an adviser, had been that the election would show "whether Afghanistan was taking a turn for the better or whether it was going in a downward trajectory." And another aide worried, "It's hard to say that we are sending your children off to fight and die for a guy who steals elections."[31] Karzai had enjoyed a good relationship with George Bush and frequent teleconferences with the president. Obama had stopped that, which the Afghan president interpreted to mean that he was no longer considered indispensable and could no longer count on unconditional support from the United States. But instead of making him more amenable to Washington's demands, this "tough love" made him all the more recalcitrant, as would become clear over the next several months.

Against this troubled background—reminiscent of the struggles with earlier American-imposed strong men, who often proved to be weaklings at crunch time or, conversely, unwilling to allow the United States to pull their strings when it wished—the first assessment of the new policy was due. Secretary Gates told interviewers that he wanted that assessment to be an honest endeavor. But he left himself plenty of room: "That is not to say we will accept all of their recommendations." Gates had insisted military commanders would have to try hard to convince him to fulfill any more requests for additional troops. Setting a date for McChrystal's report, therefore, was supposed to be a way of keeping control of the situation, but in the event it had the opposite effect. When McChrystal's sixty-six-page assessment arrived on Gates's desk at the end of August, it immediately flew out a Pentagon window to the front pages of the *Washington Post*. The White House saw in that maneuver a Pentagon plot to deprive the president of any real choice but to send more troops. That interpretation was too simple, however. It had not been McChrystal and his sponsors in the Pentagon who had outlined the full-scale plan to rebuild Afghanistan from the bottom up and to guarantee how Afghan women would be treated. The president's dilemma was largely of his own making, and when he came up against a blank wall, on the other side would be the drones.

The very first paragraph of the "Commander's Summary" of the report was meant as a stark warning, but what it did was perfectly capture the assumptions policy makers (and pro-war commentators in the media and think tanks) worked from, and the real costs a counterinsurgency strategy would exact.

The stakes in Afghanistan are high. NATO's Comprehensive Strategic Political Military Plan and President Obama's strategy to disrupt, dismantle, and eventually defeat al Qaeda and prevent their return to Afghanistan have laid out a clear path of what we must do. Stability in Afghanistan is an imperative; if the Afghan government falls to the Taliban—or has insufficient capacity to counter transnational terrorists—Afghanistan could again become a base for terrorism, with obvious implications for regional stability.[32]

Neither success nor failure could be taken for granted, the report continued, because Afghanistan faced a resilient and growing insurgency, while at the same time "a perception that our resolve is uncertain makes Afghans reluctant to align with us." Doubling down on previous strategies was no answer. The momentum of these intertwined threats required a new strategy to bring together all aspects of an "integrated civilian-military counterinsurgency campaign"—just, the author might have added, as outlined in the new Petraeus manual, which built on the "new" history of the Vietnam War. "If only Gen. Creighton Abrams had been allowed the time to finish the job" had now become the rallying cry for counterinsurgency enthusiasts about Afghanistan.

It seemed almost surreal. In this nearly invisible thread stretching across the decades from the Pentagon to think tanks and back again, *Afghanistan would prove that the Americans had actually prevailed in Vietnam.* The conflict in Afghanistan had become a war to redeem the greatest lost victory in American military history. Would Americans show the world that its mistakes in Vietnam would not be repeated?

There were two fights that had to be won, said McChrystal's report: a long-term struggle, which required patience and commitment, and a short-term fight. The latter was the one he worried most about. "Failure to gain the initiative and reverse insurgent momentum in the near term (next 12 months)—while Afghan security capacity matures—risks an outcome where defeating the insurgency is no longer possible." Even without a specific request for additional troops (as it turned out, that would come later), the report posited the need for many more American boots on the ground, perhaps as many as 80,000 additional military personnel. Keeping the top number that high was a strategy designed to take advantage of the "gulp factor"—once civilian policy makers got past the initial gulp, getting approval for a smaller number would be much easier. By highlighting as critical the next twelve months, the phrasing of McChrystal's report did appear to offer President Obama a little leeway to put a time limit on any surge. But such predictions about the capacity of the Afghans were more on the order of a sideshow barker's promises of astounding sights inside the tent than serious statements about the outlook for either the short-term or the long-term struggle.

On the other hand, McChrystal was candid about the difficulties of achieving an integrated counterinsurgency strategy in coalition warfare, which of course was another reason more troops from the allies could not satisfy the needs of a new strategy. In the past, in addition to the inherent problems of coalition warfare, the United States had run a strategy that "distances us—physically and psychologically—from the people we seek to protect," McChrystal said in the report. Tactical wins that caused civilian casualties or unnecessary collateral damage threatened strategic defeat. "The insurgents cannot defeat us militarily; but we can defeat ourselves."

Nor did the general shy away from talking about a problem that bedeviled any efforts to win over the population: the rampant corruption of the Afghan government, starting with the president's family. "The weakness of state institutions, malign actions of power-brokers, widespread corruption and abuse of power by various officials, and [the coalition's] own errors, have given Afghans little reason to support their government." The coalition "requires a credible program to offer eligible insurgents reasonable incentives to stop fighting and return to normalcy, possibly including the provision of employment and protection."[33]

George Packer, the *New Yorker*'s frequent in-depth commentator and a onetime supporter of the Iraq War, called the report an unsurprising document. While the noise in the Washington debate would be all about the troop increase question, its real emphasis was on developing a better approach to counterinsurgency—in essence, the "better" war the United States did not fight in Vietnam until it was too late. It was an impressive effort, Packer said, filled with self-criticism and fully cognizant of Karzai's great shortcomings, and consequently demonstrating a greater understanding of the situation than most journalists and academics had achieved. Packer himself was torn about the Afghan War, he said. On one hand, there was the question of whether Obama was more like JFK or Lyndon Johnson, with the former standing up at critical moments against the military's desire for a wider war in Vietnam and the latter paying no heed to warning signs. His comparison left out the roles of the advisers who would have pressured Kennedy, and who did press LBJ hard, such as McGeorge Bundy and Robert McNamara, but Packer was more troubled about other issues. "The McChrystal report is a shining example of intelligent military thinking—of the military's capacity for learning and self-transformation through the searing events of the past eight years. Its authors will have a right to feel a little bitter if it appears at the very moment when the political class has decided that it just doesn't work."[34]

Packer added in closing that the Obama administration had considered alternatives when it decided on the new strategy in March, and had rejected them. "Since then no one has made a persuasive case why [those alternatives] would work any better." One of Petraeus's advisers, David Kilcullen, made Packer's point another way, by positing the problem as having only two solutions, either getting out at once or doing it the right way. Having ruled out abandoning the fight in Afghanistan, he then said the worst option would be to compromise on the number of troops to send. "You either commit to D-Day and invade the continent or you get Suez. Half measures end up with Suez."[35]

Looking at the analysis made by Packer and Kilcullen is a good way to make the argument that Obama was not "jammed" by the Pentagon, as his defenders would later insist, but followed a neoliberal agenda from the beginning. Perhaps he had been trying to stave off the moment of decision. Now it was too late to turn back. Kilcullen's injection of the supposed analogy between D-Day and Suez was especially an almost perfect example of the abuse of history to make critical judgments about the future. It brimmed with "can do" salesmanship rather than a realistic understanding of the limitations of military power.

The Days Dwindle

The initial White House meeting to discuss the McChrystal report was held on September 13, 2009. Reports of what went on suggested there had been "a wholesale reconsideration of a strategy the president announced with fanfare six months ago." Vice President Joe Biden led the charge, questioning the premise of the counterinsurgency strategy in Afghanistan and offering instead the alternative of scaling back the overall American military presence to concentrate on a counterterrorism approach: "Rather than trying to protect the Afghan population from the Taliban, American forces would concentrate on strikes against Qaeda cells, primarily in Pakistan, using special forces, Predator missile attacks and other surgical tactics." Pentagon officials were worried, it was said, that President Obama might be having "buyer's remorse" after ordering twenty-one thousand troops there "within weeks of taking office before even settling on a strategy."[36]

The theatrics around the White House bull sessions on the Afghan War grew as the process drew out, allowing for plenty of speculation in the press. Hillary Clinton was quoted as saying that the military was using the "Goldilocks option"—a phrase that also had been invoked about the Vietnam War. One was not supposed to say anything about Vietnam, but that was inevitable as word leaked out about the president's reading of Gordon Goldstein's *Lessons in Disaster: McGeorge Bundy and the Path to War in Vietnam* (2008); revealing his choice of reading matter was aimed at showing that the president was aware of the slippery slopes on the Afghan mountains. Another portrayal of the debates put the onus on counterinsurgency advocates, in much the same manner as the argument that Afghanistan would redeem Vietnam. "It was clear to McChrystal, Petraeus, and all the other commanders that soon Afghanistan would be the only war in town," a White House adviser told David Sanger. "And so it was the last testing ground for counterinsurgency, and the last place where they could prove that this is the only strategy that would work."[37] But that was not really true—as the rapid growth of the secretive Special Operations Command (SOC) would demonstrate about war planning for the present and future.

Biden's position in the debate, which he held on to throughout the discussions until President Obama went to West Point on December 1 to announce he was sending an additional thirty thousand troops to Afghanistan, had been shaped in large part by the Afghan election debacle and other evidence that an essential element in the success of counterinsurgency was missing: a reliable and honest government in Kabul (a point also made by McChrystal). "Part of the reason you are seeing a hesitancy to jump deeper into the pool," Bruce Riedel observed, "is that they are looking to see if they can make lemonade out of the lemons we got from the Afghan election." Another leaked document, a cable from Ambassador Karl Eikenberry—a former military commander—in Kabul, briefly shook up the debate but did not have nearly the impact the McChrystal Report did. Eikenberry cabled the State Department on November 6, 2009.

Madame Secretary,

As we near the end of our deliberations on the way forward in Afghanistan, I would like to outline my reservations about a counterinsurgency strategy that relies on a large infusion of U.S. forces. I fully agree that the security situation in Afghanistan is serious and that additional troops will help reverse the worsening trends in areas where the troops are deployed. There is an unassailable logic to the argument that a robust counterinsurgency approach will yield measurable progress, at least in the security realm.

But I am concerned that we underestimate the risks of this expansion of our mission and that we have not fully studied every alternative. The proposed troop increase will bring vastly increased costs and an indefinite, large-scale U.S. military role in Afghanistan, generating the need for yet more civilians. An increased U.S. and foreign role in security and governance will increase Afghan dependency, at least in the near-term, and it will deepen the military involvement in a mission that most agree cannot be won solely by military means. Further, it will run counter to our strategic purposes of Afghanizing and civilianizing government functions here.

Perhaps the charts we have all seen showing the U.S. presence rising and then dropping off in coming years in a bell curve will prove accurate. It is more likely, however, that these forecasts are imprecise and optimistic. In that case, sending additional forces will delay the day when Afghans will take over, and make it difficult, if not impossible, to bring our people home on a reasonable timetable. Moreover, none of these charts displays dollar costs. Acknowledgement of the astronomical costs might illustrate the greater desirability of civilian alternatives now dismissed as too costly or not feasible.

Here are my reasons for this assessment:

1) President Karzai is not an adequate strategic partner. The proposed counterinsurgency strategy assumes an Afghan political leadership that is both able to take responsibility and to exert sovereignty in the furtherance of our goal—a secure, peaceful, minimally self-sufficient Afghanistan hardened against transnational groups. Yet Karzai continues to shun responsibility for any sovereign burden, whether defense, governance, or development. He and much of his circle do not want the U.S. to leave and are only too happy to see us invest further. They assume we covet their territory for a never-ending "war on terror" and for military bases to use against surrounding powers.[38]

From the outset, the top pro-surge participant in the debate was Secretary of State Hillary Clinton, who appeared to refer to Vice President Biden's position in an interview on PBS: "Some people say, 'Well, Al Qaeda's no longer in Afghanistan.' If Afghanistan were taken over by the Taliban, I can't tell you how fast Al Qaeda would be back in Afghanistan."[39]

No sooner had such reports filtered out of the initial discussion than Bob Woodward's article "McChrystal: More Forces or 'Mission Failure,'" along with the leak of McChrystal's report, appeared in the *Washington Post*. McChrystal rejected any inference that a rift had developed between the military and the White House. He welcomed the "fierce debate," he said. "A policy debate is warranted," he said in a telephone interview. "We should not have any ambiguities, as a nation or a coalition." It had been "whispered around the Pentagon" that he would resign if his recommendations were not accepted. No, he said, he was committed to whatever mission "Mr. Obama ultimately approved."[40]

Despite the general's assurances that he was committed to whatever mission was approved, he intervened from afar. After a speech in London he was asked if Vice President Biden's alternative could succeed. "The short answer is no," McChrystal replied. This brusque exchange set off another round of speculation, prompting Gates, who had held his own counsel during the early White House debates, to tell a gathering of army officers that the Pentagon would follow any strategy the president ordered: "Speaking for the Department of Defense, once the commander in chief makes his decisions, we will salute and execute those decisions faithfully and to the best of our ability." In addition to this pledge, the secretary warned that military and civilian advisers should provide "our best advice to the president candidly—but privately."[41]

Gates had played his cards exactly right, promising absolute loyalty, then shifting his position to the pro-surge side in the debate. Obama looked around for some way of limiting the mission before it became his albatross and weighed down both his domestic agenda and his legacy. Outside the White House, some of the original backers of the Iraq surge urged that the only way the United States could gain leverage over Karzai and force him to change his ways was by sending more troops.

> If the Afghan government were fully legitimate, there would be no insurgency. U.S. and international actions must aim to improve the Afghan government's ability to provide basic services such as security and dispute resolution nationwide, building the legitimacy of the government in Kabul sufficiently to dampen a large-scale insurgency. They must persuade and even compel Afghan leaders to stop activities that alienate the people and create fertile ground for insurgents.[42]

A more perfect definition of "social imperialism" could hardly be coined. Meanwhile, Gates had taken charge of the effort to find a way to satisfy both the president and his generals. Eventually he came up with a paper that the National Security Council fiddled with so as to be able to call it a "consensus" memo. The memo concluded that the United States should focus on diminishing the Taliban insurgency (but not attempting the more difficult task of completely destroy it), building up certain critical ministries, and transferring authority to Afghan security forces. Instead of forty thousand U.S. troops—McChrystal's magic number halfway between failure and success—he would get thirty thousand Americans and another ten thousand to be picked up from the NATO allies. Obama was not yet satisfied and declared that he wanted the whole process of the entrance and exit of U.S. troops speeded up. "I want this pushed to the left," he said referring to the bell curve on charts he had been shown. Turning to Petraeus, he said, "What I'm looking for is a surge. This has to be a surge."[43]

According to Jonathan Alter, author of *The Promise*, an insider's account of the first year of the Obama presidency, Hillary Clinton had a strong belief that the "reluctant Democratic Party should be dragged along into an expanded commitment," something that Biden's counterterrorism proposals specifically sought to avoid. She was, in many ways, a worthy successor to Madeleine Albright, with her conviction that America was the indispensable nation. Obama, meanwhile, had apparently changed the most. He had opposed the surge in Iraq, but now he knew he had been wrong. As he told Petraeus, "it was time to see if [the surge] could be applied in Afghanistan."[44]

What was it particularly that had given the Iraq surge a special place in American military, along with boosting Petraeus's reputation to the heights? Perhaps it was also a legend out of Vietnam: that if the enemy could be forced to fight a set-piece battle, the war could be won. Of course, that was not precisely counterinsurgency's way, but it was certainly part of the mystique attaching itself to successful generals—the "Ike" factor, going back to World War II. The French had tried the set piece once at Dien Bien Phu—with terrible results. An increase of American troops by thirty thousand in a country the size of Afghanistan with its very difficult terrain was hardly a likely testing place for either the set-piece scenario or, especially, the new and improved counterinsurgency strategy, as it came without a long-term commitment that would have implied constant mission creep and more troops—a situation Obama was desperate to avoid. And yet what most bothered the surge advocates about Biden's alternative strategy, when it came right down to it, was that Biden's proposal would not really extend or maintain America's influence in the region. The protection of Afghan women was highlighted, of course, as it always had been, going back to the March announcement of the new strategy and even earlier. Opposition to Biden was also expressed as a fear that if the Taliban triumphed in Afghanistan, that would somehow lead to the fall of the Pakistani government and let al Qaeda gain control of that country's nuclear arsenal. Here was a domino thesis for the Middle East to rival the Southeast Asian original.

Obama made his intentions clear when he announced that any alternative for leaving Afghanistan was off the table. His advisers took that to mean that military force as defined by counterinsurgency theories would lead the way, providing leverage to change Afghanistan in fundamental ways. National security adviser James Jones, a retired Marine general, had warned that counterinsurgency in rural areas would require large numbers of troops and cost a fortune, but—like Biden's concern that the end would never be in sight—Jones's fears went unaddressed except in Obama's effort to put a time limit of eighteen months on the commitment of new troops. Still, this new deadline was really only about "beginning" the transition to Afghan control.[45]

In a final go-round at the White House before he went to West Point, Obama confronted the major players in the discussion, extracting promises to the effect that a drawdown of American forces could be achieved in eighteen months. Biden came out of the final meeting to say that there would be an actual drawdown in July 2011. And the story grew that Obama's conversation with the military side justified the vice president's feeling that instead of being boxed in by the military, Obama had actually turned the tables. With these assurances in his pocket, the president addressed the cadets at West Point in a long speech during which many appeared to nod off. But, of course, they were not his real audience. His key point was that the Afghan front against terrorism had been under-resourced because of the war in Iraq—the wrong war—and hence there was a real danger the entire region would slide backward because of Taliban control, offering a space in which al Qaeda could once again "operate with impunity." Then the threat of terrorists reaching American shores would increase. This assertion was not really different from President Bush's insistence that Iraq had become the central front in the war on terror; only the name of the country had changed. Having built up the threat, Obama went off on a different tack: that the military had promised him it could all be brought under control within a few months.

> The 30,000 additional troops that I'm announcing tonight will deploy in the first part of 2010—the fastest possible pace—so that they can target the insurgency and secure key population centers. They'll increase our ability to train competent Afghan security forces, and to partner with them so that more Afghans can get into the fight. And they will help create the conditions for the United States to transfer responsibility to the Afghans.

In a strange sort of way, the speech echoed Richard Nixon's Vietnamization hopes for the survival of South Vietnam. That was not what Obama meant, obviously, but the idea that what had taken years to reach this point—years of Russian occupation, years of violent guerrilla war, followed by more years of civil war and the ruination of much of Afghanistan's infrastructure—could be put on the right road in eighteen months defied all serious reflection.

Not surprisingly, Obama aides rushed to media outlets to deny what most observers could see with one eye closed. Almost immediately, there were qualifications forthcoming in congressional testimony, with Gates and Petraeus given chances to "correct" impressions about "deadlines." The general asserted that withdrawals would be conditions-based—the usual code words for ignoring presidential rhetoric. "There's no timeline, no ramp, nothing like that," he said. "This doesn't trigger a rush to the exits. It triggers a beginning of transition to Afghan security forces and, over time, a beginning of transition to Afghan government elements as well."

The purpose of the president's stipulating a date for pulling out troops was to send a message of "resolve" along with a message of "urgency" to officials in both Afghanistan and the United States. A doubter might reply, "So what if the Taliban lies low and bides its time?" And there were plenty of doubters. Secretary Gates also responded to an inquiry from Senator Joseph Lieberman about the deadline "meaning an all at once withdrawal of our forces from Afghanistan" by denying the deadline was a deadline at all: "We're not just going to throw these guys into the swimming pool and walk away." Secretary Hillary Clinton threw in her two cents, echoing Gates: "I do not believe we have locked ourselves into leaving."[46] The congressional postscript was a fitting conclusion to a debate that had actually begun in 2002 when Barack Obama first challenged the rationale for a war in Iraq and embraced Afghanistan as the "good war." Another way of putting it would be to say that participants in the final deliberations claimed only that this was the day of the lesser evil. "There are no silver bullets," said Michele Flournoy, undersecretary of defense for policy. "We looked for them."[47]

But the Suez-obsessed David Kilcullen now predicted that if Obama set deadlines on a planned new troop increase in that country, he risked a major defeat: "I think this is a recipe for Dien Bien Phu in the Hindu Kush." Withdrawing American forces in July 2011, he added, would leave Afghanistan up for grabs. "People are clearing the decks for renewed civil war."[48] Kilcullen's conjuring up the French debacle at Dien Bien Phu was only one of several references to Vietnam ghosts that returned to walk in the Afghan mountains in recent years, stirring deep anxieties. Seizing on an even more disturbing Vietnam memory, McChrystal warned President Obama that the only alternative to sending more troops to Afghanistan was the dreaded "helicopter on the roof of the embassy."[49]

Obama's first year saw no outright disasters such as those Kennedy suffered with the Bay of Pigs fiasco, and there would be no second-year crisis to match anything like the Cuban missile crisis. But looming ahead were tests that, if less immediately dramatic, would be every bit as fateful. When McChrystal fell from grace less than a year later, the tortured process that had produced the Afghan surge became a desperate embrace of drone warfare with its unresolved implications—all put aside in the persistent belief Americans have in technological "breakthroughs" that eliminate political obstacles.

3

A TALE OF TWO SPEECHES

*The notion of American exceptionalism is as old as the writings of
Alexis de Tocqueville, the first analyst to describe the United States'
significant differences from European states. He pointed to its love affair
with liberty, its deep-seated commercialism, its revolutionary birth as
a "new nation" and its zeal for technological modernization sitting
alongside widespread religiosity.*

    —Jonathan Steele, *Ghosts of Afghanistan*

Lurking behind Obama's Afghan surge speech at West Point was
the problem of domestic support for a war that had dragged on in
the shadow of Iraq for almost a decade. Back in February 2009
Obama had promised he would end the American military role in
the Iraq War by bringing the troops home in a responsible fashion.
But he also echoed Kennedy's 1961 inaugural address with its ring-
ing message that America would pay any price to defend a friend or
defeat a foe. His Afghan plan, said Obama in this early preview of
his policy, was the best way to *increase* American influence across
the region. "Every nation and every group must know—whether
you wish America good or ill—that the end of the war in Iraq will
enable a new era of American leadership and engagement in the
Middle East. And that era has just begun."[1]

One need not doubt every word insofar as he thought ending
Iraq would free American power from its "imprisonment" in the
Iraq debacle. But how did that vision square with his vow to start
bringing the troops home from Afghanistan after eighteen months?
It puzzled both supporters and critics. Anders Fogh Rasmussen,
NATO's secretary-general, rushed to the pages of the *Washington
Post* to assure readers President Obama had "made clear to any

doubters that the United States is determined to do what it takes to finish the job." NATO would do its part with an additional five thousand troops, he promised, but the strategic mission was to transfer responsibility to the Afghans themselves "as soon as possible," not to build up an overwhelming force for a long-term occupation. Again, that sounded almost contradictory; but Rasmussen had an answer, even if it failed to convince skeptics: when citizens in the countries contributing these troops saw the transition happening, and when the Afghan people actually saw it as well, the progress would inspire the needed confidence "to continue to support this mission."[2]

Prior to assuming the NATO post, Rasmussen—almost a permanent fixture at NATO and its chief cheerleader—had been the center-right prime minister of Denmark. Obama had pushed him for the job over Turkish objections that his attitude toward Muslim concerns (a result of his support for the right of political cartoonists to caricature religious figures, an issue that had exploded with a Danish cartoonist's portrayal of the Prophet Muhammad) had stirred some notice. But the most interesting thing about his commentary was that, try as he might, he was unable to acknowledge that citizens in NATO countries—including, of course, the United States—had serious doubts about not only the surge but the war itself. Aware of the pervasive skepticism, Rasmussen did not set a precise date for the transition to Afghan control, but asserted, "I'm confident we can start next year." Yet Obama *had* put a date on his surge. American troops would start coming home in July 2011, he had promised at West Point, a pledge that quickly became the focus of intense debate and criticism. Indeed, Rasmussen's op-ed piece triggered that debate with its closing sentence: "Next year we will start to see light at the end of the tunnel."

Light at the end of the tunnel? Of all the images not to use about Afghanistan, surely that was number one with its Vietnam echo banging at the doors of policy makers who wanted to hear nothing that sounded like Pentagon press briefings from that era. Why in the world, one must ask, would Rasmussen bring up an echo of Vietnam and stir memories of the false promises about eventual military success? It is hard to understand how a politically experienced person could have failed to see that this one sentence undermined his credibility—and damaged the president's as well. Rasmussen's denial that Obama's speech in any way indicated an exit strategy was at the heart of his message, insisting on "transition" as the proper word to describe the strategy. But eighteen months? That deadline was hardly beyond the time the last of the surge troops would have arrived in Afghanistan and gotten unpacked for duty. Taliban spokesmen mocked Rasmussen's "light at the end of the tunnel" optimism and the persistent reports of progress, noting, "If Rasmussen and all his allies leave Afghanistan completely then the attacks on them will reach zero, and he can propagate the notion even more and say that the number of Taliban attacks have fallen further."[3]

Before things completely went off track, Secretary of State Hillary Clinton and Secretary of Defense Robert Gates took the first opportunity they could, NBC's *Meet the Press*, to back up Rasmussen—and back away from any deadline. Clinton: "We're not talking about an exit strategy or a drop dead deadline. What we're talking about is an assessment that in [July] 2011, we can begin a transition." And Gates: "We're not talking about an abrupt withdrawal. We're talking about something that will take place over a period of time. . . . *Because we will have 100,000 troops there.* And they are not leaving in July of 2011."[4]

That figure was important. Obama had insisted at West Point that there were no valid parallels with Vietnam, especially because the Taliban lacked the popular support the Vietcong had enjoyed. But whether there would ever be enough troops to carry out a counterinsurgency strategy was the real question. Obama had also made it appear, abetted by Rasmussen's one-man cheering section, that he had a grand alliance operating in Afghanistan, unlike George Bush's cobbled-together "coalition of the willing" for Iraq, but the forty-three nations he claimed as partners had sent very few soldiers, some numbering barely above single digits. France's president, Nicolas Sarkozy, quickly rejected the idea of any more troops, even after Obama spoke with him at length for forty minutes on the telephone. Instead, he told the American president, Paris would focus on an upcoming conference in London to discuss the whole problem. British prime minister Gordon Brown promised that his nation would send five hundred additional troops, bringing its force up to ten thousand.[5]

But these numbers were far from the ten thousand the allies were supposed to send when Obama set the new number of American troops at thirty thousand. The Pentagon's only idea about how it would all work out was that the Afghan "surge" would somehow replicate what had been achieved in Iraq when Petraeus took over in 2007. The first order of business then had been to secure Baghdad and work outward from there. Thus the plan was for Afghan surge troops to begin arriving in "opium rich" Helmand Province, a Taliban stronghold, in January 2010, followed by "a steady flow of tens of thousands" of American marines. But most of the troops would be sent to Kandahar: "With more forces we should be able to lock down the security in Kandahar and the surrounding areas of Kandahar."[6]

Something like Baghdad, redux, then. But there was something wrong with the math, for if tens of thousands of marines were headed to Helmand Province, not all that many would be left to lock down security in Kandahar. But that was hardly the only reason to be skeptical about the Pentagon's vision of things to come in Afghanistan, or to believe that everyone in the administration was on the same page. It was plain to see that the military really did not believe it had signed off on any "transition" (read "withdrawal") plan that was not "conditions based," while others in the administration, led by Vice President Joe Biden, who had opposed the surge in the early White House debates, did not back down from statements that beginning in July 2011 there would be lots of troops coming home. What, then, *was* the president's plan? And how did he hope to achieve it?

Obama's West Point speech had touched on long-term problems beyond Afghanistan, if only in a glancing way, in a paragraph discussing the limits of his proposals.

As President, I refuse to set goals that go beyond our responsibility, our means, or our interests. And I must weigh all of the challenges that our nation faces. I don't have the luxury of committing to just one. Indeed, I'm mindful of the words of President Eisenhower, who—in discussing our national security—said, "Each proposal must be weighed in the light of a broader consideration: the need to maintain balance in and among national programs."

And yet he insisted failure in Afghanistan would be catastrophic.

I am convinced that our security is at stake in Afghanistan and Pakistan. This is the epicenter of violent extremism practiced by al Qaeda. It is from here that we were attacked on 9/11, and it is from here that new attacks are being plotted as I speak. This is no idle danger; no hypothetical threat.

If the United States had a vital interest in protecting itself against attacks already being planned, how could one put any limits on the national response? Here again were the seeds of controversy. Another 9/11 was simply unthinkable, let alone the possibility of a terrorist nuclear attack—that seemed a real danger even to some in the administration. While critics focused on the "withdrawal" paragraphs of the speech, the president's answer to the problem of "the epicenter of violent extremism" was in the process of solidifying around his concept of just-war theory, as he would develop it in his Nobel Peace Prize speech—and, unbeknownst to the public, drone warfare. Meanwhile, the president allowed the pundits to do some of the missing math in counterinsurgency for him, while he did other calculations.

The Pundits Weigh In

Parsing the West Point speech quickly occupied a surge of commentators. The highly quoted conservative pundit George Will titled his contribution "This Will Not End Well." Obama had vowed to finish the job in Afghanistan, Will wrote, but his speech revealed that he thought the job was to get out of the country as soon as he could—and that was "an unserious policy." His readers might have expected that, as a conservative, he would criticize the president for not promising to stay on until the threat was eliminated once and for all. But Will surprised them. "A case can be made for a serious— meaning larger and more protracted—surge. A better case can be made for a radically reduced investment of resources and prestige in that forlorn country. Obama has not made a convincing case for his tentative surgelet."[7] In fact, Will had earlier bailed out on Afghanistan as a winner and did not see anything in Obama's speech to change his mind.

A few days later, former senator and Democratic presidential candidate George McGovern warned that the West Point speech constituted "a sharp turn toward another Vietnam." Remembered as the Democratic "peace candidate" who lost to Richard Nixon in a landslide, his reasoning was akin to Will's conclusion: "Even if we had a good case for a war in Afghanistan, we simply cannot afford to wage it. With a $12 trillion debt and a serious economic recession, this is not a time for unnecessary wars abroad. We should bring our soldiers home before any more of them are killed or wounded—and before our national debt explodes."[8]

Then there was a very surprising comment from Eliot Cohen, one of the most influential proponents of the original surge in Iraq. It was surprising as much for what he did not say as what he said. He doubted that anything he had heard from either the president or the military indicated understanding of what it would take to mount a successful counterinsurgency strategy for Afghanistan. At the top of his list of missing ingredients was "deep knowledge of the other side." That could be acquired only by long years of experience, like the efforts British colonial officers made to learn the ins and outs of Pashtun tribes in the nineteenth century. "In a world of rotating military and diplomatic assignments, three-month think tank projects and moving on to the next hot topic, it is difficult to develop that experience."[9]

Though Cohen seemed to be disparaging "think tank projects," he had played a key role in the think tank projects and White

House brainstorming sessions that produced the Iraq surge that supposedly saved America's skin when the war went bad. What he did not say in this article, however, was whether the United States could or even *should* attempt to emulate the British in what was now that "wild frontier," as Obama had labeled the Afghanistan-Pakistan borderlands—the area where the surge would concentrate its efforts—in his 2007 speech.

Perhaps it was Niall Ferguson, the expat British expert on imperial fortunes and follies who held a chair at Harvard and was very worried about the fate of the American empire, who had the most interesting thing to say—even if it was not directly about the surge. The real issue, he said, was not wars in Iraq and Afghanistan but the inevitable decline in money available for the military in budgets that were designed to trim the federal budget and in which cuts today would have a multiplier effect in future years. The culprits were entitlements—chiefly health care and social security—and inadequate tax revenues. Congress and the White House, regardless of party, had collaborated in creating a situation that inevitably spelled the decline of American power and, therefore, its ability to protect its influence over global affairs.[10]

Obama's emphasis on Pakistan in the West Point speech did not receive the attention it deserved in any of the comments quoted here, however, although it provided important clues about how the president expected things to turn out—because while supposedly tens of thousands of troops would be heading to Helmand Province and the rest to Kandahar, there were no troops going to Pakistan. Well, that was not quite true: Special Operations Command had launched Taliban-hunting raids into Pakistan's border areas. But Obama had already become impressed with the possibilities of a long-term technological solution—and being infatuated by technology was a very common American trait that, as *Guardian* reporter Jonathan Steele points out, had always been inextricably linked to other historic zeals.

There were drones going to remote places inside Pakistan, however, and elsewhere, and many more already than President Bush had authorized. Americans had been introduced to decapitating drone strikes back in 2002, when a CIA RQ-1 Predator launched a Hellfire missile attack on six Yemenis suspected of being members of al Qaeda, blowing them up in their car. But as the debate over Obama's West Point speech demonstrated, the media were not much occupied with the drone story, despite the fierce critiques offered by counterinsurgency enthusiasts that drones could quickly undo the work of thousands of soldiers operating on ground level. David Kilcullen and Andrew Exum, for example, as noted in chapter 2, had argued vigorously in the *New York Times* that drones created more enemies in the very places where it was important to curtail Taliban or al Qaeda recruits, insisting that "the drone war has created a siege mentality among Pakistani civilians."

Kilcullen and Exum made an excellent point. There was great danger in putting civilians in a country such as Pakistan into a siege mentality, not least because it highlighted once again that drones were the latest iteration in the series of weapons the advanced powers had used in past colonial wars, and although Islamabad was a nuclear power, its outlook (like those in other areas where drones were used) was still bound up in the dynamics of that earlier era. Indeed, in the spring of 2009 there was a related intelligence scare that the Taliban in Pakistan were planning an attack on a uranium stockpile near a research reactor. The uranium had been supplied to Islamabad under the old "atoms for peace" program in the 1960s. Efforts to get the material back proved unavailing, as Islamabad warned that would only excite public opposition to the United States amid rumors that Washington was trying to take away Pakistan's nuclear weapons.[11]

Washington's policy toward the Middle East and South Asia seemed to be a series of ad hoc solutions to immediate problems, in an effort to exert the most leverage possible, but instead of freeing up options, it always seemed to cause a backlash. First there had been Iran and the effort to use the shah as a regional stabilizer, and, when that failed, Pakistan's turn came. But the results were hardly better, as Islamabad sought its own path regardless of American wishes. It would still be some time, nevertheless, before Congress or the public caught up with all of what was happening at the moment of the West Point speech. And that was a deliberate administration strategy, as carefully thought out as the events leading up to the troop decision. The administration played down the increasing drone attacks, even as it searched for ways to square this new kind of warfare, carried out inside countries far removed from the actual battlefronts in Afghanistan (not only Pakistan but also Somalia and Yemen), with accepted interpretations of international law. When the justifications came, moreover, they would put the president in the center of "targeting" decisions, in a fashion that made the drones appear to be mandated not by an extraordinary grab of power by the White House but instead somehow granted under a remarkably broad interpretation of the Authorization for Use of Military Force passed by Congress in the week after 9/11. As explanations and rationale slowly emerged over the next two years, through leaks and carefully worded speeches, the stepped-up pace of drone warfare exceeded—by a wide margin—public knowledge of the legal arguments. The leak process by unnamed officials was, of course, a way of building acceptance of a controversial program that set precedents beyond those where any president had gone before. In a sense, what was being created was a stealth imperial presidency. Yet public opinion polls continually demonstrated public support in the range of 80 percent in favor of the use of drones, however; on that level at least, the Obama administration's leak strategy was a success. It began to show serious cracks by the end of his first term, as the idea occurred to some legislators that maybe there was something to charges that the Constitution was being set aside for viewing only by visitors to the nation's capital.[12]

Hammer and Anvil

Meanwhile, in much-anticipated testimony before Congress, the current American commander in Afghanistan, General Stanley McChrystal, assured legislators that he was perfectly content with the number of troops Obama had promised—and with the timetable. The strategy was reasonable and fully achievable. Republican critics from the House and Senate repeatedly challenged McChrystal on both points. "I don't believe the July 2011 time frame, militarily, is a major factor in my strategy," he replied. If the enemy attempted to wait out the Americans, they would be making a serious miscalculation, because that would allow American trainers to build up a more capable Afghan army. And as the Afghan population became more secure they would also become a less vulnerable target politically. "So they really can't afford to wait."[13]

In essence, McChrystal's testimony simply rephrased Rasmussen's op-ed piece. It was not all going to be easy, of course, because the Taliban would likely turn to coercing the population by means of suicide bombers and other attacks—but those terrorist methods would backfire as well, as they would only drive a wedge between insurgents and the population. That was counterinsurgency-speak right out of the manual. Appearing with McChrystal, Ambassador Karl Eikenberry, who, as we have seen, had fired off cables opposing new troop deployments so long as Hamid Karzai's government failed to bring corruption under control, now claimed he had no quarrel with the decision, none at all.

Both men were anxious to show there was no daylight between them on Afghan strategy. During testimony they put their dueling pistols back in their cases and exchanged compliments. Eikenberry denied he had at any time during the review opposed additional troops. His concern had been about numbers, he said, and the context of where the troops would operate. Asked about Osama bin Laden and the prospects for victory if he remained an active leader of al Qaeda, McChrystal hesitated a bit. Bin Laden was an iconic figure, said the general. Killing him would not ensure victory, but probably ultimate victory would not be possible without killing him. McChrystal's view was typical of the uncertainty—indeed, confusion—about the connection between the Taliban and al Qaeda, and about the counterinsurgency aspects of the war. And indeed, once McChyrstal was back in Afghanistan, he continued to resent Eikenberry's presence as a sign of no confidence in his mission.

Obama's evident commitment to increased use of drone aircraft to target al Qaeda leadership hiding away in Afghanistan near the

border with Pakistan, or even over the border, suggested that counterterrorism approaches were being relied on more than a surge approach; the balance between the two had yet to be determined.
Republicans—as well as other critics—had some justification in
suspecting that McChrystal was being set up for failure, not because
Obama wanted him to fail, but rather because the president could
not have gotten Congress to provide the general with an open-
ended commitment. Besides, maybe Secretary Gates was right, the
United States had not fought one war in Afghanistan, but nine
different wars, none of them with the right inputs.

While all such questions awaited serious exploration, there was
general agreement that the president's plan required Pakistan's full
cooperation, a fraught problem.[14] An American military officer who
served in the frontier area in the early years, for example, recalled
seeing Taliban fighters waving their rifles from the Pakistani side to
taunt his troops. The rules then were that the Americans could not
shoot unless they were shot at first, he told *New York Times* reporter
Scott Shane. "But when we saw them over the border, we knew we
should expect an attack that night. The only ones who recognized
the border were us, with our G.P.S."[15]

Up until now, explained Shane, the border had been so porous
and Pakistani governments "so squeamish about a fight, that the
American hammer in Afghanistan was pounding Taliban fighters
there against a Pakistani pillow, not an anvil." But that would
change when the new American troops arrived in Helmand Province, a Taliban stronghold around Kandahar, while at the same
time a major intensification of drone strikes began inside Pakistan
and the Pakistani army stepped up its campaign against militants
in South Waziristan. Or so it was hoped. "We finally have an opportunity to do a real hammer-and-anvil strategy on the border,"
agreed analyst Michael O'Hanlon, picking up on the favored image
of Obama's plan.[16]

A big supporter of the 2003 Iraq invasion, O'Hanlon had criticized postinvasion policies as wrongheaded, but he believed Obama
had gotten it right this time. A Brookings Institution senior fellow,

O'Hanlon co-authored a book, *Toughing It Out in Afghanistan* (2010), expressing confidence that the mixture of more troops and more drones would turn the tide. For a time the hammer-and-anvil image popped up everywhere. The next to use it was General David Petraeus of Iraq surge fame and now the head of Central Command. "While certainly different and in some ways tougher than Iraq, Afghanistan is no more hopeless than Iraq was when I took command there in February 2007," Petraeus told the Senate Foreign Relations Committee. "Indeed the level of violence and number of violent civilian deaths in Iraq were vastly higher than we have seen in Afghanistan, but achieving progress in Afghanistan will be hard and the progress there likely will be slower in developing than progress was achieved in Iraq."[17]

Senate Foreign Relations Committee chairman John Kerry pressed Petraeus on the border question. Sending more troops into Afghanistan, the general admitted, might result in more Taliban in Pakistan. "That is why we're working very hard to coordinate our operations more effectively with our Pakistani partners, so that they know what our operational campaign plan is, and can anticipate and be there with a catcher's mitt, or an anvil, whatever it may be, to greet these individuals."[18]

Secretary Gates was the first high-level visitor to Kabul after the West Point speech. His visit was an opportunity for Karzai to tell the Americans something about what they had bought into and what he expected in the way of support. It was clear that the Afghan president stood with those who believed that Obama's goal was finding the exit gate. Like other local leaders in the days of the old colonialism, he feared being dumped. He could see, for example, that Obama had called the recent election a fraud in his speech.

> In Afghanistan, we and our allies prevented the Taliban from stopping a presidential election, and—although it was marred by fraud—that election produced a government that is consistent with Afghanistan's laws and constitution.

And Obama had not stopped there.

> This effort must be based on performance. The days of providing
> a blank check are over. President Karzai's inauguration speech
> sent the right message about moving in a new direction. And
> going forward, we will be clear about what we expect from those
> who receive our assistance. We'll support Afghan ministries, gov-
> ernors, and local leaders that combat corruption and deliver for
> the people. We expect those who are ineffective or corrupt to be
> held accountable.

So if Karzai did not perform, could he, too, be replaced? McChrystal had already built up a relatively good relationship with the Afghan leader, but Karzai no longer had regular video conferences
with the president, as he had had with his friend George Bush. The
election had been a big factor in the growing doubts that what had
worked in Iraq could be repeated in Afghanistan. Karzai's behavior
in the immediate aftermath of Obama's announcement—however
much it could have been anticipated—was not encouraging except
to those who were committed to the long-haul counterinsurgency
required, and was another reason to look for ways of preempting the
need to work outside the difficult task of nation building.

It turned out that Hamid Karzai should not be underestimated.
Gates had no sooner arrived in Afghanistan than he was shocked
by President Hamid Karzai's blunt statement that his country would
not be able to pay for its own military until 2024. The shock was not
so much because Gates was unaware that Afghanistan could not
come up with the money, one suspects, as that the Afghan president
would be a tattletale a few days after President Obama had announced his "surge" on December 1, 2009, along with its supposed
time limit designed to hold steady the left wing of his party. Yet
there was another way to see the situation: Karzai understood perfectly well the bet Obama had placed on counterinsurgency as the
roulette wheel started spinning, and he put down his own wager.

The secretary revealed another well-known "secret" in a Kabul
press conference, confirming that Washington paid for organizing

and training the Afghan army and police (as had the colonial powers at the height of the imperial era in Asia and Africa), and admitted as well that the United States was in a cash bidding war with the Taliban for recruits, something that had been the case in Iraq as well. Only recently, Gates told reporters, had he "learned the 'eye-opener' that the Taliban were able to attract so many fighters because they paid more. Generals in Afghanistan said the Taliban dole out $250 to $300 a month, while the Afghan Army paid about $120. So Gates has made sure that the recruits get a raise to $240."[19]

New York Times columnist Maureen Dowd, who noted that Gates had been on the wrong side of history in the past, called him "the Cold Warrior who helped persuade the Reluctant Warrior to do the Afghan surge." How did he make decisions, she asked, that would "determine his reputation and that of the young president he serves?" Gates's answer suggested that he may not have noticed the implication in her question that he had been wrong before. "Anybody who reads history," he replied, "has to approach these things with some humility because you can't know. Nobody knows what the last chapter ever looks like."[20]

The Nobel Laureate

The announcement from Oslo, Norway, that President Barack Obama had been awarded the 2009 Nobel Peace Prize came as the greatest shock of the decade. The right—but not only the right—criticized the act as a preposterous move by the "lefties" on the peace prize committee to commit Obama to their agenda. It even seemed to be a none-too-subtle piece of interference in American politics, one that logically followed from Obama's choice of Berlin during the 2008 campaign to deliver what amounted to a major partisan campaign address. To those who thought this way, it was the Anti-Bush Prize, awarded to anyone who drove out the Republicans. In a strange sort of way, as we will see below, Obama (and especially certain advisers) did worry about the implication that he was being "jammed" from the other side by the Nobel Prize committee in the same way he supposedly had been by the Pentagon.

He would prove once again, however, that he understood the stakes of all the players in the game.

Candidate Obama had come to Berlin after a whirlwind trip to the Middle East. He netted pictures with Petraeus in a ten-minute helicopter ride that immensely pleased aides, and neatly trumped John McCain's challenge that he go to Iraq and see for himself how well the surge was working. Although denied a platform at the Brandenburg Gate where John Kennedy had shouted in 1961, "Ich bin ein Berliner!," and Ronald Reagan in 1987 called out a challenge, "Mr. Gorbachev, tear down this wall!" Obama channeled both men from a nearby spot.

Before a crowd of about a hundred thousand on July 24, the prospective nominee of the Democratic Party called for a new era of European-American unity on a whole series of issues. Those who saw him as the true spirit of America come to save the world from George Bush's minions who had thrust forward their version of liberty on bayonets focused on his promises to end torture and provide the world with new examples of enlightened leadership like the Marshall Plan and Berlin airlift, while also tackling questions of global warming. Obama's surrogate Robert Gibbs pushed the envelope of great expectations and told reporters that in private talks with German chancellor Angela Merkel the candidate had praised her leadership in international affairs and on the climate issue in particular, and in return had pledged "to pursue an 80% reduction in US greenhouse gas emissions by 2050."[21]

These were the headlines reporting on the speech in the press. But it was also a speech about the sterner duties of Europeans in the immediate present.

> This is the moment when we must renew our resolve to rout the terrorists who threaten our security in Afghanistan, and the traffickers who sell drugs on your streets. No one welcomes war. I recognize the enormous difficulties in Afghanistan. But my country and yours have a stake in seeing that NATO's first mission beyond Europe's borders is a success. For the people of Afghanistan, and for our shared security, the work must be done.

America cannot do this alone. The Afghan people need our troops and your troops; our support and your support to defeat the Taliban and al Qaeda, to develop their economy, and to help them rebuild their nation. We have too much at stake to turn back now.[22]

This speech, as well as his proposal on entering office to reset Russian-American relations and his Cairo speech six months earlier that called for new beginnings with the Arab world, were all fodder for embittered Republicans, who, just as much as Obama's most ardent supporters, brought to Obama's every pronouncement what they thought they heard and what they knew they believed. And therein was the dilemma posed by the speech Obama had to give in accepting the Nobel Peace Prize.

The award was just too much for the *New York Times*'s designated conservative, David Brooks, who called it a "travesty" and a "joke" on the *PBS NewsHour* on October 10, 2009. And Brooks did not stop there. "He wrote a book. That's literature. He has biological elements in his body. He could win that prize. He could have swept the whole prizes." On the same program, the *Washington Post*'s Ruth Marcus (not a conservative) said she was stunned and amazed, and seemed to agree when Brooks said that he ought to turn it down. How could he do that? Lehrer asked. People do it, insisted Brooks, and Marcus added an almost snide comment: "Marlon Brando not going to the Academy Awards."[23]

It occurred to not a few that the prize was indeed meant to guide the president's behavior, since he had no accomplishments yet on any peace front one could name. James Fallows of the *Atlantic Monthly* picked up on that notion, pointing out that the chairman of the prize committee introduced Obama by saying,

Commenting on the award, President Obama said he did not feel that he deserved to be in the company of so many transformative figures that have been honoured by the prize, and whose courageous pursuit of peace has inspired the world. But he added that he also knew that the Nobel Prize had not just been used to honor specific achievements, but also to give momentum to a set of causes. The Prize could thus represent "a call to action."

President Obama has understood the Norwegian Nobel Committee perfectly.

Fallows gave the president high marks for the acceptance speech that followed, noting first of all that it did not attempt to slide over "his predicament as a war president getting a peace prize." He continued, "I don't think he provided even a five-second passage of the speech that could be isolated by U.S. opponents to show that he was 'apologizing' for America."[24] Fallows concluded that Obama's Nobel speech, delivered two weeks after the president announced the Afghan surge, would repay close inspection, embracing as it did the contradiction of war as a means to peace.

More than any other individual besides himself, Harvard professor Samantha Power, a strong believer in the use of force to save endangered peoples from cruel rulers, was responsible for much of the wording and tone of the speech. An immigrant from Ireland as a child, Power began her adult career as a freelance writer in Bosnia during the period of Serbian atrocities against Muslims. She wrote for various magazines as she reported crimes against civilians from Rwanda, East Timor, Sudan, and Kosovo. Her first book, A Problem from Hell: America in the Age of Genocide, won the 2003 Pulitzer Prize and catapulted her into Harvard, where she established the Carr Center for Human Rights Policy. Soon after he took his seat in the Senate, Obama called Power and told her how much he liked her book. Over a four-hour dinner the two bonded, and she became what one author said was a "charismatic presence" in his Senate office and then in the campaign.[25]

Early in the campaign she made a bad error that sidetracked her for a short time. An intense foe of the Iraq War, she called Hillary Clinton a "monster" for her tactics in the Ohio primary. She resigned from the campaign, but after the election things were patched over and Power was named to the National Security Council as an adviser on human rights. Her first year in that role was largely uneventful until she sent a memo to the president suggesting that the first draft of the Nobel Prize speech could be improved; she was invited into meetings, where she was not shy about advancing her own ideas. "Power accompanied Obama to the Nobel ceremonies. Afterward, she put up a large photograph of his handwritten draft on the wall of her office. Her pride was understandable: Many of the ideas in the speech bore her distinctive imprint, particularly his emphasis on the use of force for humanitarian purposes."[26]

One can get a pretty good idea of what her private memos to Obama said from a piece Power wrote for the *New York Times Book Review* in 2007, reviewing several books on counterinsurgency and discussing the problems of meeting the terrorist challenge. Opening with a short history of how the Bush administration had fought the war on terror, including that president's dismissal of old-fashioned restraints on presidential power, Power argued that the way that president had gone about things was wrongheaded: "Six years later, most Americans still rightly believe that the United States must confront Islamic terrorism—and must be relentless in preventing terrorist networks from getting weapons of mass destruction. But Bush's premises have proved flawed, and the war-on-terror frame has obscured more than it has clarified."[27]

Most grievously, Bush had used the war on terror to "smuggle" his obsession with Saddam Hussein into a full-blown invasion that had actually done great harm to the effort to quash al Qaeda's terrorist threats and the wider effort to put an end to all such activities. The bogus war made many of America's friends dismiss genuine American concerns about terrorism as stemming from the same impulse. Even worse, some of these friends feared any association with Washington at all, wrote Power: "Many of our friends believe that too close an association with American objectives will make them electorally vulnerable and their cities potential targets." The question had become how to reclaim the moral high ground, and in doing so strike the blows needed to defeat this new enemy of freedom. She stated, "We must urgently set about reversing the harm done to the nation's standing and security by simultaneously reasserting the moral difference between the United States and Islamic terrorists and by developing a 21st-century toolbox to minimize actual terrorist threats."

In what would become a massively ironic twist on the timing of the Nobel speech, President Obama and close aides in the White House were picking out their favorite weapon from that twenty-first-century toolbox precisely at the time of its delivery. But Power's main concern was that Bush had carried things so far that his successor would have great difficulty in keeping presidential prerogatives intact so that they could be used to fight the good fight: "One question in particular hangs over this discussion: Are the American and international publics so disenchanted with Bush's effort to curb terrorism the wrong way that they will deprive his successor of the resources he or she needs to change course?"

As both Power's supporters and critics noted, the basic formulation of the issues facing a new administration and how it would go about claiming for "right" use the powers Congress had granted George Bush after 9/11 were all here. Henry Kissinger had once put the question in similar terms as he tried to explain the problems facing the Nixon administration as it sought to disentangle American foreign policy from the Vietnam debacle. After World War I, he wrote in his memoirs, the United States isolated itself from the world because its people thought they were too good for the world; after Vietnam there was a feeling among critics that America should isolate itself because it was too evil for the world.

Power was actually voicing a variation on that realist theme. But some conservative critics saw her as little more than a mouthpiece for the radical critic Noam Chomsky, using her seat on the National Security Council to direct the president's decisions toward what had once been called by an earlier generation of conservatives "one-worldism." In the *National Review*, Stanley Kurtz claimed that the whole point of the Power-Obama foreign policy was to subsume American interests into a worldwide crusade against injustice everywhere. The result would be to so dilute American power that it would be unable to fight for national interests anywhere. "Her goal is to use our shared horror at the worst that human beings can do in order to institute an ever-broadening regime of redistributive trans-national governance."[28]

However much Obama's Nobel speech reflected Samantha Power's insight and contributions, others saw different antecedents. To his surprise, David Brooks suddenly discovered—after bashing the Nobel Committee—good old Cold War antecendents he could trace to George F. Kennan and Reinhold Niebuhr and shouted something like *Bravo, bravo!* "His speeches at West Point and Oslo this year are pitch-perfect explications of the liberal international-ist approach. Other Democrats talk tough in a secular way, but Obama's speeches were thoroughly theological. He talked about the 'core struggle of human nature' between love and evil."[29]

Brooks thus labeled Obama a proper heir of "Cold War liberal-ism," and put him alongside Senator Scoop Jackson and other Democrats who shared such views of man's divergent yet simultane-ous capacities for good and evil. Samantha Power might have blushed a bit at such praise from David Brooks, but he was essen-tially right about the emerging Obama "Doctrine" in these speeches.

Former Bill Clinton speechwriter Ted Widmer was equally ful-some in his praise of the speech. He definitely knew a Clinton "centrist" when he saw one. The speech might have lacked sound bites, but the Nobel oration is not really a speech, but a lecture. And in that vein it deserved high marks. "It threw down gauntlets left and right, challenging lazy assumptions of his liberal base (that war is avoidable) and his conservative opposition (that war is glori-ous). It gently chided his European audience, reminding them that the remarkable achievement of 64 years of relative peace has been possible because America 'helped underwrite' it."[30]

The quotation marks around "helped underwrite" were meant, of course, to convey the point that without the United States nothing would have happened to save the world from Communism and/or chaos. Widmer did, however, have some little problems with the historical record as Obama cited it. "It is regrettably true that the United States has on occasion undermined the democratic aspira-tions of other countries, from the Philippines to Iran and Guatemala. But historical elisions are very much a part of the speechwriting business, and a lapse or two should not detract from the overall message."[31]

The Speech Itself

So what did Obama actually say in his Nobel speech?

"I would be remiss," the president began, "if I did not acknowledge the considerable controversy that your generous decision has generated." That remark was greeted with laughter.

He noted that there were many people around the world struggling and suffering for having committed acts of courage. Of past prize recipients, he acknowledged especially his debt to the Reverend Martin Luther King Jr., whose resistance to segregation and commitment to peace and nonviolent mass protests drew upon Gandhi's writings and example.

What came next in the speech showed how much difference there was between King's post-award actions and Obama's sense of his duties to the United States and the world. King's path had taken a sharp turn from previous causes when he expanded his concerns to include public criticism of American foreign policy and the war in Vietnam. On April 4, 1967, King had delivered a message from the pulpit of a well-known New York church that caused tremors among his allies and infuriated his enemies. He said that the award he had received commanded its recipient to work harder than ever for peace. "I cannot forget that the Nobel Peace Prize was also a commission, a commission to work harder than I had ever worked before for 'the brotherhood of man.' This is a calling that takes me beyond national allegiances."[32]

Obama's path from his antiwar protests in 2002 before the invasion of Iraq through his speech at the 2004 Democratic National Convention and then into the 2008 presidential campaign had gone in a very different direction. It was evident in the acceptance speech, as Brooks and Widmer understood, that his true mentor on foreign policy was not King but the über-realist of the Cold War years, another theologian, Reinhold Niebuhr. He did not invoke Niebuhr by name, but he insisted it was his duty as the American president to recognize that evil existed in the world and to meet its threat to the United States. These were words perfectly pitched to appeal to those who doubted his West Point speech actually meant a serious commitment to defeating the insurgency in Afghanistan. Nearly all comments on his lengthy decision-making process suggested—indeed, insisted—that it had been a soul-searching time for the president, who only came around to a conclusion to send more troops reluctantly and without full conviction because there was no other alternative. Those who had doubts, on the other hand, that he was a master of assessing mood and political temperature were well taught a lesson by the Oslo speech.

> Perhaps the most profound issue surrounding my receipt of this prize is the fact that I am the Commander-in-Chief of the military of a nation in the midst of two wars. One of these wars is winding down. The other is a conflict that America did not seek, one in which we are joined by 42 other countries—including Norway—in an effort to defend ourselves and all nations from further attacks.

Invoking the forty-three-nation alliance, it will be remembered, had been his opening image at West Point, and here he used it again as the launching pad for an exploration of just-war theory. Even if the image echoed aspects of Bush's "coalition of the willing" or even LBJ's "many flags" campaign for Vietnam, Obama was employing it here to bolster the idea of a just war by counting up the numbers. Indeed, after the initial reference to King's work and accomplishments, Obama turned almost immediately to just-war theory, emphasizing that even in World War II the number of civilian casualties exceeded the number of soldiers who perished. In that most just war in the modern era, there was no escaping the limitations of the human situation. "As a head of state sworn to protect my nation, I cannot be guided by [King's and Gandhi's] examples alone. I face the world as it is, and cannot stand idle in the face of threats to the American people." He asserted the right to act unilaterally, if need be, to protect the nation. That was to be his key observation: the human condition itself was the cause of wars, and no leader could escape the requirement to meet evil with force.

> Make no mistake: Evil does exist in the world. A nonviolent movement could not have halted Hitler's armies. Negotiations cannot convince al Qaeda's leaders to lay down their arms. To say that force is sometimes necessary is not a call to cynicism—it is a recognition of history: the imperfections of man and the limits of reason.
>
> I raise this point, I begin with this point because in many countries there is a deep ambivalence about military action today, no matter what the cause. And at times, this is joined by a reflexive suspicion of America, the world's sole military superpower.

A little later on, in describing American leadership after the end of World War II, Obama suggested that the American role had always been one of enlightened self-interest: "We have borne this burden not because we seek to impose our will." This statement seemed to imply that the world's sole military power was also the world's sole exception to the constant struggle between good and evil. Then, a few paragraphs later, came another troubling statement that confused the message he sought to convey. "So part of our challenge is reconciling these two seemingly irreconcilable truths—that war is sometimes necessary, and war at some level is an expression of human folly." *Folly?* The whole emphasis in Obama's Nobel lecture was on the need to accept just-war theory, as it had evolved from the Middle Ages, to combat evil. *Folly* is defined as a foolish act, such as a strike against the world's sole military superpower? It was an odd word to choose.

What was the basis for juxtaposing the al Qaeda challenge with Hitler? Surely there were questions of scale involved, to say the least. But it was a familiar rallying cry from the time of the first Gulf War, when George H.W. Bush compared Saddam Hussein to Hitler. Such comparisons risked flattening out the complex historical experience Obama wished to call upon into a two-dimensional world where just-war theory disintegrated into name-calling. But there was a rationale based on the threat to a structure of peace that held evil at bay. After World War II, Obama said, the world had been led by American efforts in "constructing an architecture to keep the peace." The American-inspired architecture was both a material and (within the limits of human imperfectability) moral fortress against evil. A decade into the new century, however, "this old architecture is buckling under the weight of new threats." In other words, while al Qaeda and/or other terrorist groups did not have the Wehrmacht to threaten the world, the challenge was just as great. The threat of nuclear war between superpowers might have faded, "but proliferation may increase the risk of catastrophe." Bunched together here were references to the Iranian nuclear program and a rationale for the Afghan War. "Terrorism has long been a tactic, but modern technology allows a few small men with out-sized rage to murder innocents on a horrific scale."[33]

Al Qaeda might be few in numbers, small men with outsized rage, but they were linked to the Taliban insurgency in a synergetic fashion that made it essential to prevent the defeat of the Karzai regime in Kabul, for there was no third alternative available. Here then was the motive for the American-led coalition, the International Security Assistance Force (ISAF), which he had just increased by thirty thousand troops to bring Washington's contribution to a hundred thousand. The objective was to deny al Qaeda any space in Afghanistan to prepare new terrorist attacks on the United States, but Obama's speech might just as easily be taken to mean future campaigns beyond those already being carried out by the ISAF in Afghanistan, to include not only Pakistan but Yemen and Somalia—or anywhere else where a few small men with outsized rage might gain access to modern technology such as box cutters. That might be the way Jon Stewart would put it, of course, but the speech itself challenged belief in the ability of any nation, however powerful, to maintain a global watch sufficient to deny determined terrorists a base of operations.

Therefore, despite all the energy it put into just-war theory, the Nobel speech did not answer serious questions about the purpose of the Afghan War. Instead, Obama said that the world had rallied around the United States after 9/11 "and continues to support our efforts in Afghanistan, because of the horror of those senseless attacks and the recognized principle of self-defense." Military force could be justified, he said, on humanitarian grounds. "That's why all responsible nations must embrace the role that militaries with a clear mandate can play to keep the peace. . . . And sadly, it will continue to be true in unstable regions for years to come." Still, it was necessary always for the United States to be "a standard bearer in the conduct of war. That is what makes us different from those whom we fight. That is the source of our strength. That is why I prohibited torture. That is why I ordered the prison at Guantanamo Bay closed."

Meanwhile, in the Oval Office

At the time of the Nobel Prize speech, of course, the decision not to pursue the closing of Guantánamo Bay had not yet been made. Two accounts of his presidency blame congressional opposition, mixed with a failure to do prior analysis of what it would take to close the facility. In the Nobel speech he had said that he had to face the world as it was—a very dangerous place, as he pictured it, requiring all nations to join in the effort in Afghanistan. One commentator, James Mann, also blamed the apathy of public opinion, which no longer felt the urgency it once had for closing the facility: "Sometimes, bringing about change takes more than a president." Another suggested that caring about Guantánamo and other international issues had slipped because of something much deeper in American history: "Obama finds himself fighting an undercurrent of isolationism in his own party—that has driven America, once again, to look away from a number of the global challenges it faces."[34]

So according to those views, the people who voted for Obama in 2008 either had grown apathetic about moral questions or were really isolationists, following in the footsteps of those who were responsible for all the mistakes made in American foreign policy from the time of Wilson's League of Nations fight at the end of World

War I to (in the Republican view) losing the war in Vietnam and hampering the president's power to do good and protect the American people at the same time. Blaming unreal expectations became a major theme of the Obama administration whenever it stepped back from a confrontation over Guantánamo or, on the other hand, adopted the habit of justifying its actions on the basis of the immediate post–9/11 Authorization to Use Military Force. But at the same time he was deciding he could not do anything about Guantánamo Bay, the president was engaged in expanding the drone war in Pakistan and other "unstable countries" he had referred to vaguely in the Nobel Prize speech. Reporters for the *New York Times* interviewed three dozen of the president's current and former advisers to write their story about his evolution. "They describe a paradoxical leader who shunned the legislative deal-making required to close the detention facility at Guantanamo Bay in Cuba, but approves lethal action without hand-wringing." Dennis Blair, for example, the director of national intelligence until he was fired in May 2010, told the reporters that long-term strategy against al Qaeda was sidelined by the intense focus on drone strikes. "The steady refrain in the White House was, 'This is the only game in town'—reminded me of body counts in Vietnam." White House officials dismissed the former admiral's criticism as sour grapes at being let go. Thomas E. Donilon, the national security adviser, remarked that what surprised him the most about Obama in office was that "he's a president who is quite comfortable with the use of force on behalf of the United States."[35]

From his first days in office, then, one was supposed to believe that Obama was always "a realist who, unlike some of his fervent supporters, was never carried away by his own rhetoric. Instead, he was already putting his lawyerly mind to carving out the maximum amount of maneuvering room to fight terrorism as he saw fit." The reporters' conclusion was that he had succeeded in reaching out to conservatives with an argument about evil as an abstraction, the favorite theme of conservatives.[36]

Barack Obama's soul-searching about authorizing signature strikes will be examined in chapter 5. But back in May 2010, even as the program remained unacknowledged officially, the president made a jaw-dropping drone-related joke at the annual White House correspondents dinner: "The Jonas Brothers are here; they're out there somewhere. Sasha and Malia are huge fans. But boys, don't get any ideas. I have two words for you: 'Predator drones.'"[37]

4

ON TO MARJA!

*It doesn't matter how stupid your thesis is as long as you have the right
adviser.*

> —General David Petraeus giving the punch
> line to a joke, November 2010

We have to be careful not to believe our own bullshit.
> —David Axelrod, adviser to President Obama

Professing themselves in testimony before Congress to be fully satisfied with the president's decision to commit more troops, and fully
unified among themselves, the three generals—Karl Eikenberry,
the former commander and now American ambassador to Afghanistan; Stanley McChrystal, the current commander on the ground;
and David Petraeus, Iraq War hero and now head of Central Command and future commander in Afghanistan—prepared for the
"momentum-changing" campaign that would begin with an assault
on Marja. The ultimate object, everyone said, however, was to clear
out the area around Kandahar, a city founded in the fourth century
BCE by Alexander the Great. Through succeeding ages Kandahar
became a trading center on key routes across Central Asia, making
it a strategic target for all future would-be empire builders. In 1747
Ahmad Shah Durrani, an Afghan empire builder, made it the capital
of modern Afghanistan. Although Kabul eventually won out on
that matter, Kandahar never lost its significance as a crucial objective
for Afghan supremacy, symbolically and materially.

In 1994 the Taliban captured the city after a fight with a local
warlord, Gul Agha Sherzai. Seven years later an American invading force drove the Taliban out of Kabul and Kandahar during the

failed search for Osama bin Laden. Having installed Hamid Karzai as the new president of Afghanistan, however, the Americans left in a rush to go in search of Saddam Hussein's supposed weapons of mass destruction. That quest turned into a prolonged struggle that ruined George Bush's goal of birthing Middle East democracy, while Afghanistan slipped deep into the shadows. Meanwhile, the Taliban regrouped and threatened to regain the upper hand. With President Obama's blessing, American strategists now saw Kandahar as a key testing ground for wars of the twenty-first century carried forward under the counterinsurgency banner. Time was of the essence now, because the Pentagon had to beat the Taliban back and, unless the campaign showed real promise, Obama's timetable for bringing the troops home would come into play.

So a lot was riding on the outcome. Marja was, said Petraeus, "the first salvo" in the fight to control Kandahar. The city was not only important symbolically to the Taliban, who considered it their birthplace, but also a crucial point in the struggle to control all of Afghanistan, with accompanying international implications. Without Kandahar, it was said, Hamid Karzai could only claim to be mayor of Kabul. Karzai had himself been born in the city and had lasting connections there through his family, especially a half brother, Ahmed Wali Karzai, a politician and drug lord. Americans were never sure whether the president's brother was a necessary evil in the fight against the Taliban or a detriment to their plans. Ahmed Wali Karzai "had his unsavory side, but he was someone we could work with and he kept a lid on things in Kandahar," one U.S. official told the BBC. But others felt he was a major obstacle to American plans. Another anonymous "senior U.S. military official" told reporters he had paid a visit to Karzai to put him on notice. "I told him, 'I'm going to be watching every step you take. If I catch you meeting an insurgent, I'm going to put you on the JPEL.'" The Joint Prioritized Engagement List was reserved for the most-wanted insurgents. "That means," the official said he told Karzai, "that I can capture or kill you."[1]

The Ahmed Wali Karzai "challenge" was but one part of what Obama had undertaken—a Sisyphean endeavor with many boulders on many hills. And Ahmed Wali Karzai was present on many of those hills, collecting American money from the CIA for helping it push the boulders—when he chose to help, that is. The American military hated him, and the interagency feuds over the president's half brother resembled, wrote Mark Mazzetti in his book *The Way of the Knife*, something of a cross "between a Graham Greene novel and *Mad* magazine's *Spy vs. Spy*." McChrystal detested him as the very sort of corrosive influence that undermined counterinsurgency operations. The supposed legend of General Creighton Abrams getting everyone on the same page over Vietnam was apparently just that: a legend.[2]

Despite the reality of ethnic divisions deeply embedded in Afghan history, military policy makers held up the new counterinsurgency manual, Field Manual 3-24, as a guide to the way forward in dealing with insurgencies of all sorts. Yes, it was true, there was a crucial missing piece: a strong central government in Kabul that could guarantee Afghans a better choice than the Taliban. But stabilizing Kandahar—even as people worked to correct what was wrong in Kabul—was deemed a high-priority objective, not only for thwarting the Taliban but also for influencing the country's immediate neighbors, Pakistan and Iran, to leave Afghanistan alone.

Beyond those two, furthermore, India and China both had a big stake in any final settlement of the Afghan situation. Discouraging international rivalries began with Pakistan. Islamabad was already the most active player in the new Great Game, fearful of losing out when the Americans finally decided it was time to go home. Like Obama's domestic critics, Pakistani leaders took the president's West Point speech—no matter what the White House (or the Pentagon) said afterward—as signaling a determination to give the war one last try. Pakistan had a ringside seat as American leaders struggled mightily to produce a functional Afghan national security force to take over when the surge ended.

American political and military leaders were aware, on the other hand, of the known and suspected contacts the Pakistani intelligence service, ISI, had not only with Taliban leaders but also with the offshoot Haqqani terrorist network. Relations with the Haqqani network had to be the greatest irony of the American Afghan War. The network, originally led by Jalaluddin Haqqani, had been a Cold War ally. All during the 1980s, the CIA funneled arms and cash to the Haqqanis via Pakistan to counter Soviet forces. But now American officials expended a great deal of time and effort trying to convince Islamabad's leaders to see that their best interests did not reside in promoting such a nasty counterweight to Indian influence in Afghanistan. "It is really beginning to irk and anger us," complained an American security official familiar with efforts to convince Islamabad to cut off its complicit relations with the Haqqanis. If Islamabad did not take care of the problem, he warned, "Americans will by resorting to broader and more frequent drone strikes in Pakistan."[3]

The Marja-Kandahar offensive would relieve pressure on key issues—or so it was hoped. Most of all, it would show that the United States finally had, in counterinsurgency-speak, the proper military-political "inserts" to change not only the military equation inside Afghanistan, but also the good "outputs" from Afghanistan to correct the regional political balance of forces so that Afghanistan's future would not become a permanent scramble for power. In Washington, however, war rhetoric stayed focused on the line that the surge had been necessary to make sure al Qaeda had no place to launch a new attack on the United States. The president also continued talking about not sacrificing the gains for women, casting that goal as a major war objective. Yet most savvy observers knew there were limits to Obama's commitment. Above all he was determined to avoid another Vietnam. That determination, therefore, shaped the outer boundaries of what could be accomplished—at least by boots on the ground. And while he might not be around to enforce a final withdrawal of American forces should he not be reelected, the nation's tolerance for a long war was not something the Pentagon cared to put to the test. "Nobody," admitted a senior official, "wants to abandon the women of Afghanistan, but most Americans don't want to keep fighting there for years and years. The grim reality is that, despite all of the talk about promoting women's rights, things are going to have to give."[4]

"How much?" was always the question. What could the Americans leave undone and still consider the mission achieved? The beginning of a final answer to that question, it was said, would depend on the success or failure of the Marja campaign. General David Petraeus had put a bet on Marja as the "initial salvo" in a hard fight to reverse the Taliban momentum of recent years, and he had encouraged McChrystal's confidence that here was a real test for counterinsurgency theory.

Government in a Box

The most famous boast as the campaign for Marja began was McChrystal's claim that he had a government in a box ready to roll out as soon as the area was pacified—or even as coalition and Afghan troops advanced. He was bringing with him, in other words, a cadre of new civilian authorities from Kabul prepared to give citizens security and needed services. As a prelude to the military campaign there had appeared a brief flurry of statements emanating from a variety of sources about the possibility of a political settlement to the war. For example, McChrystal himself said, "Any Afghan can play a role if they focus on the future and not on the past." But this was again counterinsurgency-speak, referring to the notion that only a certain percentage of the enemy was actually fully committed to the cause, while others were simply waiting for a better deal.

In the Afghan War, the debate about a political settlement had suddenly become all about "reintegration" of individuals versus "reconciliation" with the Taliban as a whole. These were code words, of course, and they did not make understanding the different positions easy—on purpose. In one sense, it was little more than an updating of the Vietnam War debate over negotiations with the Vietcong circa 1965–67 when Washington offered "unconditional talks" as soon as the enemy gave up its effort to shoot its way into power, as Secretary of State Dean Rusk put it, and came in out of the jungle to participate as individuals in the political process. Just as Rusk had not expected the Vietcong to respond to any offer he made, American policy makers did not expect negotiations with the Taliban until the momentum in the war had shifted completely. "'Talking to the Taliban,'" writes Jonathan Steele, who reported from Afghanistan for many years for *The Guardian*, "was not intended as a genuine move toward negotiations. It was a weapon of war and a counterinsurgency tool, designed to undermine the Taliban by encouraging defections and breaking the movement into more easily defeatable fragments."[5]

The debate about "reconciliation" and "reintegration" was, however, considered a useful tactic to meet some of Hamid Karzai's proposals for reaching out to midlevel Taliban officials, a proposal he put before a January 2010 London conference of ISAF bigwigs. British and American officials were afraid Karzai would jump out ahead of the military with a proposal for talking with Mullah Muhammad Omar, at the top of the Taliban high command, or other "hard-core" types that Washington had declared "not reconcilable." The conference did decide on a $100 million investment in trying to encourage defections, but like so many other initiatives little was heard of it ever after. In any event, said dubious American officials, nothing could be expected from the other side until the thirty thousand soldiers of the surge made a serious dent in the Taliban's aspirations. Even then, as in the Vietnam "offer," any "reconciliation" would require Taliban leaders to renounce violence. "That's a pretty high bar for the Taliban leadership," commented Brian Katulis of the Center for American Progress, a think tank with ties to the Obama administration.[6]

Karzai's behavior offered a reason, therefore, to launch a military campaign to reverse, or preempt, any surfacing of a Karzai "peace offensive." Early in January, the Afghan president had invited about two dozen prominent Afghan media and business figures for a lunch at the palace. During the meal he said some things and outlined a theory of American motives and plans that leaked out. Their goal, he said, was not to build up an independent Afghanistan but to exercise power over regional issues. He bore a heavy burden, he told them, of standing up to the Americans. Left alone, he could strike a deal with the Taliban, but the United States refused to allow him to do so. They wanted to keep the war going so as to allow American troops to stay indefinitely.[7]

Deciding how serious Karzai was about such maneuvers sounded another echo of Vietnam. In 1963 American suspicions that South Vietnam's president, Ngo Dinh Diem, was entertaining, or actually engaging in, negotiations with North Vietnamese contacts as a last-ditch effort to prevent a large number of American troops coming into the country—and with them political demands for "reform"—had been a factor in Washington's decision to encourage South Vietnamese generals to move against the presidential palace in the fall.[8] At least one difference from the Vietnam experience stood out, however. In that conflict, set against the background of the Cold War, the enemy was the Vietcong/North Vietnam alliance; in Afghanistan the constant conflation of al Qaeda and the Taliban confused the issue of war and peace negotiations almost beyond understanding.

Similar confusions abounded about Marja itself. Although it was described in a military briefing on February 2, 2010, as a "city" or "town," it was really an unincorporated agricultural district with about eighty thousand inhabitants spread out over a large area in the southern province of Helmand. At its center was a collection of farm markets and a few mosques. Ahead of the military advance it was reported that thousands of residents had fled the area waiting for the dust to settle. That was just fine with McChrystal, for he said it would limit civilian casualties and perhaps lure some "lukewarm" Taliban to the government side. "We're not interested in how many Taliban we kill," he said. "We'd much rather have them see the inevitability that things are changing and just accept that."[9]

McChrystal elaborated several times on that theme, with one eye on Obama's pledge to start bringing the troops home in July 2011. "This is all a war of perceptions. Part of what we've had to do is convince ourselves and our Afghan partners that we can do this."[10] Operation Moshtarak (meaning "together" in the Dari language of Afghanistan) almost didn't get started—at least on the scheduled D-Day. There were supposed to have been last-minute negotiations with a Taliban figure, but another explanation is that McChrystal could not get President Karzai's permission to start the battle on time because the Afghan leader was "napping." He had a cold and was staying in bed, said aides, while the American general fumed over a leader who seemingly had no interest in the biggest moment of his career. The awful truth was that Karzai did not really have a lot of faith in counterinsurgency, McChrystal, or Obama. Presenting himself at the palace, McChrystal told Karzai, "This is your insurgency, but I'm your general." Well, said, Karzai this was the first time anyone had asked his permission to launch an offensive. After forty-five minutes the general left with his permission slip.[11]

McChrystal had given a pep talk two weeks before to more than a hundred American and Afghan officers. "Now we are real partners and fighting this war together," he said. For years there had been a struggle to get people to pay attention to Afghanistan. "Now everyone is paying attention. The people of Marja will watch this operation carefully. People from every corner of Afghanistan . . . will watch this operation carefully. There will be people in [the Taliban's high command in] Quetta who watch what happens carefully. And in every capital of the world, they will watch what happens carefully. What they will see is a complete change from what they have seen in the past."[12]

These brave words once again put the Afghan War at the center of world events, with momentous outcomes at issue. It seemed that the American military spent a great deal of effort simply to convince itself that the war was crucial—no matter what the rest of the world, including NATO allies, thought about the American obsession with "credibility." Things had indeed changed, however—but not quite the way McChrystal imagined would happen. Instead of the usual "softening up" by bombing, McChrystal had given plenty of warning that he was coming. Brigadier General Ben Hodges explained in an interview with National Public Radio's Judy Woodruff that there were indicators the senior Taliban leadership had left town. "The insurgency, really, you need to think about that as 80 percent little-t Taliban, 20 percent capital-T Taliban. In other words, a fifth or less are probably full-fledged, ideologically motivated Taliban insurgents." Well, that was what Field Manual 3-24 said about insurgencies, and that was what Hodges and his superiors wanted to believe—sort of a reverse transubstantion, wine to water. But not everyone in the Pentagon agreed. A writer for *Time* magazine interviewed one planner—anonymous as usual—who thought that the Marja Taliban were local and less easy to sort out from the population. "It's harder to separate the enemy from the people," he said, "when they are the people."[13]

Such warnings were rare, however. "The Afghan forces all have Marine haircuts right now," McChrystal quipped as the troops began the assaults.[14] At the outset there were plenty of flag raisings over "captured" territory. But officers warned their soldiers that, unlike what often happened in Iraq, there were to be no American flags raised, only Afghan flags, and no end zone touchdown dances. As early as February 26, Admiral Mike Mullen, chair of the Joint Chiefs of Staff, declared that the offensive had transformed the Marja area from the "clear" phase to the "hold" phase. "The raising of the [Afghan] flag is a significant symbol that's changed." And he praised McChrystal's "playbook" strategy of announcing the impending attacks in order to warn civilians and to allow low-level Taliban to flee. "We clearly informed the population before the operation," he said. "One of the signature events, as far as I'm concerned, was a meeting of 450 Afghan elders from the area, and they all signed up to this."[15]

By "this," he apparently meant American strategy. Deputy defense secretary William Lynn III said Marja had emerged as an area where hope was returning. "Because of our new strategy, and President Obama's deployment of additional troops," Lynn told an American Legion assembly in Washington, "Marja is one of many cities in Afghanistan that has begun to have hope." Now the focus will change, said Mullen: "Kandahar will be next."[16]

But after the early days, the fighting got tougher, with many casualties from improvised explosive devices, or IEDs. "We're not through Marja," Mullen said, tempering his optimism. "It's been a very tough operation, [and] will continue to be."[17] While the Taliban had melted away in large numbers, as hoped, there were snipers. The biggest and most enduring problem was that the locals did not really trust the Americans to protect them, especially not so long as they feared going out for their normal everyday activities for fear of being shot. The offensive "had frightened and disoriented them." The Taliban were cruel (or at least strict), but they were predictable. Americans swooped down into the mud-walled compounds in pursuit of the elusive enemy that had disappeared into the shadows. "We are innocent people," complained one elder in a meeting with Marine officers. "We have a lot of expensive things in our homes. Please do not break our things or take them."[18]

Worse was to come. Twelve people—five children, five women, and two men—were killed in a rocket attack on a house. Marine battalion commander Lieutenant Colonel Brian Christmas stood with a local elder, a relative of the victims. "I bring my deepest condolences and will provide all of my support," he said, referring to the problem of getting the bodies buried quickly according to Afghan custom when so many routes had been sealed off by the fighting and destruction of bridges. American helicopters were used to transport the bodies, while ISAF and Afghan authorities investigated the "incident." There were hints that a poorly trained Afghan unit had fired the rockets. At a news conference, however, the Afghan interior minister claimed that only nine of the twelve killed were civilians; the other three were Taliban insurgents who had forced their way into the house. The minister quoted a local tribal leader, who, he said, was saddened but not angry: "If nine civilians have died, hundreds of thousands will get freedom." Skeptical reporters who wrote the story of the rocket attack and the aftermath commented that the Marines found no weapons in the house and that the Marja area had a population of only eighty thousand.[19]

American military brass from Washington visited Marja and declared that its markets were open and people could feel safe on the streets. As for the government in a box, Hodges said that the goal had been to bring in a district governor and district chief of police who could deliver basic services, "like water, roads, some health care," and other things to help an agricultural economy be able to get its goods to market. The reporter with whom Hodges spoke sounded skeptical: wasn't Karzai bringing in as officials men who had lived outside Afghanistan for years, such as one who had been in Germany for fifteen years? "The selection of who is coming in to take government positions, of course," replied the general, "is the decision of the Afghan government."[20]

Whatever Hodges thought about Karzai's decisions, or whatever the elders had previously told Mullen, the locals were not happy about what they found wrapped inside the box. McChrystal and Eikenberry had persuaded Karzai to come to Marja for a "victory lap." Several hundred residents crowded into a mosque to hear the president talk about how he was restoring security to the country. But the speech did not go down well, and neither did his choices to run the local government. "We will tell you," thundered one elder, "that the warlords who ruled us for the past eight years, those people whose hands are red with the people's blood . . . they are still ruling over this nation." Another screamed at Karzai that the new police chief's minions preyed on young boys. "You sent these people here!"[21]

Not only did the mosque audience call out Karzai, but there were shouts about the Americans as well. Farmers were being arrested by the Americans. Schools and homes had been taken over by American troops. They destroyed irrigation canals. "You have said on the radio that you wanted our children to be educated," said a local leader, apparently not one of the 450 Mullen talked to who supposedly approved the campaign. "But how could we educate our children when their schools are turned into military bases? The Taliban never built their military bases in the schools."

Karzai attempted to cut off the "dialogue" with a warning. Afghanistan cannot shun the Americans, he said, or the country would fall under the influence of neighboring states. "We need their help to rebuild ourselves," Karzai explained. "As soon as we rebuild ourselves they will leave." A man shouted from the crowd, "Are they promising to leave?"[22]

As tempers simmered in Marja—and Washington—McChrystal faced another setback. Military officials in Kabul let it be known that American and NATO troops firing from passing convoys and military checkpoints over the past year had killed thirty Afghans and wounded another eighty—but in no instance had the victims proven to be a danger to the safety of the ISAF. The number was actually larger because private security contractors hired by the military did not keep tabs on how many Afghans they shot over the same period of time. "We have shot an amazing number of people," confirmed the American commander, "but to my knowledge, none has ever proven to be a threat." The persistence of these shootings had turned villages firmly against what Richard Oppel of the *New York Times* now called "the occupation"—not a term used about friendly territory in any previous American war. ISAF public relations officers could not have been very happy reading such articles. Embedding reporters had been thought to be the solution to the negative stories filed by reporters during the Vietnam War, but apparently that strategy did not always work.

Quickly, then, the symbol of flag raising promising independence turned into the reality of an alien force controlling events. Alas, McChrystal was caught in the middle, seemingly in a lose-lose situation. He had tried bringing the special operations forces in Afghanistan under his direct control in an effort to minimize such errors. Special ops units staged night raids, knocked down doors, and searched private quarters hunting for Taliban. One unit could be doing counterinsurgency properly, McChrystal admitted during a videoconference, while another carried out "a raid that might in fact upset progress."[23]

That was one way of describing the situation facing the general, a former special ops guy now trying to carry out the population-friendly mandates of the counterinsurgency manual. He had headed the team that discovered Saddam Hussein hiding away in his "spider hole" in December 2003. He was also credited with getting the number two al Qaeda man in Iraq, Abu Musab al-Zarqawi. Along with these feats, however, he had come under fire for abetting the false story of Pat Tillman's death and had been implicated in stories of torture in Iraq (see chapter 2).

While McChrystal had dodged those earlier bullets, now in Washington the general's critics complained that the new rules McChrystal had instituted put American soldiers at greater risk of being wounded or killed. With Marja beginning to backfire, the president decided he must call on Karzai in person to set things going again. In a lightning visit to Kabul on March 28, Obama met with the Afghan president during the evening hours before going on to Bagram Air Base to address American soldiers and then flying out at dawn. Karzai had been given less than a week's notice that he was expected to host the American president and his entourage. Obama had sent word ahead, moreover, that he expected to meet not only with President Karzai but also with the major players in the Afghan president's cabinet. The "request" conveyed in private what Obama's national security advisor James L. Jones told the press immediately after the meeting broke up. The American president, Jones said, wanted Karzai to understand "that in his second term, there are certain things that have not been paid attention to, almost since Day One."[24]

Standing alongside Karzai, Obama had not praised the Afghan leader or talked much about "progress." Yes, there had been military gains, but "we also want to make progress on the civilian process." What Obama had said in private about the continuing corruption rampant in Kabul, the failure to appoint effective members to the Afghan cabinet, the constant issue of opium revenue funding for the Taliban, and failures to achieve results in improving local governments, we do not know. Transparency International had ranked Afghanistan 176th out of 180 countries in corruption among public officials. Only Haiti, Iraq, Myanmar, and Somalia ranked lower. In his briefing, Jones stressed that Karzai needed "to be seized with how important that is . . . We have to have the strategic rapport with President Karzai and his cabinet to understand how we are going to succeed this year in reversing the momentum the Taliban and opposition forces have been able to establish since 2006."

One member of the parliament, Noor ul-Haq Ulumi, who headed the defense committee, agreed that it was a critical moment. He hoped, however, that Obama would focus less on big military operations. "Our problem needs a political solution," he said. "Karzai became president through fraud, and it's still a corrupted government inside Afghanistan."[25]

As Obama stood beside Karzai that day, the Afghan leader may well have been smiling at the suberterfuge going on behind the rhetoric. For over a decade he had been receiving private funds from the CIA totaling tens of millons of dollars to pay off warlords; when finally questioned about the money, he said he also used it to help out other people in dire need. Asked about these payments later, Karzai treated them as purely matter-of-fact transactions, not worthy of serious concern. As Matthew Rosenberg reported in the *New York Times,*

> Asked why money that was used for what would appear to be justifiable governing and charitable expenses was handed over secretly by the C.I.A. and not routed publicly through the State Department, Mr. Karzai replied: "This is cash. It is the choice of the U.S. government."
>
> He added, "If tomorrow the State Department decides to give us such cash, I'd welcome that, too."[26]

Which U.S. government was in command: the White House or the CIA? When it came to Karzai, it appeared the intelligence agency had its own policy—either that or Obama felt he had to play the role of plausible deniability for the audience at home.

A Bleeding Ulcer

No sooner had Obama returned to Washington than Karzai was at it again with provocative statements, this time denouncing the "West" for demanding that "foreigners" oversee parliamentary elections. The Americans wanted a weak parliament, he told a gathering of election officials, "and for me to be an ineffective president." He castigated Americans for saying he had perpetrated a fraud in the presidential election. All those accusations, he said, were aimed at diminishing him in the eyes of his countrymen. "They wanted to have a puppet government. They wanted a servant government."[27]

On April 16 Obama met with the National Security Council for its monthly update on the situation. McChrystal's report on his progress was not what Obama wished to hear. The model had been to clear, hold, build, and then transfer. The general had to admit that he had not yet been able to transfer authority to the Afghan national security forces anywhere in the region. "Are we on time-line?" Obama asked. Yes, replied the general. Obama then ran down the list of places where the model had stalled at the "hold" level. Were any of them close to being transferred? Not one, the general said. As Bob Woodward put it, "The model had become clear, hold, hold, hold, hold and hold. Hold for years. There was no build, no transfer."[28]

At the end of April a new Pentagon report requested by Congress offered up a very mixed picture of where matters stood. It reaffirmed faith in the "reintegration" process for peeling away foot soldiers in the Taliban, but the enemy's momentum had not been halted, let alone reversed. Despite the Taliban's having killed more than twice the number of civilians than had been killed by ISAF forces, the Karzai government was less popular in more than 90 of 120 key districts considered essential to success. And despite the growing number of American troops arriving with their new technology, better even than that used during the Iraq War, the report said that the insurgency had the advantage of drawing upon poverty, tribal friction, and lack of governance, as well as access to small arms and explosives for roadside bombs, to support "robust" military operations.[29]

The report also suggested that the effort to implement counter-insurgency through reintegration had failed to produce any measur-able successes. Instead, special operations forces—carrying out the nighttime raids that McChrystal had roundly criticized only weeks before as the Marja campaign got under way—had accomplished the most of what had been achieved. Then came this list of bad indicators for the future: peeling away midlevel Taliban had not been effective; separating out the population from the Taliban had not succeeded; forcing Karzai to provide competent, honest officials for local government had not worked. It did not mention his CIA "slush fund," a topic much too hot to handle. Perhaps, however, what we now know about Obama's "private army" (as the CIA

would become known as among insiders) the Pentagon authors
were unaware of at the time.

On May 1—as if to accentuate the impotence (or irrelevance) of
the counterinsurgency strategy in Afghanistan—a naturalized
American citizen from Pakistan, Faisal Shahzad, attempted to set
off a bomb in Times Square, New York. The bomb did not go off,
but Shahzad nearly escaped before being taken off a flight out of
JFK airport at the last minute. Investigations and interrogations led
back to contacts and training Shahzad had obtained from the Pakistan branch of the Taliban, and more shadowy connections with
the Pakistan military. He revealed that he had had several choices
of targets and had decided on the center of New York City, where
memories of 9/11 would maximize the explosive power of his crude
device. Shahzad failed in his mission because his training was not
perfect, nor even highly professional. But how many more like him
were out there, seething with anger and ready to strike a blow against
their adopted country? Here was something very new. In the past,
expat groups schemed against the rulers of the country they had
left; now they were plotting against their host countries.

Shahzad's bomb attempt was headline news for a few days. But its
real impact probably was in nudging Washington faster away from
reliance on the McChrystal-Petraeus strategy. The Pentagon report
had already hinted at the shift before the Times Square incident,
and its sober tone provided the background for the upcoming visit
of President Hamid Karzai. Instead of another upbraiding from national security adviser James Jones, however, Karzai was treated to a
walk with Secretary of State Hillary Clinton in a private garden in
Georgetown, and then to a full state dinner at the White House.

What accounts for the dramatic change? Washington was not at
all convinced that Karzai had suddenly seen the light about the
need to change his ways. When Obama and Karzai held a joint
press conference at the conclusion of the Afghan visit, on May 12,
the American president talked about how important success in
Afghanistan was for American security. But the frame of reference
he used was the May 1 attack and how it demonstrated al Qaeda's
determination to foster plots originating "in the border regions

between Afghanistan and Pakistan. And a growing Taliban insurgency could mean an even larger safe haven for al Qaeda and its affiliates." There was a lot in that sentence to think about. The Marja campaign was still important. "We have taken the fight to the Taliban," said the president, and "pushed them out of their stronghold in Marja." And "we are working to give Afghans the opportunity to reclaim their communities." So it is too much to say that the Pentagon report and the abortive May 1 attack caused priorities to shift away from counterinsurgency, but the enthusiasm for what could be accomplished by troops working with Afghan national forces had begun to wane. Clinton's hospitality and the wording of Obama's comments suggested not a warming of relations but a kind of public display reserved for visiting Indian princes in the days of the British Raj.

At the press conference Obama talked about his recent flight into Kabul, declaring there was no denying that progress had been made in recent years, "as I saw in the lights across Kabul when I landed—lights that would not have been visible just a few years ago." American policy makers were addicted to "light" metaphors in describing evidence of progress in winning the wars against dark forces of the world, but the operations that were working the best, the Pentagon report had said, were those carried out by the special ops forces, who struck at night in the darkness. Obama also reinforced the hard-line position on "reintegration" versus "reconciliation," declaring that while the United States supported the upcoming "peace jirga," or peace conference, that Karzai planned for Kandahar, the basic requirements for a settlement had not changed: before anything could happen, the Taliban's momentum had to be reversed. "The United States supports the efforts of the Afghan government to open the door to Taliban who cut their ties to al Qaeda, abandon violence, and accept the Afghan constitution, including respect for human rights. And I look forward to a continued dialogue with our Afghan partners on these efforts."[30]

Around the edges of the Karzai-Obama meeting, McChrystal secured a commitment to supply $200 million worth of diesel generators to Kandahar and, to his great satisfaction, to keep control over their delivery and installation. The general and his aides thought Obama had made a deeper commitment at this press conference than in even his West Point speech. Only one of the aides expressed doubts to a reporter about the stability of the relationship with the Afghan president: "This is just a honeymoon period. I doubt if it's going to last two weeks."[31]

Three weeks later senior *Washington Post* writers Karen DeYoung and Greg Jaffe described the expansion of U.S. "secret war" capabilities. Special operations commanders, they wrote, had become a far more regular presence in the White House than they had been during the George W. Bush years.[32] The advantage of a surge in special operations deployments in various places inside Afghanistan, but also in Pakistan and Somalia and Yemen, was that these forces seldom talked about what they were doing. For a Democratic president facing criticism from left and right, the journalists asserted, the unacknowledged raids and drone attacks in Somalia and Yemen "provide politically useful tools." "We have a lot more access," said one special ops commander. "They are talking publicly much less but they are acting more. They are willing to get aggressive much more quickly."

There were many signs that special ops and drones were becoming President Obama's weapons of choice. He increased budget requests for the special operations forces by nearly 6 percent for fiscal 2011. But perhaps more important, an issue that had been brewing since Donald Rumsfeld's efforts to make special ops capable of acting inside a country without the ambassador's approval or even knowledge had now resurfaced. The secretaries of state in those years, Colin Powell and Condoleezza Rice, had successfully held off Pentagon efforts to bypass the civilian representatives of the president in order to pursue their own agenda; now, it appeared, Obama was close to making advocates of such stealth operations his own personal representatives outside traditional chains of command.[33]

Admiral Eric T. Olson, head of Special Operations Command, acknowledged as much in a speech, though he placed the emphasis

on the supposed wishes of host countries: "In some places, in defer-
ence of host-country sensitivities, we are lower in profile. In every
place, Special Operations forces activities are coordinated with the
U.S. ambassador and are under the operational control of the four-
star regional commander."[34]

The place where authority seemed to overlap—at the level of
"the four-star regional commander"—was also the area where Special Ops wanted more independence. And the regional commander
they were concerned about was, not surprisingly, McChrystal.
While all military personnel were supposed to be working for Central Command under Petraeus, one of the special ops people told
reporters, "our issue is that we believe our theater forces should be
under a Special Operations theater commander." Obama seemed to
agree. What began under George W. Bush as a Pentagon grab for
independence now seemed to have evolved into something else,
thanks to the "close relationship" between Bob Gates and Hillary
Clinton, who have "smoothed out the process."[35]

What the "process" had led to—at least in detail—remains a
classified matter, but Obama's wishes coincided with changes going
on even in the midst of the Marja campaign. In effect, he was
gaining a private army and air force to use in an unacknowledged
manner. Meanwhile, the May 1 attack added impetus to Obama's
desire for a weapon to counter what counterterrorism adviser John
Brennan saw arising out of the investigation of Faisal Shahzad's
background in the Pakistan Taliban: the threat of American citizens being recruited to carry out terrorist attacks inside the United
States. Shahzad was only the latest, Brennan said, in a series of
"American terror suspects." He added, "They took advantage of
their U.S. citizenship and were operating in many respects not necessarily alone, but in manners that made it more difficult for us to
detect. These are the ones I am concerned about."[36]

"Not necessarily alone" would turn out to be a key to understanding what was coming. It was not a long way from setting out
the rationale for drone strikes on American citizens in foreign
countries suspected of receiving (or giving) terrorist instructions.

Meanwhile, in Afghanistan, Gen. McChrystal made another visit to the Marja district and offered up another highly quotable comment: "This is a bleeding ulcer right now." As a reporter traveling with the commander described the moment, the general sat gazing at maps of the area as the marine battalion commander, Lieutenant Colonel Brian Christmas, pleaded for more time to oust Taliban fighters from their strongholds.

> "You've got to be patient," Lt. Col. Brian Christmas told McChrystal. "We've only been here 90 days."
>
> "How many days do you think we have before we run out of support by the international community?" McChrystal replied. . . .
>
> "I can't tell you, sir," [Christmas] finally answered.
>
> "I'm telling you," McChrystal said. "We don't have as many days as we'd like."[37]

Describing his access to the commander's encounter with Colonel Christmas and a British major general named Nick Carter, the head of coalition forces in southern Afghanistan, as a rare opportunity to hear the frank conversations, reporter Dion Nissenbaum called the sessions a wake-up call that drove home the hard fact that Obama's plan to start bringing home American troops had collided with the realities of the war. There simply weren't enough U.S. and Afghan forces to provide the security that's needed to win the loyalty of wary locals. "The Taliban have beheaded Afghans who cooperate with foreigners in a creeping intimidation campaign," Nissenbaum wrote, and the government in a box held too few crayons to draw even a rough sketch of a workable local government. Carter backed up the Marine colonel: there had been too few troops to lock down the place. McChrystal was not impressed with that explanation. "You're going to feel that way," he said, "It's your plan."[38]

"What we have done, in my view," McChrystal said, winding up the conference, "we have given the insurgency a chance to be a little bit credible. We said: 'We're taking it back.' We came in to take it back. And we haven't been completely convincing."

There Will Be No Tanks

The setbacks in Marja had an immediate impact on the Kandahar objective. The NATO Office of Communication called down the McClatchy Newspapers for printing the "bleeding ulcer" comment out of context. Overall, wrote Admiral Gregory Smith to the managing editor, McChrystal felt—and had told Nissenbaum—that the campaign was "largely on track." "It's that it's misperceived to be going badly." McClatchy wasn't buying—and neither were a lot of people in Afghanistan and Washington. Even before his trip to the Marja front line, McChrystal was in the process of shifting to more reliance on the night raids and other non-counterinsurgency methods of keeping the Taliban from gaining ground in Kandahar. First there was the change of attitude about the problematic Ahmed Wali Karzai. McChrystal's intelligence chief, Gen. Michael T. Flynn, had once said about Wali Karzai and Kandahar, "The only way to clean up Chicago is to get rid of Capone."[39]

By the end of March that assertion was already out of date. Wali Karzai had become essential because he had sources of intelligence that were critical for the success of the night raids. The Marja experience had demonstrated, moreover, that it was unlikely Kabul would come up with new local leaders capable of running a much bigger show in Kandahar. "There isn't time for risky experiments in Kandahar," said a *Washington Post* correspondent with inside sources in the Pentagon.[40]

But Wali Karzai was himself a risky strategy and a symbol of the inability of the American agencies involved to develop and agree on a strategic plan, particularly since he could use his intelligence sources to pinpoint personal enemies and political rivals. On the other hand, the American military had stopped using the term "offensive" to describe planned operations for Kandahar. In other words there would be no "clear, hold, transfer" progression. Instead, the military would work around the Taliban to start projects, and continue using special ops raids to take out specific targets. It was described to the press as a "civilian surge" accompanied by a "quiet increase of American troops to provide security for them." The operation, originally to be called Moshtarak Phase III, was renamed Operation Hamkari (meaning "cooperation").

This change resulted in part from a visit President Karzai had made to Kandahar in early April, where he solicited advice from the crowd that had gathered to hear him, and promised them there would be no broad-scale military advance. "You don't want an offensive, do you?" he called out to general acclamation. "There will be no operation until you are happy." He did this flanked by American military brass, who, it appeared, were on board with the Afghan president, if only because there was no other choice. Yes, agreed General Nick Carter, Karzai had taken away the impression that people did not want to see another Falluja "on the streets of Kandahar, and I think we all said 'Amen' to that." What was coming to the Kandahar region instead was a surge of $90 million. "It's huge," said one official. "We've employed 40,000 people in cash for work."[41]

The new strategy envisioned wrapping "Kandahar City in a circle of assistance and development projects," but the risk was always the same as with earlier troubles. The ones administering all this aid were the old power brokers who were not trusted by the people, or new ones from Kabul also not trusted. Secretary of State Clinton declared that there would be no "tanks rolling into the city." Whatever the strategy, care would be taken so that the effort "doesn't destroy Kandahar in the effort to save Kandahar." Her words were taken (and meant to be taken) from a scene in Vietnam in the aftermath of the Tet offensive when an American military commander said that it had been necessary to destroy a city to save it. General McChrystal added a rueful note that captured the mood of the moment perfectly: "I actually think the U.S. military would love to find an enemy that was dug in on a piece of terrain, that we could establish a D-Day and we could attack with no civilians around, because that would play to every strength that the coalition has."[42]

But Afghanistan was not Vietnam with lessons learned, let alone World War II in Europe. *Washington Post* writer Rajiv Chandrasekaran talked about the perils of soft power when applied to the situation confronting American policy makers. It had unleashed "unintended and potentially troubling consequences . . . sparking new tension and rivalries. . . . It is also raising public expectations for handouts that the Afghan government will not be able to sustain once U.S. contributions ebb." Buying victory was thus also a mirage. "Those cash-for-work men—half of them used to be Taliban," said a district governor. "If the Americans stop paying for them to work, they'll go back to the Taliban."[43]

The "cash surge" in Afghanistan was based on two doubtful assumptions beyond the matter of whether any government in Kabul could afford to continue supplying the money. One was the recent experience in Iraq where cash payments to the "Sunni awakening" had been a big part of the Petraeus "success story" in turning around the critical situation there. The second was the more theoretical arguments made in Field Manual 3-24 that only a minority of insurgents were true believers, while the great majority were simply soldiers for hire in a situation in which there were few opportunities. The problem with both assumptions was, as the district governor said, what happens when the money dries up?

Karzai's flirtations with a negotiated settlement took a new turn in early June when he fired two officials who were favorites of the Pentagon and CIA. The firings occurred after explosions and a rocket attack near the place where Karzai had summoned a peace jirga. After the excitement died down, the Afghan president refused to hear any evidence that the Taliban had been responsible. "He treated it like a piece of dirt," said one of those who brought the information to him. Instead, he blamed the two men for not preventing the attacks, or secretly encouraging them because they opposed negotiations. One of these was the interior minister, Hanif Atmar, who, it was said, opposed the Karzai policy of "reintegration" of former Taliban into the national police. Here again the confusion between "reintegration" and "reconciliation" surfaced, because Washington was not happy about Karzai doing much of either. Pentagon spokesman Geoff Morrell said Atmar and national director of security Amrullah Saleh were both "people we admire and whose service we appreciate." Saleh was an ethnic Tajik, a member of the Northern Alliance, which had helped the United

States drive out the Taliban during the 2001 invasion. Karzai apparently saw him as an obstacle to any effort at serious negotiations. A member of the parliament confirmed that impression: "Intel has a very important role in reconciliation. Saleh was not the right person for this job. No Taliban would ever trust this man."[44]

Saleh was convinced that the president's motivations stemmed from a belief that the West could not defeat the Taliban and that it was up to him to make a deal with them, operating through contacts with Pakistan. He believed as well that the assertions he stole the election all had to do with a desire to get rid of him. American commanders had given Karzai an alternative explanation for the attacks on the jirga—it had been organized by the Haqqani network, which, of course, they insisted was acting for elements of the ISI in Pakistan. Karzai did not believe that assertion, either. But above all, said an Afghan general, "he doesn't think the Americans can afford to stay."[45]

Almost on cue, it seemed, a new Pentagon release described a great discovery in Afghanistan: there was nearly $1 trillion in mineral deposits in the country, "enough to fundamentally alter the Afghan economy and perhaps the Afghan war itself." A small team of "Pentagon officials and American geologists" had discovered the vast scale of this mineral wealth, and then briefed President Hamid Karzai. The implications of this discovery suggested that American subsidies would not be necessary over the long haul, while for the immediate future what was needed was a little more patience. "There is stunning potential here," Gen. Petraeus said in an interview. "There are a lot of ifs, of course, but I think it is hugely significant." An Afghan minister chimed in, "This will become the backbone of the Afghan economy." The Pentagon had already started trying to set up a system for mineral development. International accounting firms had been hired to help oversee mining contracts, and technical data were being prepared, to be turned over to "multinational mining companies and other potential foreign investors." Finally, the Pentagon was helping Afghan officials arrange bids for mineral rights—starting as early as the fall of 2011 (when American troops from the surge were to start coming home).[46]

It turned out that the Americans had not exactly been the first ones to latch on to the vast mineral deposits in Afghanistan, which included "huge veins" of iron, copper, cobalt, gold, and lithium—a veritable treasure house of minerals essential to modern industry. The Russians had collected preliminary data during their occupation in the 1980s before they withdrew. But in any event, the Pentagon would play the role of overseer to manage a new mining and extraction branch of the Afghan government. (This was not exactly new either, as the Pentagon had had a task force in Iraq that created business development firms before the task force was transferred to Afghanistan.)[47]

Then it turned out that American geologists had not been in the dark about Afghanistan's mineral deposits before the Pentagon's sudden announcement after all. Accounts of the mineral resources had been published by both American and British geological surveys three years earlier. It took very little time for various reporters to start making connections between the report and worried policy makers' concern that there was very little time left for political leaders in the United States and NATO countries to convince their publics, as Defense Secretary Gates admitted to a Brussels conference, that the McChrystal/Petraeus strategy for reversing Taliban momentum was working.[48]

McChrystal was at the Brussels meeting, and both he and Gates insisted that progress was slow but steady; the important thing was to keep up a sense of urgency. Yet the attendees in Brussels, including the press, learned that whatever offensive was being planned for Kandahar had now been postponed for at least three months. "The key," said Gates, "is not that there's going to be some end state by the end of December where we suddenly declare victory or say that Kandahar is done. Kandahar is a project that will take a number of months." McChrystal implied that Karzai himself was behind the delay, telling reporters, "When you go to protect people, the people have to want you to protect them." This was both counterinsurgency dogma as well as an admission that so far it hadn't worked because the Afghan president had not done his job.[49]

Bad news continued to pour in from Afghanistan with stories about how NATO convoys guarded by Afghan mercenaries were paying bribes to Taliban insurgents along the way to let them pass. The amounts paid, investigators asserted, had mounted up to tens of millions of dollars. Some of this money was being funneled into the hands of Afghan officials. "People think the insurgency and the government are separate, and that is just not always the case," said a NATO official in Kabul. "What we are finding is that they are often bound up together." The U.S. was supporting both sides in the war, said the official. There were literally thousands of private guards involved, with more than fifty security companies allegedly providing protection to the convoys. Hanif Atmar, the former interior minister Karzai fired, told Dexter Filkins, the top *New York Times* reporter in Afghanistan, that there were thousands of these guards running around in Kandahar and other places, not in uniform and with no identification, operating virtually under no government control. Hashmat Karzai, a cousin of the president, controlled one of these security companies.[50]

When the surge was announced, Obama had said the troops would start coming home in the summer of 2011. His cabinet officials and the Pentagon immediately jumped in to say there would be no rush to the exits, but a gradual transition phase. By June 2010 the Taliban's momentum had been slowed down in some areas— but nobody had really expected they could take Kabul. Columnist Bob Herbert suggested that the real issue had become "the courage to leave": "There is no good news coming out of the depressing and endless war in Afghanistan. There once was merit to our incursion there, but that was long ago. Now we're just going through the tragic motions, flailing at this and that, with no real strategy or decent end in sight."[51]

The Return of General Petraeus

The cascade of bad news from Afghanistan caused Capitol Hill to stir uneasily, like a heavy sleeper who hears noises out in the hallway and finally has to get up to see what the matter is out there. As the number of dead in the Afghan War passed one thousand, the headlines spoke of a dysfunctional and corrupt government in Kabul not worthy of American support. Summoned to a Senate hearing to explain what actually was going on, Pentagon officials took their turns providing explanations. Undersecretary of Defense for Policy Michele Flournoy, a strong defender of counterinsurgency from the outset, cited the number of times Afghans reported to Americans where IEDs had been placed along roadsides. This development, she asserted, indicated that there were "growing pockets of confidence" among local Afghans and increasing willingness to support ISAF efforts to establish security and governance. It was true that insurgent attacks had resumed in Marja, but they were less effective in terms of casualties per incident, indicating a "possible reduction in some of their operational capacity."[52]

Pentagon press secretary Geoff Morrell pled for greater recognition of the fact that this would be a tough fight and that casualties would increase as progress was made. Then he said part of the problem was that reporters wished to be embedded in the worst trouble spots and not with military units in the north, where conditions were more stable. The result was a skewed picture of the overall war effort. "While Helmand and Kandahar are important provinces," he said, "they do not comprise the entirety of Afghanistan. There are many places where security is improving and life is getting better. . . . Let's at least allow them the next six months to prove that General McChrystal's strategy will work."[53]

Whatever had happened to the pre-Marja campaign assurance that thirty thousand troops were enough because only some provinces needed to be cleared of Taliban? Morrell's plea suggested that reporters should go only to less dangerous places and report on the measurable progress there. Even before the hearings, Defense Secretary Gates had told reporters that he was unhappy with their coverage. "I, frankly, get a little impatient with some of the coverage because of the lack of historical context. So as far as I'm concerned, this endeavor began in full, and reasonably resourced, only a few months ago."[54] Gates's plea was a familiar one; he had made it several times. And again at the hearings he complained about press coverage being "too negative." The man everyone wanted to hear from, however, was David Petraeus. His testimony came in two parts. On the first day, shortly after giving his opening statement, he collapsed—a result, it was said, of dehydration. He recovered within thirty minutes and asked to continue, but his testimony was put off until the next day.

Senator Carl Levin of Michigan had not been happy with the general's response on the first day to a question about whether he supported the president's determination to start withdrawing troops in the summer of 2011; Petraeus had indicated that he did support the president, but also that he was wary about timetables. On the second day Levin, who stood in for the administration in these hearings as a defense attorney confronting Republicans who sought to turn the hearings into an indictment of the White House's time-table, pressed Petraeus for a stronger affirmation of his support. The general came prepared with a statement that he did "support and agree" with the decision to begin drawing down the surge as planned, with the pace determined by security conditions a year from now. Satisfied, Levin said he was glad to hear Gen. Petraeus express his support for the timetable. "I strongly believe it is essential for success in Afghanistan that everyone understand the urgency with which the Afghans need to take responsibility for their own security."[55]

Admiral Mike Mullen added a note of caution. "We all have angst" about Afghanistan, he said, but "I think we will know by the end of the year, obviously, where we are with respect to reversing the momentum." What happened next, however, sent a tremor through the entire war front, from Afghanistan all the way to the Pentagon and then to the White House. A *Rolling Stone* article, "The Runaway General" by Michael Hastings, set it off. Even before it appeared in print on June 25, 2010, the shock wave from leaks had reverberated around the world, and General McChrystal was on the verge of being relieved of his command. In an almost dream-like sequence of rambling comments delivered around a Paris din-ner and during interviews with Hastings, McChrystal and his closest aides had vented their anger about the White House's idea of how to run a war.

McChrystal started by saying his meetings with the president left him feeling Obama did not really have any inclination to understand the problems Afghanistan presented. When McChrystal got the job, Obama gave him ten minutes. "It was a 10-minute photo-op," one of the general's advisers was quoted as saying. "Obama clearly didn't know from anything about him, who he was. Here's the guy who's going to run his fucking war, but he didn't seem very engaged. The boss was pretty disappointed."[56]

The general and his aides then joined in on a verbal strafing of the president's top advisers, from Vice President Biden on down through the list. McChrystal and his aides believed that no one on the civilian side was really up to his or her job. National Security Advisor Jim Jones, a retired four-star general, was called a "clown" stuck in a 1985 Cold War mind-set; Richard Holbrooke was intelligent enough but behaved like a wounded animal because he was afraid of being fired. And Biden? Months earlier, while the surge decision was supposedly still up in the air, McChrystal had responded to a question about Biden's opposition by saying that was a surefire way to get "Chaos-istan"—a comment that had not pleased Obama. Now, in the interview, McChrystal speculated about what he would do if he got another Biden-like question. As Hastings reported:

> "I never know what's going to pop out until I'm up there [at the podium], that's the problem," [McChrystal] says. Then, unable to help themselves, he and his staff imagine the general dismissing the vice president with a good one-liner.
>
> "Are you asking about Vice President Biden?" McChrystal says with a laugh. "Who's that?"
>
> "Biden?" suggests a top adviser. "Did you say: Bite Me?"

These throwaway lines were a culmination of sorts to a longstanding feud with the civilians in the administration. McChrystal had been unhappy ever since it had been leaked to the press that Ambassador Eikenberry had sent cables opposing sending more troops to Afghanistan. The general felt that since he had "won" the

debate, Eikenberry should have stepped aside; instead, his continued presence in Afghanistan indicated to McChrystal the president's
skepticism about the mission. The general blamed civilians, especially the State Department, for failing to provide the necessary
resources for reconstruction purposes. "If we lose," said an American at NATO headquarters in Kabul, "it's going to be because of
civilians."[57]

Why had McChrystal allowed Hastings, a reporter for a left-
leaning magazine, to record all of those statements? No completely
clear explanation has emerged yet. On Hastings's side, his purpose
was clear: he wanted to get McChrystal. "I'd liked hanging out with
McChrystal and his team, yet I hated the war. . . . [T]hey were an
unchecked force, steamrolling the civilian leadership. . . . What
they told me, I realized, revealed the attitudes behind one of the most
brazen assaults on civilian control of the military that the Pentagon's
generals had ever attempted."[58]

Like many others who voted for Obama in 2008, Hastings believed that what the Democratic candidate said about Afghanistan
was really more of a slap at George W. Bush than any real conviction about Afghanistan. "Obama resisted doing so [tripling the
number of soldiers], but the military leadership pushed hard and
played dirty to get the war in Afghanistan they wanted." Hastings
apparently believed that he was offering the president a way out of
a bad decision that had been forced on him. The problem with that
interpretation of what had happened to Obama on the way to the
Oval Office was that at the outset of his campaign in 2007 he had
endorsed counterinsurgency in his opening speech on foreign policy at the Wilson Center in Washington, D.C. It might well be that
he now rued having listened to Robert Gates and Hillary Clinton,
but Obama's problems were not the result of a supine surrender to a
bullying military.

After the article appeared, Obama accepted McChrystal's apolo-
gies, but also his resignation. Hastings recounts that Gates and
Clinton urged Obama to scold the general and then send him back
to duty to complete the mission. Instead—with Hastings's help (at
least in Michael Hastings's opinion)—Obama stood up to the mili-

tary. Within minutes of announcing the firing of General Mc-
Chrystal at a National Security Council meeting, Obama summoned
Petraeus to the Oval Office. According to Hastings, the general had
been in the White House basement mulling over who might replace
McChrystal if the decision was to fire him.

As Petraeus walked up the stairs he passed CIA director Leon
Panetta, as well as Secretaries Gates and Clinton, all of whom
avoided eye contact "like physicians about to give a grim diagno-
sis." Once Petraeus was seated in the Oval Office, Obama asked
him to take over command in Afghanistan, and Petraeus agreed
to do the job for thirteen months.[59] Few noticed that the end of
that thirteen-month period coincided neatly with the target date
for withdrawal.

Journalist Tom Ricks wrote in the *Washington Post* that the new
commander would have a hard time repeating the success of the
Iraq surge because Petraeus could not count on the same degree of
teamwork and cohesion as he had in Iraq. Obama had not taken
the critical next step in firing Eikenberry and Holbrooke, Ricks argued, "so it is likely that the same nettlesome quarrels that exasperated McChrystal also will fatigue his successor."[60]

Ricks then predicted, "The president of the United States may
have signaled the beginning of the end of the war in Afghanistan.
In a year or two, President Obama will be able to say that he gave
the conflict his best shot, reshaping the strategy and even putting his
top guy in charge, the general who led the surge in Iraq—but that
things still didn't work out." The problem, according to this thesis,
was that the civilians in Washington had failed to hold up their
end of the counterinsurgency endeavor. The idea that Afghans
might well resent what was happening in their country, and even
blame Americans for the misery inflicted upon them by Taliban
outrages, was not to be entertained by the once skeptical journalist
who now filled the end seat in the pew of Petraeus rooters.

Republicans in Congress took up the charge against civilian in-
competence as well, with Senator Christopher Bond of Missouri
saying on Fox News that he agreed Eikenberry and Holbrooke
should be ousted—and "a muzzle put on the vice president when it

comes to this war." South Carolina's Lindsey Graham said Obama should tell Biden to "shut up." Here was a chance to put new people on the ground, but if they had to drag old baggage around, the results would be the same, "and if we don't change quickly we're going to lose a war we can't afford to lose."[61]

Before leaving for Afghanistan, Petraeus told Congress that the war must be won, as doing so was "vital" to United States security. Yet he also tried to allow no daylight to appear between himself and the president on the timing of the beginning of the end of the surge. It was an uncomfortable perch, to say the least. The U.S. commitment to Afghanistan would be "enduring," he promised Congress. No territory must be available for al Qaeda to use in another attack on the American homeland. "July 2011 is the point at which we will begin a transition phase. . . . July 2011 is not a date when we will be rapidly withdrawing our forces and switching off the lights and closing the door behind us."[62]

He promised the legislators that he would look very carefully at the issue of whether McChrystal's implementation of a counterinsurgency strategy put American soldiers at greater risk of being wounded or killed. "I want to assure the mothers and fathers of those fighting in Afghanistan," he told a Senate Committee holding hearings on his confirmation, "that I see it as a moral imperative to bring all assets to bear to protect our men and women in uniform." He felt so strongly about this point that he had already consulted with President Karzai and other Afghan leaders, "and they are in full agreement with me on this." And he went on to emphasize, "I mention this because I am keenly aware of concerns by some of our troopers on the ground about the application of our rules of engagement and the tactical directive."[63]

In a sense, by joining the crowd that had criticized McChrystal's efforts to implement counterinsurgency and put special ops under tight control, Petraeus was backing away from the approach he had fathered at Fort Leavenworth half a decade earlier and which was enshrined in Field Manual 3-24. What was at the heart of the debate was whether counterinsurgency was actually a workable strategy.

Arriving in Kabul, Petraeus used remastered Cold War rhetoric to describe a war reaching its "critical moment." "We must pursue the insurgents relentlessly. . . . We must demonstrate to the Afghan people, and to the world, that al Qaeda and its network of extremist allies will not be allowed to once again establish sanctuaries in Afghanistan from which they can launch attacks on the Afghan people and on freedom-loving nations around the world." He had not come to Afghanistan to negotiate a surrender. Speaking to American soldiers, he repeated what he had said to Congress about protecting them from unnecessary risks: "We must demonstrate to the people and to the Taliban that Afghan and ISAF forces are here to safeguard the Afghan people, and that we are in this to win. That is our clear objective."

Although he had begun by saying what had happened was only a change of personnel and not strategy, it was impossible to ignore the repudiation of the Marja approach—that is, of counterinsurgency. Petraeus went on to suggest that there had been less than full cooperation from the civilian side, just as McChrystal had claimed. "To our diplomatic and international civilian partners here today: We are all—civilian and military, Afghan and international—part of one team with one mission. Indeed, we all recognize the grave threat that the Taliban, al Qaeda, and the associated 'syndicate' of extremists pose to this country, to this region, and to the world." Here was a coded reference to Pakistan's support of various Taliban offshoots—and the dawn of the drone age.

5

THE WAR OF THE DRONES

The problem with the drone is it's like your lawn mower. You've got to mow the lawn all the time. The minute you stop mowing, the grass is going to grow back.

—Bruce Riedel, quoted in the *Washington Post*,
October 24, 2012

Whatever part frustration with the ground war in Afghanistan played in the decision to go hard with UAVs, it also remains the case that real public attention to President Obama's stepped-up drone campaign did not come into focus until the firing of Gen. Stanley McChrystal. But thereafter things moved quickly. Upon replacing McChrystal, David Petraeus immediately assured the troops that he had not been sent to lose the war: "We are in this to win. That is our clear objective." He also reaffirmed the commitment to counterinsurgency: "My assumption of command represents a change in personnel, not a change in policy or strategy."

When he arrived in Afghanistan, however, in the dismal aftermath of Marja, Petraeus was already under pressure from Congress to show progress and hold down American casualties. And with midterm elections just ahead, the president's expectations for Petraeus centered on relieving pressure on the White House. As Spencer Ackerman would later write, "By the time President Obama tapped Petraeus to run the Afghan War in 2010, something had changed. Petraeus' mouth was saying 'counterinsurgency,' with its focus on protecting civilians from violence, but in practice, he was far more reliant on air strikes and commando raids. He was even touting body counts as a measure of success, which was completely antithetical to counterinsurgency doctrine, and his staff's insistence that nothing had changed sounded hollow."[1]

In July 2011, after only a year in Afghanistan, Petraeus was recalled to head the Central Intelligence Agency (though the job he had been coveting was chair of the Joint Chiefs). After thirty-seven years in an army uniform, Petraeus appeared in a civilian suit for the swearing-in ceremony. His first order of business, he announced, was to have the civilian analysts pay more attention to the opinions of soldiers in the field about how the war was going. But even as he spoke about more input from the front lines, Petraeus must have known that was really past history. One former CIA official told the *Washington Post* the agency had already been transformed into "one hell of a killing machine." Since 9/11, he said, it had had a new role launching drone strikes and engaging in other paramilitary operations. Then, noted the reporter, the official "blanch[ed] at his choice of words" and "quickly offered a revision: 'Instead, say "one hell of an operational tool."'"[2]

"Just War" and Drones

In July 2001, two months before the terrible events of 9/11, the U.S. ambassador to Israel, Martin Indyk, condemned Israel's targeted killings of presumed Palestinian terrorists. "The United States government is very clearly on record as against targeted assassinations. . . . They are extrajudicial killings, and we do not support that."[3] But that would change. By 2010 Obama had abandoned the wider notion of a war on terror for a supposedly more targeted effort against al Qaeda, in line with his insistence that the United States was not at war with Islam. He had also vowed to go after Osama bin Laden. "I don't believe in assassination," he said as a candidate, "but Osama bin Laden has declared war on us, killed 3,000 people, and under existing law, including international law, when you've got a military target like bin Laden, you take him out."[4]

The use of unmanned aircraft had a history going back to the days of President Bill Clinton, who used cruise missiles to strike at al

Qaeda sites in Afghanistan and to bomb a factory in Sudan on August 20, 1998, in retaliation for the bombing of two American embassies in Kenya and Tanzania that had killed twelve Americans and three hundred Africans. At the time, though, the president was reeling from revelations about his intimate relations with a White House intern, and some Republicans saw the attacks as a smoke screen to shield Clinton from possible impeachment proceedings. There were real questions, moreover, about whether the chemical factory in the Sudan had even the slightest thing to do with al Qaeda—and, as it turned out, it didn't. But evidence that the al Qaeda leader had been responsible for the bombings satisfied Clinton's secretary of defense William Cohen, who responded to questions about whether it was right to say bin Laden was a legitimate military target this way: "To the extent that he or his organization have declared war on the United States or our interests, then he certainly is engaged in an act of war."[5] Gen. Hugh Shelton, chair of the Joint Chiefs of Staff, added that bin Laden's network had "been actively seeking to acquire weapons of mass destruction, including chemical weapons for use against U.S. citizens and our interests around the world." Even with these statements by Cohen and Shelton on record, however, Clinton attempted to differentiate between attacks on a suspected training site and a planned assassination. Presidents Gerald Ford and Ronald Reagan had both issued executive orders against assassination, and Clinton no doubt did not wish to become involved in a second debate on ethics at that moment.

Richard Clarke, chief White House counterterrorism adviser to both Clinton and George W. Bush, recalled that the CIA and Pentagon initially shied away from the use of drones. He did not say the reason was the previously issued executive orders against assassination, but that seems the logical explanation. In any event, Clarke claims he convinced Clinton that the only way to find Osama bin Laden was by using drones. As noted in the introduction, Clarke claimed that an unarmed Predator drone had spotted bin Laden in October 2000. After that experience, Clinton gave orders to create an armed drone force, though under George W. Bush the CIA and Defense Department balked at using drones to target bin Laden,

even in the days leading up to 9/11.[6] After 9/11, of course, everyone
wanted in on the action. But even then, after achieving a major
success with the killing of a top al Qaeda operative in Kabul, says
Clarke, President Bush proved "reluctant" to use this new weapon
very often.

Richard Clarke's claim to be the godfather of drone warfare may
not become the official narrative, and certainly it reflects his personal disagreements with President Bush over going after Saddam
Hussein. Yet Clarke is certainly right in arguing that Clinton's use
of cruise missiles throughout his terms in office—from 1993, when
he bombed an Iraqi intelligence center to retaliate for a supposed
assassination attempt on former president George H.W. Bush, to the
1998 attacks in Sudan and Afghanistan—demonstrated a preference for UAVs over soldiers.

When a full history of the drone is written, Clinton's memorandum of notification amending the Reagan ban on assassinations
will be one starting point. The memorandum permitted "lethal"
counterterrorism actions against a short list of named targets, including Osama bin Laden and his top lieutenants. Killing could be
approved only if capture was not deemed "feasible." "A week after
the Sept. 11 attacks," reported Karen DeYoung in the *Washington
Post*, "the Bush administration amended the finding again, dropping the list of named targets and the caveat on 'feasible' capture."
As a Bush administration official told DeYoung: "By design, it was
written as broadly as possible."[7]

While the president already had authority to authorize covert
activities, including lethal action on a case-by-case basis, what the
CIA gained with the September 17, 2001, memorandum of notification was blanket authority, changing forever its role in American
life. The memorandum not only provided the president with plausible deniability for secret intelligence operations, including drones
and death squads, but also relieved him of requirements to consult
with more than a handful of congressional leaders—after the fact—
concerning any specific operation. With this, the thin gray line that
had once separated legal and illegal actions became a mile-wide
freeway for lethal actions.

John Yoo, author of the 2002 Office of Legal Counsel's memos on torture, asserted that the president's powers always expanded dramatically in wartime—even, he argued, to action inside the United States, as it would be absurd to stop pursuing an enemy simply because he crossed the border from Mexico or Canada during wartime. While it was true that the president had never asked Congress for an actual declaration of war, that did not matter, said Yoo, as the United States was in a war with al Qaeda and its affiliates.

> I think we have moved from a world of holding people responsible for attacks that have already happened to trying to stop them—to pre-empt Al Qaeda from attacking us again as they did on September 11. The place I think you see it most clearly and sharply is in the use of force to kill people. We, the United States, apparently launched an attack, using missiles fired from a drone to kill an Al Qaeda leader driving a car in Yemen who's not about to attack some American citizen; he was just a legitimate target because he was a member of Al Qaeda. There was an American citizen in the car with him who was also a member of Al Qaeda.[8]

Despite Yoo's contentions (and those of succeeding presidential advisers), the question of whether UAVs constituted assassination or legitimate targeting in the age of nonstate enemies continued to engage policy makers' lawyers through the years, reaching a peak in the Obama administration's still-classified fifty-page memorandum justifying the killing of American citizens by such weapons without an open court hearing. How far one could follow this down the ladder—"he was just a legitimate target because he was a member of Al Qaeda," as Yoo put it—is part of the ongoing debate. By Yoo's reckoning, the United States would be justified in using drones to kill every single member of al Qaeda inside or outside any recognized war zone, in any country, and whether or not the target was engaged in actual warlike activity at the time.

Richard Clarke has never had qualms about this kind of war, and dismisses objections without a moment's thought. "The fact that those pilots [of drones] are safe and they are not engaged in a 'fair fight,' which troubles some critics, has always struck me as positive. As an American, I do not like putting our military personnel at unnecessary risk."[9]

It still worries others, however; indeed, the announcement after Obama's reelection that the administration would now attempt to write a code of behavior for drone warfare illustrated the dilemma, if not the outright fear of how far down a dangerous path the drone had already taken political leaders. Even before 9/11, drones posed an irresistibly seductive way to project American power without worrying about congressional prerogatives under the Constitution. But even back then it would have been possible to see at least one of the consequences of such actions: the 1998 cruise missile strikes missed their target in Afghanistan, but the blowback produced a closer alliance between the Taliban and al Qaeda.[10]

Rationalizations

During the pre–Iraq War hype about Saddam Hussein's supposed weapons of mass destruction, Bush administration figures tried to frighten senators and representatives by bringing them into secure rooms in the Capitol complex to deliver secret briefings warning about the Iraqi leader's supposed capability of delivering biological and chemical weapons via unmanned drones. Recalling the episode in 2004, Senator Ben Nelson explained that he had voted to give the president the authority to go to war based on those images conjured up for skeptics. "I was looked at straight in the face and told that UAVs could be launched from ships off the Atlantic coast to attack eastern seaboard cities of the United States. Is it any wonder that I concluded there was an imminent peril to the United States?"[11]

Instead of Saddam Hussein using UAVs after 9/11, however, it was the Bush administration that sent a Predator drone in 2002 to kill a suspect in the 2000 bombing of an American warship. When the Hellfire missile vaporized a car on a desert road in Yemen and killed Yoo's "legitimate" targets, Qaed Salim Sinan al-Harethi and five others, Deputy Secretary of Defense Paul Wolfowitz praised the new tactic: "One hopes each time you get a success like that, not only to have gotten rid of somebody dangerous but to have imposed changes in their tactics, operations, and procedures."[12]

Wolfowitz was right about how attractive drone warfare seemed; in 2012, David Ignatius would write, "The CIA's Counterterrorism Center has become proficient in managing drone attacks to the point that they've made assassination from 10,000 feet an almost addictive covert tool of policy."[13] It soon became apparent, moreover, that the goal of imposing changes on the enemy's perception of American abilities was as important as the actual number of high-level kills, *if not more so*. Intimidation, then, loomed large from the beginning as a positive result of drone warfare. And, as Rahm Emanuel, one of Obama's closest advisers, realized, "the muscular attacks could have a huge political upside for Obama, insulating him against charges that he was weak on terror."[14]

It is worth repeating here the early criticisms lodged by two well-known counterinsurgency advocates and military advisers, David Kilcullen and Andrew McDonald Exum, who in May 2009 were the first to write about the potential blowback in an op-ed article for the *New York Times*. Kilcullen and Exum readily acknowledged the seductive attractions of drone warfare: the disruption of terrorist networks, the sense of insecurity created among militants and their interactions with suspected informers, the avoidance of American casualties. To this list they might have added the enduring romance of Americans with technological "fixes" in all aspects of their lives, war just as much as politics, business, and entertainment. But drone warfare was self-defeating, they claimed, because for every terrorist eliminated, fifty noncombatants were killed. The result was to guarantee an ever mounting desire for revenge, "and more recruits for a militant movement that has grown exponentially even as drone strikes have increased."[15]

Until Kilcullen and Exum's piece, there had been no public acknowledgment that a drone campaign even existed. A peek-a-boo charade had been put in place, it was said, in order to protect the governments of the countries where the attacks took place from the wrath of their people. The pretense served another purpose, too:

keeping down questions about how the offensive was being run, especially the CIA's active role. Civilians who carried out acts of war were (to say the least) in an ambiguous position. Recognized laws of warfare called for transparency as to both responsibility for conducting warlike acts and accountability for possible war crimes. By contrast, the CIA specialized in opaqueness.

Two days after Kilcullen and Exum's op-ed appeared, CIA director Leon Panetta gave a "rare public acknowledgment of the raids." They were "very precise," he informed a meeting of the Pacific Council on International Policy in Los Angeles. He could not get into specifics, but he "could assure" everyone that they were "very limited in terms of collateral damage." Having dismissed the major Kilcullen-Exum objection, Panetta asserted there was no other way to go. "Very frankly, it's the only game in town in terms of confronting or trying to disrupt the al Qaeda leadership."[16]

Panetta's assurances were not likely to persuade skeptics. While public opinion polls consistently showed a big—indeed, overwhelming—vote in favor of using drones against terrorists, the way the question was asked largely determined the answers. When it came to the question of whether the president needed to consult Congress on drones, the results were less lopsided: 50 percent said no in one poll, while 37 percent said yes.[17]

In the meantime, administration supporters began to engage Exum and Kilcullen's arguments in an effort to convince liberal elites who might have been puzzled by Obama's wholehearted embrace of drone warfare. Journalist Steve Coll—a very bright star in Eastern intellectual circles, and author of *Ghost Wars*, a Pulitzer Prize–winning account of the origins of the Afghan War from the Soviet invasion until 2001—rationalized Obama's drone policy as aimed at bringing Osama bin Laden to justice while degrading al Qaeda in the meantime. It was a matter of bringing closure to the trauma of 9/11, something that the nation could not go forward without. And Obama could not win reelection without having taken every step he could to get Osama bin Laden.

Kilcullen and Exum were right, Coll said, to pose the issue of a serious backlash caused by the drone attacks. But the Kilcullen-Exum argument underestimated the value drones had as a response to the political, moral, and legal obligations of any president to identify and respond to a "clear and present danger." In short, so long as the al Qaeda network existed and had plans to carry out terrorist attacks, Obama could not overrule his generals and intelligence advisers and end the drone attacks "immediately." Suppose he did so, asked Coll, and, "six weeks later, a manic-depressive Pakistani-American living in New York City, who happened to visit his cousins in Karachi earlier this year, decides on his own volition to walk into a New Jersey shopping mall with an automatic rifle and kills a dozen shoppers." What would happen then? The advisers who had disagreed with Obama's decision would immediately leak their memos supporting the continuation of drone attacks, and Republicans would once again claim that Democrats were weak on national security, starting a flap that would consume American politics once again, leaving no room for an Obama agenda.[18]

With its suggestion that the increased drone strikes were meant to bring closure to the mishandling of the aftermath of 9/11—a wrong war, against a wrong enemy—Coll's response to Kilcullen and Exum stopped short of any long-term consideration of where the drone policy might take the president or his successors. He did not say that drone strikes would end after Osama bin Laden had been found, but one could certainly read here an expectation that the situation Obama faced would look very different. "To put it reductively, if Bin Laden and Zawahiri [the number two figure in al Qaeda] are removed from the narrative, Obama's options in the region will expand considerably."[19]

Coll also did not reckon with the American romance with technological fixes. Once drones were in use, there were always new uses to be found, and an eager group of defense contractors to point out where they were. As the months went by there were several obvious markers indicating the direction things were going. In early December 2009 the White House authorized a wider use of drones in Pakistan's "lawless tribal areas . . . to parallel the president's decision" to send thirty thousand additional troops to Afghanistan.[20] Here was confirmation—if any were still needed—that drone war-

fare had other missions and was aimed at improving Pakistan's stability as much as fighting a war in Afghanistan. No one was ready
to say quite yet that counterinsurgency had become a strategy
without a mission, but that was becoming more obvious every day.
Pakistani leaders would tolerate no American "boots on the ground,"
but so long as the drones were not officially "recognized" by any party
to the secret contract between Washington and Islamabad, they
could be useful to both sides.

Drone warfare in Afghanistan was Pentagon-run because the
country was an actual war zone. Things were different in Pakistan.
Drone warfare there and in other places had to be managed by the
CIA for reasons of "plausible denial." But what had been a quiet
campaign inevitably grew noisier as Pakistan's previously "complicit" government had to state its objections in the face of public
protests that would continue to grow. In an interview with a German newspaper, the Pakistani prime minister reacted with apparent
concern, as if he had opposed drones all along. The strikes did no
good, he claimed, "because they boost anti-American resentment
throughout the country."[21] Reviewing the evolution of drone warfare, Micah Zenko, a fellow at the Council on Foreign Relations,
observed that despite such disclaimers, by the summer of 2008 the
CIA had become, "in effect, the counterinsurgency air force of the
government of Pakistan." When the strikes began, Zenko noted, with
the permission of the Pakistan government, the targets were always
non-Pakistanis, Arabs or Uzbeks. But quite soon pressure increased
to attack "targets which are a threat to the Pakistani regime."

For Zenko the problem was not merely legal but whether the
spreading use of drones reduced the number of terrorists or actually
caused an increasing number of active terrorists in Pakistan and
elsewhere. So far there had been no national debate about drones,
said Zenko. "I like to describe it in terms of U.S. nuclear weapons. I
know roughly the size of the U.S. nuclear weapons arsenal, their
type, the warhead lifecycles, where they're deployed, what the military doctrine is for them." None of these things was available for
drones.[22] By some estimates, such as the New America Foundation's, one third of those killed in the strikes were "civilians"—but

the government, without officially acknowledging the existence of the supposedly secret program, insists both that the calculation was wrong and that smaller missiles and better targeting procedures had limited collateral damage.

Harold Koh's Speech

Panetta's almost casual comments about drones being "the only game in town" clearly were not going to be enough to satisfy critics. So the administration gave long thought to how to make a more serious effort to reconcile its positions with international law. David E. Sanger's book *Confront and Conceal* provides the best source available on the internal debates leading to a speech by Harold Hongju Koh, the State Department's legal adviser, about the legality of drone strikes. A "jovial liberal former dean of the Yale Law School," Koh was the best man for the task if the administration was "going to have a prayer of convincing Obama's liberal base." After all, here was someone who had shredded the arguments in John Yoo's infamous torture memoranda, and many thought he would be the perfect choice to become the first Asian American on the Supreme Court.[23]

Koh told Sanger, "Almost as soon as I came in I raised the issue about why we hadn't clarified what our standards are" on drone warfare. It seemed to be taken for granted that should a standard be set forth, all but the most obdurate leftists would be satisfied. Koh's self-designated assignment was, in effect, to be a character witness for President Obama. What he would show was how drone warfare differed from attempting to take out Fidel Castro with an exploding cigar—and how a program aimed at "eliminating al-Qaeda's middle management" still qualified as protecting the United States from a clear and present danger.[24] However, when he proposed giving the speech, there was considerable opposition from the intelligence agencies. "You can't talk about our covert programs," said one official. "In World War II . . . the civil liberties community wasn't saying we want to see targeting lists of what you're hitting. George Washington did not turn over his targeting list of the British."[25]

The problem for Koh and other defenders of the drone warfare was in that last statement. Whom exactly the drones were targeting was the only thing "covert" about the drone attacks, not the false issue of where they were launched from and who was launching them. It was the key issue because there was already much uncomplimentary talk about how Obama's determination to close down secret CIA detention sites and not to put any more suspects in Guantánamo meant drones were the only alternative left for dealing with a "targeting list" that kept extending further down the ladder of al Qaeda foot soldiers. The "targeting list" problem was often alluded to cautiously, but sometimes bluntly as the ironic result of Obama's efforts to "clean-up America's act" after the Bush years.[26]

The State Department's legal adviser had been a skeptic about targeted killings, especially about President Obama's decision to put an American citizen, Anwar al-Awlaki, on the CIA's kill list in early 2010. What would be the consequences? Could, for example, the Russians or Chinese use an American precedent to take down dissidents on the streets of Washington, D.C.? Koh's doubts were put to rest, he told Daniel Klaidman, after he was ushered into a small room where he spent almost five hours reading "stacks of intelligence" on Awlaki's plans to poison Western water and food supplies, "as well as attack Americans with ricin and cyanide." Awlaki's ingenuity at coming up with plots stunned Koh: "Awlaki was not just evil, he was satanic."[27]

No one else has seen the intel supplied to Koh that day, but there is good reason to believe that much of it came from a Danish double agent, Morton Storm, who now claims that he has not been given his proper due in providing the CIA with data and targeting information that clinched the ability of UAV pilots to get their man. According to an article by three Danish reporters,

> for almost 10 years before this story begins, Storm was an internationally well-known figure in radical Islamist circles, known by the nickname Murad Storm. A convicted criminal who had converted to Islam, Storm visited mosques throughout Europe and the Middle East, speaking openly about the need for armed jihad.

Storm was studying, he says, in Sana, the capital of Yemen, and there met and became close to Awlaki. Storm is somewhat vague about what prompted his "loss of faith," but one day he had had enough—more than enough, apparently—for he was prompted to call the Danish secret service and offer to infiltrate Awlaki's inner circle. Storm was instructed to bring Awlaki various weapons from contacts in the West, which were tracked by the Danish secret service in cooperation with the CIA, eager to get hold of all this information on the radical cleric's plots and sources of supply. "He wanted to attack the big shopping centers in the West . . . by using biological weapons. But I said that I didn't want to take part in killing civilians— I could only agree to attacking military targets," Storm said. "Of course I wouldn't have helped him carry out any kind of terrorist actions. But I had to let him think that I was on his side."[28]

Whether the Danish agent was the only source of the reports Koh read in that "crappy little room" under the watchful eye of John Brennan or one of his aides, or whether he was one of several sources, is not known. Nor is it likely that anyone outside the innermost circles of U.S. intelligence will soon see any of this material. But it convinced Harold Koh to put aside his doubts and give the speech.[29]

The occasion for Koh's long anticipated speech was a meeting of the American Society of International Law, and his speech was entitled, "The Obama Administration and International Law." He began by relating his long experience attending meetings of the society, and how as a young lawyer he stood in awe, like someone watching Hollywood stars arrive at the Oscars to walk on the red carpet as the famous figures he knew only by sight passed by in the halls. Now it was his turn at the podium.[30]

His job as legal adviser combined four roles, he said, "counselor, conscience, defender of U.S. interests, and spokesperson for international law." He interpreted these roles to mean that his job required him to speak "lawfare to power." *Lawfare* was a sometime dirty word in the Bush administration, especially in the OLC, where it referred to international organizations eagerly hoping to ensnare in a legal web Americans dutifully engaged in defending national interests. The great irony of lawfare, of course, was that many of the human rights conventions that these activists wanted to use against the United States in international courts had been proposed and supported by the United States originally. He was there, Koh assured his audience, as a spokesperson for the U.S. government on why international law mattered. What followed, however, was a long exegesis on how the American interpretation of international law made room for drone warfare, including when it was used outside of recognized war zones.

Koh was addressing what had become one of the biggest worries that had emerged concerning drone warfare—that without international rules it could be turned against the United States in retaliation, or even in other ways. Was it outlandish to consider the possibility that, say, a Spanish government drone might attack a Basque separatist riding on a car on Fifth Avenue, killing American civilians and leaving a big crater in the middle of a busy Manhattan roadway? Yes, very probably it was, but there was an obvious need to get the point settled that drones could be used only in "lawless" areas—that is, places currently defined as such by American policy makers. Hence the importance of getting out in front with the backing of international law—and especially before any confrontation with the UN Human Rights Council occurred.[31]

Koh introduced his main topic by saying that the question was how "obeying international law advance[d] U.S. foreign policy interests and strengthen[ed] America's position of global leadership." In other words, "with respect to international law, is this Administration really committed to what our President has famously called 'change we can believe in'?" Some panelists at the conference, he said, had argued there was really more continuity with than change from the previous administration. His first answer to that was that there was always more continuity than change. "You simply cannot turn the ship of state some 360 degrees from administration to administration every four to eight years, nor should you." (An unsympathetic listener might point out, of course, that because 360 degrees is a full turn back to a starting point in a circle, Koh had just admitted that there was no difference between Bush and Obama. Presumably he meant 180 degrees.)

But, Koh said, the Obama "approach and attitude toward international law" was different from Bush's by virtue of an emerging "Obama-Clinton doctrine" dedicated to following universal standards, not double standards. He had learned in the nine months he had been on board that making foreign policy was "infinitely harder than it looks from the ivory tower." Government lawyers, moreover, were obligated to start with a presumption of stare decisis—meaning that an existing interpretation by the executive branch had to stand unless there was compelling evidence for a change.

Administration efforts in this regard, he said, established the point that President Obama was to be trusted. But then Koh immediately backtracked to what he called "the law of 9/11" to explain how drone warfare fit into the corpus of international law. This "law" was embedded, he argued, in Obama's Nobel Prize speech. As the president had reminded us, "the world must remember that it was not simply international institutions—not just treaties and declarations—that brought stability to a post–World War II world. . . . [T]he instruments of war do have a role to play in preserving the peace." Despite Koh's insistence on parsing the president's Nobel rhetoric, there was a circular sound to the phrase "law of 9/11"— and about the idea that Obama could be trusted with the task of making drones legal weapons because he could be trusted to decide what "instruments of war" preserved the peace.

> There are obviously limits to what I can say publicly. What I can say *is that it is the considered view of this Administration—and it has certainly been my experience during my time as Legal Adviser—that U.S. targeting practices, including lethal operations conducted with the use of unmanned aerial vehicles, comply with all applicable law, including the laws of war.*[32]

The Debate Goes On

Harold Koh's arguments and references to President Obama's good intentions did not close the debate on drones. The president's Republican opponents—who had been criticized for supporting the waterboarding of terrorism suspects in an effort to elicit information that would help prevent new attacks—came up with an interesting riposte: you couldn't interrogate a dead man. John Yoo, often Harold Koh's favorite target in the past and now back at Berkeley teaching law students, joined several other Republicans and neocons in criticizing the drones for depriving the United States of potential intelligence sources. "The administration," he would write,

> has made little secret of its near-total reliance on drone operations to fight the war on terror. The ironies abound. Candidate Obama campaigned on narrowing presidential wartime power, closing Guantanamo Bay, trying terrorists in civilian courts, ending enhanced interrogation, and moving away from a wartime approach toward a criminal-justice approach. Mr. Obama has avoided these vexing detention issues simply by depriving terrorists of all their rights—by killing them.[33]

William Howard Taft IV, who served in Koh's position in the Bush administration, told journalist Tara McKelvey that he had originally supposed it would be possible to change that administration's mind—meaning John Yoo and the OLC—when it claimed the Geneva Convention did not apply to those captured in the war on terror, but "it turned out we could not persuade them." McKelvey then asked a pointed question that struck at Koh's reliance—indeed, insistence—on faith in Obama's judgment about such matters, phrasing her query as a general proposition: "Why does the law matter when everyone thinks something is OK?" This exchange followed:

> "That is actually a deep question. When a human life is at stake, there needs to be a process for determining that a person can be executed or shot in an armed conflict," [Taft] says. "Otherwise, we will have an individual just deciding that he wants to kill someone."
> "What if it's the president?" I ask.

"Especially," said Taft. "He's the main person who might possibly have this authority, and you've got to watch it."[34]

Koh's points would be elaborated on and supplemented several times by heavy hitters in the administration, including chief counterterrorism adviser John Brennan (who had been Obama's original briefer on drone warfare after the 2008 election), attorney general Eric Holder, and chief Pentagon lawyer Jeh Johnson. But in each instance the case rested on some variation of Obama's use of the illusive "law of 9/11." Or, more simply, "Trust me."

McKelvey questioned retired general James Cartwright about Koh's conversion to drones, a weapon the general heard Koh say in a White House conversation early in the administration constituted "extrajudicial killings," meaning assassination. When she confronted Koh, he denied he had changed his mind: "I never used that phrase." He referred her to his 2010 speech, saying, "You'll see that I said they were not 'extrajudicial killings.'" She asked him about a 2002 interview in the *New York Times* in which he was quoted as saying, "The question is, what factual showing will demonstrate that they had warlike intentions against us and who sees that evidence before any action is taken?" He still denied that he had ever changed his position. So far as the quotation was concerned, Koh had the better of the argument, because he also said in that interview, "The inevitable complication of a politically declared but legally undeclared war is the blurring of the distinction between enemy combatants and other nonstate actors."[35]

More telling than the 2002 quotation, however, was the nearly ferocious statement Koh read to a subcommittee of the Senate Judiciary Committee on September 16, 2008, that began with a blunt statement about the "sorry historical record" of the Bush administration since 9/11 in turning upside down the nation's international reputation as the global leader in defense of human rights. To repair the damage to the nation's institutions, he said, would require recognition that "constitutional checks and balances do not stop at the water's edge . . . we need an energetic executive, but checked by an energetic Congress and overseen by a vigilant judicial branch."

And that was only the beginning. He made two pertinent arguments that went beyond anything he had ever said about judicial process or presidential prerogatives to make lethal target decisions. "There are no law-free zones, practices, courts or persons," Koh said, citing Guantánamo as the worst example of an effort to establish a "law-free" zone, but the statement extended to secret CIA rendition locations, and in general, logically, to areas not recognized as "war zones." He also said in an exasperated tone, "The last straw has been the startling argument that executive action should be treated as a kind of law unto itself." The president's lawyers had argued that the policy rationale for executive action had somehow "*created* the legal justification for executive unilateralism." It had done this by relying on the Authorization for Use of Military Force Resolution as a general congressional encouragement to go as fast and far as possible. What had happened "evoked eerie memories" of a comment by Richard Nixon: "When the president does it, that means it is not illegal." If that were true, said Koh, then the president's word was above the law, and the checks and balances of the Constitution no longer existed.[36]

Harold Koh's parsing of the law on Obama's behalf in 2010 also relied on a painstaking review of evidence about the "targeting list." How the meticulous Koh must have cringed, then, to read comments such as those by Jeffrey Addicott, who served as senior legal adviser to the Army Special Forces. Addicott readily admitted that tallies of drone "misses" were almost certainly wrong, because no matter how good the technology, "killing from that high above, there's always the 'oops' factor." It was likely that for every "bad guy" killed, there were 1.5 civilian deaths. But Addicott was not upset at the thought. "This is war and we are entitled to kill them anywhere we find them. We can kill them when they're eating, we can kill them when they're sleeping. They are enemy combatants, and as long as they're not surrendering, we can kill them."[37] Such comments revealed the love affair American leaders were having with their new technology of death. Indeed, a former U.S. intelligence official told a Reuters reporter, "Everyone has fallen in love with them."[38]

The development of drone technology expanded the CIA's arsenal, which now incorporated micro-UAVs about the "size of a pizza platter," capable of monitoring potential targets at close range for hours or days at a time: "It can be outside your window and you won't hear a whisper."[39] In an effort to assuage Pakistani outrage and protests about infringement of sovereignty, the U.S. government touted the drones' smaller size and greater precision. In March 2010, a CIA missile—"probably no bigger than a violin case and weighing about 35 pounds"—tore through the second floor of a house in Miram Shah, in the Pakistani province of South Waziristan. It killed a top al Qaeda official "and about nine other suspected terrorists." These were CIA accounts of the strike, of course, and they were slanted to demonstrate how accurate the newer weapons fired from drones had become. By one measure the drone got ten bad guys; by a more skeptical measure, however, the drone got one "bad guy" and nine "passersby," so to speak.

6

THE MEANING OF TWO DEATHS

Hopefully, that "dark side" is not going to be something that's going to forever tarnish the image of the United States abroad and that we're going to look back on this time and regret some of the things that we did, because it is not in keeping with our values.
    —John Brennan, interview on *Frontline*, March 8, 2006

Only hours after President Obama told the nation that "justice has been done," details about the killing of Osama bin Laden in his Pakistani compound had become a controversy. White House aides, following the president's lead, stressed the extraordinary courage and capability of the Navy SEAL Team Six that had carried out the raid as they fought their way up to the third floor to where the author of the 9/11 attacks was ready to make his last stand. "After a firefight," said the president, "they killed Osama Bin Laden and took custody of his body."

The president's aides added details that made the story sound like a reenactment of the shoot-out at the OK Corral, with the SEALs playing the role of the Earp brothers and Doc Holliday. White House press secretary Jay Carney began the next morning by reminding reporters of Obama's vow in the 2008 presidential campaign: "We must make it clear that if Pakistan cannot or will not act, we will take out take out high-level terrorist targets like bin Laden if we have them in our sights." Then he turned the press briefing over to John Brennan, the president's special assistant for Homeland Security and Counterterrorism.

The very first question was whether any consideration had been given to taking bin Laden alive. "Absolutely," began Brennan; the SEAL team was prepared for all contingencies. "If we had the opportunity to take bin Laden alive, if he didn't present any threat, the individuals involved were able and prepared to do that [take him prisoner]. We had discussed that extensively in a number of meetings in the White House and with the president. The concern was that bin Laden would oppose any type of capture operation. Indeed, he did. It was a firefight. He, therefore, was killed in that firefight and that's when the remains were removed."[1]

Then came another question, a more specific one, about bin Laden's supposed resistance: "Did he get his hand on a gun and did he fire himself?" Brennan seized on the question, however, as an opportunity to elaborate on a number of themes he wanted to get across in this first public discussion of what had happened—and the meaning behind bin Laden's life and death. He chose his words carefully about bin Laden's active role in shooting: "He was engaged in a firefight with those that entered the area of the house he was in. And whether or not he got off any rounds, I quite frankly don't know."

Having skirted the actual question, he took the reporters along another path.

Thinking about that from a visual perspective, here is bin Laden, who has been calling for these attacks, living in this million-dollar-plus compound, living in an area that is far removed from the front, hiding behind women who were put in front of him as a shield. I think it really speaks to just how false his narrative has been over the years. And so, again, looking at what bin Laden was doing hiding there while he's putting other people out there to carry out attacks again just speaks to I think the nature of the individual he was.[2]

In other words, it was best to focus on the meaning of his death rather than the details. But the press conference was far from a completely successful venture. The very next day Carney had to explain away several of Brennan's assertions as the products of "the fog of war." For example, the story about bin Laden using a woman as a shield was simply not true. Brennan had used it to discredit bin Laden's credibility and image as a brave leader. Indeed, the original firefight story itself had begun to burn out. At the next briefing Jay Carney was confronted with Brennan's "misstatements . . . such as that the wife was shielding bin Laden and . . . there may not have been a shield and it wasn't clear whether or not bin Laden had a gun." The questioner asked, "Are you guys in a fog of war in this, or what gives?"[3]

Carney was grateful for the prompt and the exit lane it opened up out of a traffic jam of raised hands. "Well, what is true," he said, "is that we provided a great deal of information with great haste in order to inform you and, through you, the American public about the operation and how it transpired and the events that took place there in Pakistan. And obviously some of the information was— came in piece by piece and is being reviewed and updated and elaborated on." Here he caught himself before he might have said that some of the information was false or not fully accurate.

He also tried his best to find wiggle room around the president's use of the word *firefight*. "There was concern that bin Laden would oppose the capture operation—operation rather and, indeed, he did resist." Taking out "capture" after a pause avoided another near misstep. But the press secretary continued to have difficulty as he put forward a series of confusing details about bin Laden's final moments: "In the room with bin Laden, a woman—bin Laden's—a woman, rather bin Laden's wife, rushed the U.S. assaulter and was shot in the leg but not killed. Bin Laden was then shot and killed. He was not armed." Still, Carney insisted, "The resistance was throughout. As I said, when the assaulter entered the room where Osama bin Laden was, he was rushed by one individual in the room, and the resistance was consistent from the moment they landed until the end of the operation."

Despite Carney's insistence that the "firefight" or "resistance" began the second helicopters arrived at the compound and continued until the final shots into bin Laden's body, the questions kept coming.

Q: Jay, just to follow up, how did . . . Osama bin Laden resist if he didn't—if he didn't have his hand on a gun, how was he resisting?

MR. CARNEY: Yes, the information I have to [give] you—first of all, I think resistance does not require a firearm. But the information I gave you today is what I can tell you about it. I'm sure more details will be provided as they come available and we are able to release them.[4]

There were no more briefings like this one. They were not needed. Getting the first word is often more important than getting the last word. Besides, with teeming crowds in New York at the 9/11 site and outside the White House in Washington chanting "USA, USA, USA" and "CIA, CIA, CIA," the details of Osama bin Laden's death mattered very little to the public. It was easy for Jay Carney to say that the mistakes and contradictions resulted from the "fog of war" and the desire to get the story out.[5] But all the accounts agreed on one point: bin Laden himself had no weapon at hand when he was killed.[6]

When the reaction in Pakistan proved far less joyous, the White House argued that Osama bin Laden had committed the real violation of Pakistan's territory. Secretary of Defense Robert Gates went to see an Obama aide, offering up some barbed advice. "I have a new strategic communications approach to recommend," he said. What was that? asked the aide, Tom Donilon. The defense secretary replied, "Shut the fuck up." But simply shutting up was not going to win any new friends in places where American drone attacks had already caused more than PR problems.[7]

A few weeks later General James Cartwright, another close adviser to the president, talked to a reporter about other meanings of bin Laden's death, and the success of the mission, code-named Neptune's Spear. Were there other terrorists out there, he was asked, worth the risk of another helicopter assault on a Pakistani city? Yes, there were, Cartwright said, giving as examples Ayman al-Zawahiri, bin Laden's successor, and Anwar al-Awlaki, the American-born cleric in Yemen. Going after them, he cautioned, did not necessarily mean SEAL teams dropping down ropes or hustling up stairs after their targets. What was important here was the precedent the raid set for more unilateral actions in the future. "Folks now realize we can weather it. . . . penetrating other countries' sovereign airspace covertly is something that's always available for the right mission and the right gain."[8]

No matter, then, whether all the Hellfire missiles from drones were actual "hits" or not. The usefulness of the drone as intimidators—as in Obama's crude joke warning the Jonas Bothers to stay away from his daughters—was a weighty part of the calculation.

The Lead-in to Neptune's Spear

The compound at Abbottabad, a midsize city only an hour's drive from Islamabad, was where Osama bin Laden had lived in secret for six years. It was also less than a mile away from a large Pakistani military academy. Without being prompted, Brennan had brought up the latter point during his first briefing, more than implying some form of Pakistani involvement in the latter stages of his career. "We are looking right now at how he was able to hold out there for so long, and whether or not there was any type of support system within Pakistan that allowed him to stay there."[9]

President Obama had been careful in his original announcement of the raid's success to credit Pakistan with help in finding the al Qaeda leader, but journalists took Brennan's hints and pursued the leads he offered. "Signs Point to Pakistan Link," wrote three reporters in the *Wall Street Journal* almost immediately after Brennan's comments. Reaching out for background confirmation to a "high-level" European military official, they got this answer to Brennan's "question." "There's no doubt he was protected by some in the ISI," said the European official, referring to the Pakistani intelligence service. These "same elements," they were told by American officials, had connections with "other Pakistan-based terror groups, the Haqqani militant network and Lashkar-e-Taiba"—the group responsible for the 2008 Mumbai hotel raids in India that left 165 dead and more than 300 wounded.[10]

Obama's own words about Pakistani aid in finding bin Laden clashed with the reality of his aides' responses to questions about when the Pakistanis had actually been informed of the raid: not until the Americans had recrossed the border and were safely out of Pakistani airspace. Speculations about whether it was the ISI who protected bin Laden's hiding place, or some unconnected "rogue element" acting in sympathy with his anti-American agenda, led to a discussion of the problematic cooperation between the ISI and the CIA in the post–9/11 era. In the early days of the Obama administration, the president appointed Richard Holbrooke, now deceased, as his special representative for what was called the "Af-Pak" theater to stress the connections between events in the two countries and American objectives. Of course, one vital connection was Pakistan's possession of a nuclear arsenal—a situation that scared the daylights out of the administration in the spring of 2009. The Bush administration had spent more than $100 million teaching the Pakistanis how to build fences around their nuclear installations. But Islamabad had refused any technical visits to sites it thought might help Americans identify the actual location of nuclear weapons. The most frightening thing was the possibility that a bin Laden sympathizer or one of the groups "allied" to al Qaeda might sneak out of a facility with enough weapons-grade plutonium to make a bomb.[11]

The issue of Pakistan's vulnerability somehow got into the press with rumors that the local Taliban had a bead on stockpiles of highly enriched uranium—material, ironically, that had been supplied for a reactor by the United States years earlier. There followed a series of contretemps with Pakistani officials over American ambassador Anne Patterson's attempts to get the uranium back. There were questions at Obama's press conferences and testy exchanges with reporters. These led Pakistani authorities to tell Patterson that it was simply impossible to talk about sending the uranium back because the "sensational" international media coverage made it impossible to proceed "at this time." Within a short time, however, the crisis went away: it appeared that the National Security Agency—the code breakers with all the latest high-tech stuff—had misunderstood a word passed along in an unfamiliar dialect, and that the word didn't necessarily mean "nuclear."[12]

As David Sanger wrote, however, the "bomb scare" underscored the fact that Pakistan could represent a genuine strategic threat. American diplomacy toward Pakistan veered constantly between poles of "friendly persuasion" and "timely warnings," but there could never be a complete break, because each side needed the other.

The number of drone strikes inside Pakistani territory reached a peak in 2010 at nearly 120—more than double the number of the previous year, when Obama ramped up the campaign from Bush levels. The last four months of the year saw particularly intense levels, with an attack every 1.8 days after Labor Day. "That torrid pace of attacks should make it beyond debate," wrote one military affairs specialist, "that the drones are the long pole in the U.S.'s counter-terrorism tent, even if the drone program is technically a secret."[13]

The number of civilians killed in these attacks was always at issue—particularly because the "enemy" wore no regular army uniform. The dispute over "civilian" casualties centered on the so-called signature strikes, where military and CIA officials claimed that they could identify the enemy by the company they kept. At one point John Brennan even asserted that not one civilian had been killed by an American drone. "There hasn't been a single collateral death because of the exceptional proficiency, precision of the capabilities we've been able to develop." But after many reports that the drones were not infallible made it into the media, Brennan adjusted his wording—slightly. "Fortunately, for more than a year," he said in August 2011, "due to our discretion and precision, the U.S. government has not found credible evidence of collateral deaths resulting from U.S. counterterrorism operations outside of Afghanistan or Iraq, and we will continue to do our best to keep it that way."[14]

Defenders of the strikes slowly retreated from the zero civilian deaths line to a more reasonable argument that while there were no perfect bombing missions, drones caused far less collateral damage than strikes, say, by F-117s or other similar piloted aircraft. Of course, that evaded the question of national sovereignty or formal war zones, as well as the controversy over "signature" strikes. In mid-December 2010 the Pentagon completed its congressionally mandated review of the war situation in Afghanistan, one year after President Obama sent the additional thirty thousand troops to reverse the Taliban's momentum. Admiral Mike Mullen, chair of the Joint Chiefs, said in the review that there had been some "hard won security gains" over the past year, but they would not last unless cemented by "more important gains" in governance. In other words, Hamid Karzai's government was still a big part of the problem, instead of the solution. But there was also the Pakistani half of the struggle, and Islamabad had not done its part. Specifically, that government had repeatedly rebuffed U.S. pleas "to launch a ground operation in North Waziristan, the base of an alphabet soup of militant organizations" that included al Qaeda and Afghan insurgents such as the Haqqani network.[15]

Pakistan had supposedly placed 140,000 troops on its western border. What was the problem? Why the reluctance, then, to really go after the Haqqani network? The answers were really quite simple, as they had been all along. Islamabad did not want to be excluded from any final settlement of the Afghan War, and the Haqqanis were a valuable asset that could ensure a strong voice for Pakistan; that could not be forsaken in order to satisfy American demands. But Washington could not press the issue too far, officials confided to a Reuters correspondent, because Pakistan could make life difficult for the International Assistance Force by shutting down vital supply routes into Afghanistan—as it had recently done in October after a helicopter intrusion killed two Pakistani troops.[16]

The day after Mullen talked about the annual review, news broke about the removal of the "top CIA spy" from Islamabad because of death threats after his cover was blown. A Pakistani attorney representing a North Waziristan resident who claimed that two relatives and a friend had been killed by American drone strikes had named the station chief in a legal document. The resident had threatened a lawsuit against the CIA and had asked Pakistani police to file a criminal complaint against the station chief to prevent him from leaving the country. The death threats followed. These were of such a serious nature, said U.S. intelligence officials, "that it would be imprudent not to act." He was rushed out of the country the same day that President Obama issued a new warning that Pakistan's leaders must act against "terrorist safe havens within their borders."[17]

Intelligence officials also believed that the outing of the CIA station chief had been part of a tit-for-tat power game going on between the ISI and the CIA. American officials had become persuaded, it was said, that the lawyer and the lawsuit were all part of these maneuvers over drone attacks. And that game, in turn, was part of the internal struggle between the ISI and the civilian government in Islamabad. Nonsense, insisted ISI spokespeople; the station chief's name was well known throughout the capital, and the lawyer confirmed he had gotten the name from reporters, adding, "If there is an official complaint that the CIA has, then they should use official channels rather than leaking it to newspapers." What was not in doubt was that the Islamabad station was "one of the largest in the CIA's constellation of overseas posts." Neither was it denied—indeed, it was actually affirmed by Washington sources— that the station chief would have had a principal role in selecting and approving the targets of Predator drone strikes.

The outing infuriated American officials because it was doubtful that this highly competent "up-and-coming" young officer could ever regain the ability to serve overseas again. Whether a direct response or not to the blown cover, three more drone strikes in the Khyber tribal area were launched with claims that fifty-four suspected militants were killed, "an unusually large casualty count."[18]

Pakistanis chafed at American behavior all the time, and had begun calling the American embassy a fortress. The new embassy in Islamabad was said to cost $736 million when it was announced in 2009, and to be the second priciest after the Vatican City–sized one in Iraq. These vice-regal compounds designed to hold not only diplomats but contingents from various intelligence agencies displayed American power while also stirring deep-seated feelings about the colonial past. Plans had been made, for example, to buy a five-star hotel, the Pearl Continental in Peshawar, near the border with Afghanistan, to use as a "consulate," but at the height of the nuclear scare a truck full of explosives had rammed it. Whatever the Islamabad embassy cost, wrote longtime foreign policy critic Chalmers Johnson, it would more resemble a medieval fortress than a traditional embassy. Housing more spies, intelligence officers, and military than diplomats, such "embassies" will now be the visible part "of an in-your-face American imperial presence."[19] It was true that Pakistan was considered one of the most dangerous assignments for Foreign Service officers, and that while most lived outside the building, they could be seen traveling to and from in armored cars. Despite all these rumblings, American officials insisted they wanted to make their work more visible to improve the local public's impression of the United States. They wanted to make sure the symbolism was not that of a fortress, one official told foreign journalists in Islamabad, but, he added, "It's also a gesture to [the] Pakistani people that we're not scared of them."[20]

It was a very complicated business, because at the same time as the hullabaloo over the outing, there was also cooperation between American and Pakistani military units throughout the border area. Things had worsened in the early months of 2011, triggered by the arrest of Raymond Davis, a CIA contractor who shot and killed two Pakistanis on the streets of Lahore. Washington's first reaction was to claim diplomatic immunity status for Davis—an assertion that crumbled into pieces almost at once. Making matters worse, a car driven on the wrong side of the road by a consular official rushing to the scene, apparently in a failed effort to get Davis out of the area, killed a third Pakistani. In a display of the arrogance Chalmers Johnson described, an American official complained that "Pakistan became paranoid about the agency's presence," almost as if there were nothing to the incident.[21]

The Davis case had all the trappings of a spy thriller. He shot the first man through his windshield with his Glock pistol. The second man was shot in the back as he tried to run away. Davis's cover story that he had shot in self-defense during a robbery attempt didn't explain why he was careful to take pictures of the two men he had killed. When it was finally admitted that he was no diplomat but a CIA-assigned contractor charged with protecting a "safe house" in Lahore, the plot thickened. Because of the nature of his

job, there were likely ties to the drone campaign, and indeed Davis
had been known to offer CIA payments to Pakistanis willing to
name "militants." Eventually the U.S. government paid the victims'
relatives $2.2 million in blood money. The handling of the "Davis
affair" divided American officials in both Islamabad and Washington, with the CIA chief quarreling openly with Ambassador Cameron Munter about the need to strike a deal to secure his release. At
first the CIA station chief confronted Munter with a blunt statement that he was not to cut a deal, adding, "Pakistan is the enemy."
In the end the State Department pragmatists won out. But the
fallout from the Davis case left a permanent mark on everyone it
touched—and on Islamabad's relations with Washington.[22]

Almost immediately upon Davis's release, moreover, the United
States carried out an especially controversial "signature" drone
strike on March 17, 2011, that killed an estimated forty-two people.
The gathering was a jirga called to settle a dispute over a chromite
mine. Most of those killed were civilians, said an investigative report, including elders and auxiliary police. Only about four known
members of a Taliban group attended, the report claimed, quoting
survivors and news accounts. U.S. officials insisted, on the other
hand, that all the dead were militants. Inevitably, the question of
drones and intimidation came up every time: Did four Taliban justify an attack on forty-two people? What if there had been twenty?
Where *did* body counts lead in such a war?[23]

But the question of CIA funding of Pakistani "assets" came to a
full boil after the raid on Abbottabad. Pakistan arrested five suspected informants, including an army major who had noted down
the license plates of vehicles entering the compound. Another was
the owner of a safe house used by the CIA to observe the goings-on
at the compound. Then there was the doctor who agreed to pretend
he was part of the Pakistani health service offering vaccinations to
children in an effort to gain access to the compound. He would face
the most serious charge and be sentenced to thirty-three years in
prison—despite strong protests from Washington. Bruce Riedel, the
former CIA agent that Obama had called upon for his first review
of the Afghan War, commented that the arrests were about trying

to learn more of what the CIA and other agencies were doing inside the country. But they also wanted to send a warning to other Pakistanis thinking about working with the United States. "By letting this news out," he said, the Pakistanis "are intimidating anyone who might consider working for the Americans in future."[24]

Intimidation, then, could work both ways. Drones were intimidators, or so it was hoped, but working with American targeters could be dangerous, too. Riedel added that the Pakistanis wanted to go back to the "Reagan rules" of the 1980s, when Washington gave Pakistan millions of dollars to fund the mujahideen to fight the Soviets. "We are not going to go back to the 1980s but they are trying to clip the wings of the US in Pakistan and this is one way of getting closer to that." In the wake of bin Laden's death, other officials dismissed Islamabad's complaints as all part of the burden borne by being the indispensable nation, as secretaries of state from Dean Acheson to Madeleine Albright had explained the American role in the world. In a closed briefing of the Senate Intelligence Committee, CIA deputy director Michael Morell was asked to rate Pakistan's cooperation with U.S. counterintelligence on a scale of 1 to 10; he replied that it was a 3. Defense Secretary Gates quipped that most governments "lie to each other" and sometimes spy on each other: "It's the real world we deal with."[25]

In the post–Osama bin Laden world, reality apparently meant that the United States could do pretty much what it wished. "There's also much less riding on the US-Pakistan relationship than even a year ago when the Davis affair erupted," said a writer in the *Christian Science Monitor* about the doctor's sentence. "NATO has managed to keep the Afghan war effort going, despite Pakistan cutting off supply lines through its territory. Then, too, trust has evaporated since the discovery of bin Laden in Pakistan and the unauthorized US raid to kill him."[26]

Game Changer?

Despite the downgrading of Pakistani-American relations with the death of bin Laden, there was still the Afghan War. Brennan had said at the time of bin Laden's death that there had been differences of opinion with Islamabad, including "what we think they should and shouldn't be doing . . . we believe that that partnership is critically important to breaking the back of al-Qaeda and eventually prevailing over al-Qaeda as well as associated groups." Then he went on to deliver a one-sentence lecture on the meaning of bin Laden's death: "And we're hoping that this is going to send a message to those individuals who are out there that terrorism and militancy is not the wave of the future, it's the wave of the past."[27]

Getting bin Laden was "immeasurably important," agreed Lawrence Wright, author of *The Looming Tower* (2007), the authoritative history of al Qaeda. "He's been a symbol of resistance and of the failure of American policy to reach out and stop this kind of terror. It emboldened other imitators all around the globe." With all the changes that had been going on in the Arab world, "real change—in some ways—couldn't come until this moment happened."[28] Put another way, Wright's argument almost seemed to be that the United States had somehow liberated Arabs from a useless and dangerous past by killing bin Laden and dumping his corpse into the sea, thereby opening the way to modernization and Western-style democracy. Defense secretary Bob Gates also suggested that bin Laden's death "could be a game changer." "Bin Laden and [Taliban leader] Mullah Omar had a very close personal relationship, and there are others in the Taliban who have felt betrayed by al-Qaida—[they feel] it was because of al-Qaida's attack on the United States that the Taliban got thrown out of Afghanistan." Gates added, "We'll have to see what that relationship looks like."[29]

Within days of Gates's remarks there were new reports of speeded-up efforts to talk with the Taliban, to see where matters stood. Contacts were proceeding along a number of tracks involving both Arab and European governments. The Taliban was interested, said a U.S. official, in opening a formal political office in Qatar that could lead to direct talks with the American side. And reporters were reminded that Secretary of State Hillary Clinton had signaled as far back as February that talks between the two sides did not have to wait until the Taliban renounced all ties with al Qaeda. That could come as a declaration made at the end of negotiations. All this was a bit breathtaking, if not wishful thinking, coming so soon after bin Laden's demise at the hands of the SEAL team. Exactly what role the Taliban would play in a postconflict government was indeed a crucial matter, and it did not appear that Afghan president Hamid Karzai had been consulted. Certainly his opponents were making the argument that such talks could lead to the end of the democratic experiment in Afghanistan—a victim of American desires to get out as soon as possible.[30]

Secretary Gates's suggestion that bin Laden's death offered a game-changing possibility left plenty of room for speculation about the changed objectives in American policy. Instead of conditions on the ground in Afghanistan, the more important question had become the political ground in the United States. Nine days after bin Laden's death, Republican senator Richard Lugar was ready to consider alternatives for Afghanistan and scale down expectations accordingly: "The question before us is whether Afghanistan is important enough to justify the lives and massive resources that are being spent there, especially given our nation's debt crisis." Just withdrawing an arbitrary number of troops was not the right way to go about rethinking the Afghan strategy, he went on; what was needed was a new definition of success.[31]

What then of the argument that victory or defeat in Afghanistan was of crucial significance to America's future security? Had bin Laden's death made all the difference? Apparently so. Senator John Kerry, the Democratic presidential nominee in 2004, agreed with Lugar about the escalating cost of the war, saying, "It is fundamentally unsustainable to continue spending $10 billion a month on a massive military operation with no end in sight." But he worried about the "lack of clarity" the administration had exhibited about its ultimate goals—and whether or not America's allies were being read into the picture. In response, a senior administration official simply said that was because the situation *was* unclear, but bin Laden's death made it more likely the Taliban would seek to separate itself from al Qaeda, which could give "traction to reconcilia-tion efforts."[32]

Karzai might well have reason to believe that his regime had been relegated to outsider status, as had Nguyen van Thieu's in the Paris peace talks on Vietnam three decades earlier. The reports on potential peace talks even implied that by responding to American overtures, the Taliban could secure for itself a safe route out of Pakistan, one that would end interference in its affairs from the ISI and the Haqqani network. That was really breathtaking if one stopped to consider all the things Americans had supposedly been fighting for—religious tolerance, women's rights to education, et cetera. "Some people who have met with the Taliban say that among the reasons [the insurgents] want to establish their own office is so they can get out from under the Pakistanis," said a senior ad-ministration official.[33]

The hopes of direct talks with the Taliban quickly faded, but the American determination to "get out from under" the war grew stronger—as did the desire to carry on drone warfare wherever a likely target was spotted. Counterinsurgency was yesterday's top story; drones were the headliners now. Indeed, Afghanistan began to be relegated to the inside pages. If al Qaeda was knocked out, where did that leave the Taliban?

Even before bin Laden's death, however, there were comments that the drone strikes were no longer taking out major al Qaeda targets in Pakistan—there just weren't that many left. What made such reports especially interesting, of course, was the implication that for all of his threats and plans to carry out assassinations, Osama bin Laden had indeed become little more than a caged tiger venting his rage on videotapes. Former CIA officials who continued to describe the drones as essential now admitted that they recog-nized fewer and fewer among the names of the killed. The agency was increasingly firing off missiles when it saw certain "signatures," such as travel out of a "known" al Qaeda site or a group traveling in possession of explosives. "It's like watching 'The Sopranos': You know what's going on in the Bada Bing." Instead of clearing the air, bin Laden's death had filled the skies with UAVs in search of targets to vaporize. Yes, it was always more dramatic to take the bishop and, if you can find them, the king and queen, said the former official, but "pawns matter."[34]

The Real Game Changer

When the two Afghan surges were announced by President Obama in the spring and fall of 2009, it had not been expected that finding and killing Osama bin Laden would change everything all at once. Neither, however, had it been expected that drones and special ops would provide a whole new framework for thinking about the ultimate deterrence quotient in the war on terror. Drones were eliminating the need for pursuing the war on terror one country at a time. They were the technological fix for long, inconclusive wars—if political obstacles such as national sovereignty or irksome constitutional rights could be overcome. Having gotten away with the Abbottabad raid, the United States was truly ready to expand its capacity by opening up new drone bases and legal justifications for striking at anyone anywhere.

There had been the Af-Pak theater of operations; now there would be attacks on al Qaeda in the Arabian Peninsula (AQAP) as well as ventures into Somalia and eventually Libya and Mali by proxy. The *Wall Street Journal* reported that the U.S. military had reopened a base for unmanned aircraft in the Seychelles Islands, an archipelago in the Indian Ocean about a thousand miles from mainland Africa's east coast. "Defense Secretary Leon Panetta," said the *Journal* article, "and other officials have stressed a need to urgently follow up on the killing of al Qaeda leader Osama bin Laden in May with operations to destroy his terrorist organization." Or, as another "senior U.S. official" said, "We do not know enough about the leaders of the al Qaeda affiliates in Africa. Is there a guy out there saying, 'I am the future of al Qaeda'? Who is the next Osama bin Laden?"[35]

The air force and navy still commanded a large number of drone raids, probably the greater number. Drone central was Creech Air

Force Base, located outside Las Vegas. Sitting in a central control room, drone pilots dressed in flight suits were the new top guns in robot warfare. From the digital feeds on the bright screens before them that reproduced the "battle zones," the operators could unleash a Hellfire missile on a target half a world away. There were more than sixty satellite bases that housed the drones, with the overseas bases currently concentrated around the Horn of Africa and the Middle East. And they were expanding into new locations at a fast pace. "We are constantly evaluating potential operating locations based on evolving mission needs." The Department of Defense had plans to purchase about 730 new medium-sized and large drones over the next decade. Drones were the bedrock of new military planning.[36]

The CIA mother base was Langley. From CIA headquarters CIA "pilots" ran their missions, and analysts watched footage of Osama bin Laden's compound sent back by the RQ-170 Sentinel, nicknamed the "Beast of Kandahar." While all this expansion was plainly evident even to casual observers of national security policy, Obama's chief counterterrorism aide, John Brennan, described al Qaeda as on a steady slide downward. In a newspaper interview he described the recent death of an al Qaeda leader in the tribal area of Pakistan as a "huge blow." This particular leader, Atiyah Abd al-Rahman, was "reportedly" hit by a CIA drone strike. Al Qaeda was now too busy trying to hide, Brennan asserted, to plot new attacks. And this attack also showed why, he went on, U.S. intelligence had detected no attacks planned for the tenth anniversary of 9/11.[37]

So while al Qaeda was on the ropes, the mission creep of drone warfare was far more ambitious and growing more rapidly than anything seen previously—and certainly more extensive than any boots-on-the-ground wars in the Middle East and Africa. In September 2011, for example, the United States blamed the Pakistani intelligence service for supporting a new outrage by the Haqqani network operating in Afghanistan, a deadly bomb attack on the U.S. embassy in Kabul. The chair of the Joint Chiefs, Admiral Mike Mullen, made an explicit accusation before the Senate Armed Services Committee: "The Haqqani network acts as a veritable arm of Pakistan's Inter-Services Intelligence agency." Washington apparently threatened to send troops into Pakistan to chase down the Haqqanis—a practice of intruding into other sovereign states that began even before 1916 when Woodrow Wilson sent General John J. Pershing into Mexico to try to end Pancho Villa's raids into Texas. Pershing didn't find Villa, and Mexico City did not welcome the mission.[38]

Rehman Malik, Pakistan's interior minister, held a similar opinion about such an incursion. "The Pakistan nation will not allow the boots on our ground, never," he said. "Our government is already cooperating with the U.S.—but they also must respect our sovereignty." Despite these crosscurrents and bitter exchanges, and Mullen's statements to the committee that the Pakistanis had only undermined their international credibility, Mullen concluded his testimony by saying that he had not wasted his time putting so much effort into cooperation with Islamabad: "Military cooperation again is warming."[39]

Mullen's optimism rested on drone missions, for they were the only area where it appeared Islamabad's interests and Washington's concerns came together. As matters would develop, it would be even clearer in places such as Yemen that drones could be welcomed, as al Qaeda became intertwined with opposition movements there. Drones appeared to be the answer to the problem of maintaining American world leadership without bankrupting the nation in the process or forcing to the surface nationalist anger that would undermine the American presence—both devilish issues that had sent previous "whole-world" empires careening to a rapid collapse.[40]

The troubles in the Arab world that threatened chaos after Egyptian president Hosni Mubarak was overthrown now appeared to Brennan to be only a "bump in the road," as military cooperation was soon reestablished with Egypt's armed forces. Counterterrorism cooperation with Tunisia (where the so-called Arab Spring had begun) had also been good. But there was one place where the situation had become acute: Yemen. Yemeni forces were battling a serious challenge from the bin Laden affiliate al Qaeda in the Arabian

Peninsula, which has "worked with the rebel tribes to grab large swaths of territory in the south." American efforts had been hampered in part by the unpopularity of President Ali Abdullah Saleh's regime. His sons were running the government while Saleh recovered in Saudi Arabia from an assassin's attack that left him with burns over 70 percent of his body. Brennan hoped he would not return, but instead stay away so that real elections could take place. The problem was that "the political tumult" made it appear that the government was positioning itself for "internal political purposes as opposed to doing all they can against AQAP," Brennan told reporters in a wide-ranging and revealing interview. "I've told him that I do not believe it's in his interests, Yemen's interests or our interests . . . to go back to Yemen."[41]

Yemen was a "tinderbox," he ended, that could erupt into a civil war that AQAP would take advantage of to gain power. What American policy makers needed was someone to attack in the country whose anti-Americanism was so virulent that a drone strike would not appear to be interference in the domestic politics of Yemen. Fortunately, one was at hand: Anwar al-Awlaki.

The Constitution and the Preacher

Anwar al-Awlaki was then a Yemeni preacher with many followers globally. He was born to Yemeni parents in New Mexico, where his father was studying agricultural economics and business administration. That made him a native-born American citizen—a big complication when the time came to debate whether to target him for terrorist acts. The Constitution requires due process for citizens accused of capital crimes under the Fifth Amendment, without which they cannot be deprived of life, liberty, or property; and Article 3 of the Constitution defines treason as a specific overt act, namely, "levying War against [the United States], or in adhering to their Enemies, giving them Aid and Comfort." This article also requires that conviction for such an act must depend upon two witnesses in open court or a confession of treason. While the language about what actually constitutes an overt act of treason is somewhat slippery, the requirement under the Fifth Amendment seems air-tight: there must be a judgment in open court to convict.

Born in 1971, Awlaki grew up in the United States and as a young adult lived in Colorado and San Diego. In many ways he was an unusual person to claim to be a spiritual leader, as he did when he moved with his wife and son to Virginia, where he became an imam at an Islamic center in Falls Church, as he had been busted twice in San Diego for soliciting prostitutes. Even before the move to Virginia he had become a "person of interest" in a variety of FBI investigations into possible connections with various suspected terrorists and radical jihadist-oriented organizations. Eventually the FBI closed out its preliminary investigations, saying that "the imam . . . does not meet the criterion for [further] investigation." He then became for a time the Muslim chaplain at George Washington University.[42]

After 9/11 he began preaching against the United States, but he turned up at the Capitol to lead an invited service and even at the Pentagon, where he became part of an "outreach" effort by the military. His phone number was found in the room of one of the 9/11 hijackers in Germany, and it is said that one of the hijackers visited his mosque. Awlaki denied any knowledge of the plot but expressed sympathy for the Taliban. Once again he was arrested for transporting a prostitute from Washington to Virginia, but no attempt was made to prosecute him. After a time in England, Awlaki moved to Yemen. He was imprisoned there in 2006 for eighteen months, apparently at U.S. request, and interrogated by the FBI once again in search of a connection with 9/11. But the Yemeni government insisted it was not because of suspected al Qaeda links or activities, but rather on kidnapping charges and other crimes.

In a taped interview shown in Great Britain, Awlaki claimed that he did not know for certain what the interrogations had been about, and added that he would like to travel outside Yemen but would not do so "until the U.S. drops whatever unknown charges it has against me." He had built up quite a reputation in England as an inspirational speaker, one of a very few respected radical clerics who could write and speak in English. And this talent he used to the fullest. "America is in a war with Allah," he said in one You-Tube lecture, referring to the fighting in Afghanistan and Iraq. All Muslims would have to choose—President Bush or the mujahideen. The solution for the Muslim world, he said, "is jihad."[43]

The language, of course, was a play on President Bush's famous declaration after 9/11 that other nations were either for or against the United States—there was no middle ground. In November 2001, for example, Bush said after a meeting with French leaders, "Over time it's going to be important for nations to know they will be held accountable for inactivity. You're either with us or against us in the fight against terror." Awlaki was becoming something of a celebrity in certain circles for his ability to turn American claims around, and for his supposed ability to inspire—and perhaps actively recruit—people to carry out terrorist missions. In February 2008 there was a deliberate leak to the *Washington Post* about the cleric's threat. "There is good reason," asserted the usual anonymous official, "to believe Anwar Aulaqi has been involved in very serious terrorist activities since leaving the United States, including plotting attacks against America and our allies."[44]

Obama took over the Awlaki hunt and the tricky diplomacy that went with it. Awlaki gave him plenty of reasons to be upset, issuing an almost constant stream of taunts and forecasts of dire consequences for Americans who supported Israel and waged war in Iraq and Afghanistan. "I pray that Allah destroys America and all its allies and the day that happens," he asserted in February 2009, "and I assure you it will and sooner than you think, I will be very pleased." With this rhetoric he attracted Muslims in other countries—and, most astonishingly, even the U.S. Army.

Major Nidal Hasan, an army psychiatrist who would kill thirteen soldiers and wound thirty-two others at Fort Hood in Texas in November 2009, had asked Awlaki what his duty was as a Muslim. Would he be considered a martyr if he took lives? Hasan had initiated a mostly one-sided e-mail exchange—indeed, he wrote seven e-mails to Awlaki before he got any response, and in none of them did he reveal what he might be planning. The later e-mails had to do with questions of charity and finding a "proper" woman, a kind of request almost like one would write to a dating bureau. By this time, of course, the FBI was tracking Awlaki's e-mail. One agent commented:

> While e-mail contact with [Awlaki] does not necessarily indicate participation in terrorist-related matters, [Awlaki's] reputation, background and anti-U.S. sentiments are well known. Although the content of these messages was not overtly nefarious, this type of contact with [Awlaki] would be of concern if the writer is actually the individual identified above.[45]

To put it differently, Awlaki was responsible for producing dangerous threats, even if he did not initiate them directly. "Nidal Hasan did the right thing," Awlaki wrote on his website. Muslims could only justify serving in the U.S. military by eventually following "in the footsteps of men like Nidal." "Nidal Hasan is a hero. He is a man of conscience who could not bear living the contradiction of being a Muslim and serving in an army that is fighting against his own people," Awlaki wrote. This was exactly how turncoat killers were made, said American investigators. As a former FBI agent put it to ABC News: "Awlaki is known as a senior recruiter for al Qaeda. He would be the spiritual motivator. Almost like someone you would go to and say, 'this is what I'm thinking about doing.' And they join in and encourage you and basically help you rationalize your behavior."[46]

Awlaki's extravagant praise of Hasan's act as the precursor of many more attacks to come set policy makers' teeth on edge. And little wonder: it was like the fear of brainwashing in the Korean War, with a Stephen King twist about how it could be done from a distance of thousands of miles. A month after the attack, Awlaki told an interviewer:

> I did not recruit Nidal Hasan to this operation; the one who recruited him was America, with its crimes and injustice, and this is what America refuses to admit. America does not want to admit that what Nidal did, and what thousands of other Muslims do

against America, is because of its unjust policies against the Islamic world. Nidal Hasan is a Muslim before he is an American, and he is also from Palestine, and he sees the oppression of the Jewish oppression of his people under American cover and support. True, I may have a role in his intellectual direction, but nothing beyond that, and I am not trying to absolve myself of what he did because I do not support it. No, but because I wish I had had the honor of having a bigger role in what happened than the role I really had.[47]

Awlaki was doubly dangerous because of the clever way he absolved himself of initiating actual acts of violence while advocating that others emulate Nidal Hasan until America was driven out of the Middle East. In a lengthy *New York Times* review of how President Obama's embrace of drone warfare evolved as the 2012 presidential campaign began to heat up, the controversial case of Anwar al-Awlaki received special attention. Obama's first national security adviser, General James Jones, told *Times* reporters that the president "was very interested in obviously trying to understand how a guy like Awlaki developed." His fiery sermons "had helped inspire a dozen plots, including the shootings at Fort Hood." The precise number given is of some interest because Nidal Hasan's thoughts led *him* to contact Awlaki, not the other way around. There were plenty of fiery sermons out there, or at least plenty of websites and other sources of inflammatory anti-American rhetoric. The word *plots* is also a less than precise description of the Fort Hood outrage, because no one contended Hasan acted under orders from anyone.[48]

Those questions will continue to be debated, but it is certain that Awlaki became almost as much of an obsession to policy makers as Osama bin Laden had been. The *Times* reporters quoted General Jones to the effect that Awlaki had gone beyond inspirational activities to "operational" plotting with his Nigerian protégé Umar Farouk Abdulmutallab, the "underwear bomber," who attempted to blow up a Northwest Airlines jet with three hundred passengers over Detroit on Christmas Day, 2009. The crude bomb he hoped to set off by injecting a syringe into a chemical package hidden in his underwear failed to explode. But it set him afire, badly burning his groin area. An FBI interrogator quipped that the bomb may have failed to explode because Abdulmutallab had not changed his underwear for three weeks so that he could feel secure in wearing the package.[49]

The attempt was anything but a joke to Obama administration figures. "Had that plane gone down, that would have been their version of 9/11." The "their" in this sentence referred to al Qaeda in the Arabian Peninsula. "We didn't know they had progressed to the point of actually launching individuals here," John Brennan said at a White House briefing two weeks after the failed attack, before investigators were willing to single out Awlaki as the sole culprit. What made matters worse was that it soon became apparent that American intelligence actually had had enough information to have prevented Abdulmutallab from boarding that flight—had all the dots been connected properly.[50]

The Christmas Day attack, the *Times* article said, was the tipping point: Awlaki was put on the kill list. It appeared there was some ex post facto tampering with the actual chronology here to make it fit a narrative more suited to careful consideration of constitutional issues concerning the targeting of an American citizen without "normal" judicial process; as news reporters noted, a missile strike aimed at an al Qaeda group in the Arabian Peninsula that included Awlaki occurred on the same day as the attempted effort to down the airliner over Detroit.[51] The cleric admitted that he had met with the Nigerian, indeed called him his student, but said he had not ordered Abdulmutallab to use a bomb. "Brother mujahed Umar Farouk—may God relieve him—is one of my students, yes," the cleric told the Al Jazeera news service. "We had kept in contact, but I didn't issue a fatwa to Umar Farouk for this operation." Investigators said, however, that the Nigerian youth admitted during questioning that Awlaki had introduced him to a bomb maker during a visit to Yemen in the summer of 2009 and told him "to get on a U.S. airliner and detonate his explosives over the United States." The FBI had not been entirely convinced by the Nigerian's confession. "He's saying all this," commented one agent, "but we haven't determined all of it is true; whether [Awlaki] blessed it or gave the green light or was the impetus behind it . . . it's very possible and it's being investigated. But it's also possible he's saying it to give himself credibility among militants who look up to Awlaki." There were other questions about Abdulmutallab's confession as well. He told his whole story after his father and uncle arrived in the United States and spoke with him. Perhaps the advice they gave him was to claim he was under Awlaki's spell as part of a plea bargain. We will never know, for he could not be called as a witness in a trial that would never be held, as Awlaki was killed in a drone strike.[52]

But in each retelling of the sequence of events, what stands out is the care with which the administration talked about Awlaki to make a strong case, bringing together the Fort Hood massacre and the would-be bomber as Awlaki's "inventions" as parts of a string of "plots," highlighting treasonable acts to satisfy the Constitution's definition of that crime. In fact, however, there had been at least one effort to kill Awlaki—on December 24, 2009, the day *before* the Nigerian tried to set off his bomb. And Obama had come into office at the beginning of 2009 fully briefed by aides about Awlaki's ability to inspire followers within the United States. If a *Washington Post* reporter, Susan Schmidt, had been told about Canadian and American intelligence discoveries of private computer files and audio files of lectures by Awlaki promoting the strategies of a "key al-Qaeda military commander, the late Ysef al-Ayeri, a Saudi known as 'Swift Sword,'" and if CBS News obtained information about how in December 2008 U.S. Customs agents "intercepted a computer disk full of lectures that his wife sent to an Islamic publishing house in Denver," then the president-elect had certainly known what the agencies had collected. Awlaki was a dangerous man because he inspired people to act. An intelligence document obtained by the Associated Press noted ominously that about 11 percent of visitors to the cleric's website were in the United States.[53]

Rumors about Awlaki's contacts with some of the 9/11 hijackers had been circulating almost from the day of the attacks. But the FBI told both the commission investigating the World Trade Center and Pentagon attacks and Congress that it did not have reason to detain the cleric. Senator Bob Graham, chair of the Senate Intelligence Committee, believed that the FBI had bungled the investigation, and that information showed Awlaki had met with two of the perpetrators, who "shared their terrorist intentions and plans." Again, we will never know more about any role Awlaki may have played in those events.[54]

We do know that the first acknowledged (or semi-acknowledged) attack aimed at killing Awlaki was launched on December 24, 2009, and was therefore based on no overt act the cleric had committed, only assumptions about his influence. The *Washington Post* report emphasized that American officials knew Awlaki had been scheduled to be in a particular place at a particular time, and believed he had been killed. This attack and one a week earlier demonstrated the administration's "greater willingness . . . to use military force in confronting terrorists outside the traditional war zones of Iraq and Afghanistan." Whether or not American "support" went beyond providing intelligence about the meeting, the *Post* article said, was not clear.[55] And then came bad news. The number of "civilian casualties" in the Yemen drone strike, over a hundred, belied claims that only militants had been killed. Awlaki survived the attack, moreover, and quipped that apparently someone was angry with him. While rumors connected Awlaki to various terrorist plots, the raids increased fury about the Yemeni dictator's ability to take advantage of Awlaki's presence in his country to press for increased aid in the supposed fight with al Qaeda, while receiving large sums of military aid to preserve his government against opposition forces.

Saleh's cooperation was deemed essential to the process of bringing down Awlaki, and there was the rub. The United States risked causing further outrage across the Muslim world if it continued to ally itself too closely with the dictator, presenting an ugly dilemma in the murky world of post–9/11 alliances of convenience. In these circumstances, the United States did not want to admit publicly that cruise missile or drone strikes were its responsibility, only that Saleh had relied on intelligence help. But which was worse, to say the United States had been acting at Saleh's behest or to accept responsibility for the civilian casualties? Neither option looked very

good as the casualty figures were revealed. The use of the CIA instead of the military offered a shade of deniability because the
agency was less accountable for its doings under U.S. laws, but the
cover was not opaque enough, it seemed.

In a conversation with General David Petraeus in January 2010,
the problems American policy makers had let themselves in for
were fully spelled out: "Saleh lamented the use of cruise missiles
that are 'not very accurate' and welcomed the use of aircraft-deployed
precision-guided bombs instead. 'We'll continue saying the bombs
are ours, not yours.'" His preference was for drones and Hellfire missiles, which were thought less likely to cause "collateral damage."
His deputy "joked" that he had lied by telling parliament that the
bombs were American-made but Yemeni-deployed.[56]

Four days after the attempt on the airliner, Obama made a public
statement about American intentions that boxed him into a drone
campaign in Yemen as the only alternative. "This [the airliner bomb]
was a serious reminder of the dangers we face and of the nature of
those who threaten our homeland. We will continue to use every
element of our national power to disrupt, to dismantle and defeat
the violent extremists who threaten us." White House lawyers,
meanwhile, were mulling over the legality of "proposed attempts to
kill an American citizen" believed to be part of the leadership of
AQAP, Anwar al-Awlaki. One of the parties engaged in the internal debate told ABC News that opportunities to "take out" the subject "may have been missed," suggesting, of course, that there had
been other attempts *besides* the December 24 drone strike. "A spokesman said the White House declined to comment." But reporters did
not. Such a strike, said ABC News, aimed "to kill him would stretch
current Presidential authority given to the CIA and the Pentagon
to pursue terrorists anywhere in the world." And that was what
worried some inside the administration: "American officials fear the
possibility of criminal prosecution without approval in advance
from the White House for a targeted strike against Awlaki."[57]

The question of what limits applied when it came to tracking
down and killing an American, the report said, came as "hundreds
of FBI and other federal agents . . . fan out this week as part of a

secret operation to pursue leads about Americans with connections to Yemen that were previously dismissed as not significant."
But there was a new twist to this manhunt story. Awlaki's father
had learned that his son had been put on a "kill list" and publicly
appealed to President Obama not to kill his son, who he said was
in hiding.

Aside from all the noise, however, there was a serious problem
raised when the suspect's father filed a lawsuit seeking to prevent
President Obama from ordering his son's death. The American
Civil Liberties Union and the Center for Constitutional Rights argued that there was no "battlefield" in Yemen and the administration could not hide behind state-secrets privileges to carry out an
extrajudicial execution. The whole trial took on aspects of parody,
with the government's chief lawyer saying at one point that "as far
as the allegations there is a kill list, et cetera, we're not confirming
or denying." But he also observed that Awlaki would not be under
any lethal threat if he "turned himself" in to Yemeni authorities—a
strange comment that amounted to an acknowledgment of the list.
The Justice Department invoked the state-secrets privilege to ask
for the dismissal of the lawsuit in the U.S. district court in Washington. Judge John Bates agreed, saying that targeting was a "political question" to be decided by the executive branch. Bates also
ruled, in Alice in Wonderland fashion, that Awlaki's father had no
legal standing to file a suit on his son's behalf unless he was actually
killed. The reasoning was similar to the administration's insistence
that signature strikes could not be challenged ahead of time, only
after they had killed civilians.[58]

Obama had made a thicket of legal issues even denser than
before. It took six months for the Office of Legal Counsel to find a
way out with a fifty-page memorandum setting forth an opinion on
whether the president had the right to kill an American citizen
without a court trial. The authors did not like to put it so bluntly,
but that was the subject of their deliberations. Actually, no one
outside the executive branch knows even today what is written
there, because the memo remains classified. From the usual anonymous sources came teasers about its contents, such as "What con-

stitutes due process *in this case* is a due process in war"—emphasis added for two reasons: first and most obvious, the debate was definitely about Awlaki; second, the memo set a precedent in what was sure to become "a legal debate over whether a president can order the killing of U.S. *citizens* overseas as a counterterrorism measure" (emphasis added for the same reason).[59]

During the time the memo was being written, Obama found himself questioning where the policy was leading. The targets he was being asked to approve for "direct" action too often came from a wing of AQAP that was not externally focused and was uninterested in attacking the United States. Was the United States being sucked into Yemen's civil war? In a June 2010 meeting a military adviser referred to the ongoing "campaign" in Yemen. The president interrupted: "We're not in Yemen to get involved in some domestic conflict. We're going to continue to stay focused on threats to the homeland—that's where the real priority is."[60]

After bin Laden

"US intelligence had been tracking Anwar al-Awlaki for years, but in the wake of the bin Laden operation," writes Daniel Klaidman, "Obama had become fixated on taking out the charismatic cleric." He wanted him even more than he wanted Ayman al-Zawahiri, the former al Qaeda number two who had been promoted to the top spot upon bin Laden's death. Zawahiri had no charisma, and that made him less of a threat. "Awlaki had things on the stove that were ready to boil over," an adviser said. "Zawahiri was still looking for ingredients in the cupboard." And, Klaidman added, at the White House meetings on terror (where Obama chaired the sessions that selected targets), the president demanded updates from Brennan. "I want Awlaki," the president said at one. "Don't let up." Lethal operations in Yemen had been handled by the military, but by the summer of 2011 Operation Awlaki was turned over to the CIA.[61]

A drone attack on September 30, 2011, finally killed Awlaki near where he had been hiding. It also killed Samar Khan, the key figure behind *Inspire*, an English-language magazine produced by AQAP. His death was brushed aside as acceptable "collateral" damage. "An administration official said the CIA did not know Khan was with Aulaqi, but they also considered Khan a belligerent whose presence near the target would not have stopped the attack." The White House swung into action mode immediately, with rapid-fire statements from the president and others, the gist of which were to promote Awlaki to "external operations" chief for AQAP.[62]

The death of Awlaki, said the president, was "another significant milestone in the broader effort to defeat al Qaeda and its affiliates." Speaking later at the retirement ceremony for Admiral Mike Mullen, chairman of the Joint Chiefs of Staff, the president said Awlaki "took the lead in planning and directing efforts to murder innocent Americans," such as the attempt to blow up U.S. cargo planes in 2010. The killing of Awlaki was a tribute to the U.S. intelligence community and the efforts of leaders in Yemen. He also said that al Qaeda in the Arabian Peninsula remains "a dangerous but weakened terrorist organization."

The mixed volley of celebrations, justifications, and warnings continued all day: "Make no mistake, this is further proof al Qaeda and its affiliates will find no safe haven in Yemen or anywhere around the world," Obama said. But in a radio interview the president declined to say whether he gave the order to kill Awlaki, saying he could not discuss operational details. "This is something that we had been working with the Yemeni government on for quite some time," he said. "There's been significant cooperation at the intelligence levels with a lot of countries in the region. We are very pleased that Mr. Awlaki is no longer going to be in a position to directly threaten the United States homeland, as well as our allies around the world."

When he finally finished with the Tony Blair–like evasions that everyone knew were false, Obama got to what, for him, was the heart of the matter: "The fact that he is now no longer around to initiate the kind of propaganda that also was recruiting people all around the world to that murderous cause I think is something that's very good for American security."[63]

Many Republicans praised Obama's action, while criticism from Democrats was mostly centered on the awkwardness of defending a secret memorandum. The only politician of note to bring up the Constitution and due process was Ron Paul, who said, "Al-Awlaki was born here; he's an American citizen. He was never tried or charged for any crimes." But Paul was dismissed, wrote Richard Cohen, "as a constitutional kvetch." Bush attorney general Michael Mukasey put it the bluntest possible way, noted Cohen: "These militants were killed because the Obama administration, having ruled out harsh interrogations, had no use for them."[64]

On a Sunday talk show, *State of the Nation with Candy Crowley*, former vice president Dick Cheney called on Obama to apologize for his past criticism of Bush administration policies. He had no problem with killing Awlaki, of course, but what he resented was the way Obama's OLC had claimed that the cleric was not entitled to normal legal protections because he was a combatant. That reasoning "rankled" Cheney, who said, "They, in effect, said that we had walked away from our ideals, or taken policy contrary to our ideals, when we had enhanced interrogation techniques. . . . Now they clearly have moved in the direction of taking robust action when they think it is justified."[65]

Democrat Jane Harman, the former chair of the House Intelligence Community, appeared on the same CNN program. She called on the White House to release the legal memorandum. "The Justice Department should release that memo," said Harman, director of the Woodrow Wilson International Center for Scholars and a former chairwoman of the House Intelligence Committee. "The debate on the legal grounds for that strategy should be more in the open." The "targeted killing of anyone should give us pause," she added, but Awlaki was a "good case" of someone posing an imminent threat.[66] A White House official dismissed all criticism of the strike on legal grounds—or anything else: "If Anwar al-Awlaki is your poster boy for why we shouldn't do drone strikes, good fucking luck."[67]

Two weeks before sending a drone to kill Awlaki, the president sent John Brennan to Harvard University to give a talk called

"Strengthening Our Security by Adhering to Our Values and Laws." Brennan acknowledged that he was not a lawyer, but he said he had developed a profound appreciation for the roles that American values played in keeping the nation safe. The administration was committed to strengthening "our national security by adhering to those values." He then went on to say that the administration was not "rigid or ideological," but pragmatic. In the context, this was a phrase to explain how the administration was "pragmatic" when it came to deciding what was due process under the Fifth Amendment. When the U.S. government upheld the rule of law, then governments around the globe would be more willing to provide the United States with intelligence needed to "disrupt ongoing plots." The guiding principles of the administration, again, were "pragmatic—neither a wholesale overhaul nor a wholesale retention of past practices." Where they had been effective and enhanced security, they had been retained. Where they had not, "we have taken concrete steps to get us back on course."[68]

Two weeks after the drone strike that killed Anwar al-Awlaki, another raid on a barbecue site killed his son, sixteen-year-old Abdulrahman al-Awlaki, a cousin of the same age, and six or seven other boys. At first U.S. officials claimed Abdulrahman was twenty-one—even as it still claimed not to be responsible for specific antiterrorist operations with drones. Then his grandfather produced his birth certificate. Senator Carl Levin, who received a classified briefing as chairman of the Senate Armed Services Committee, said about the death: "My understanding is that there was adequate justification." How? "It was justified by the presence of a high-value target." Well, so much for Brennan's defense that there were no confirmed collateral deaths in drone warfare. Probably the most sensitive, the most perceptive writer on the lethal presidency, Tom Junod, in a long exegesis on the meaning of all that the administration's defenders have written and said, finally concludes, "There is the fog of war, and then there is the deeper fog of the Lethal Presidency. What is certain is only this: that a drone crossed the moonlit sky, and when the sun rose next morning, the relatives of Abdulrahman al-Awlaki gathered his remains—along with those of his cousin and some teenaged boys—so that they could give a Muslim funeral to an American boy."[69]

At the height of the 2012 presidential campaign, former press secretary Robert Gibbs delivered a shocking reply to a reporter's question about Abdulrahman al-Awlaki: "I would suggest that you should have a far more responsible father," he snapped, "if they are truly concerned about the well being of their children." Gibbs seemed to be saying that all children who had jihadist fathers were fair game for drone hunters. Even worse, he seemed not to know that the strike that killed the boys occurred two weeks after the elder Awlaki's death on September 30, 2011. He had elaborated by saying that Awlaki had renounced his citizenship, and had to be reminded that the boy had not. Aside from Gibbs's resentment that he was being asked these questions, what comes through so clearly was disinterest in the consequences of American actions—except that they hit their targets. No one asked the 2012 presidential candidates, Obama and Mitt Romney, about the incident during the presidential debate season, even as a writer in the *Atlantic Monthly*, Conor Friedersdorf, said of Gibbs's performance, "Killing an American citizen without due process on that logic ought to be grounds for impeachment."[70]

"I want to ask a question," said Yemen's president Saleh on the day Awlaki was killed by a drone strike. "I am addressing the American public. Are you still keeping your commitment in continuing the operations against the Taliban and al-Qaeda?" If so, he went on, then Washington should stop pressing him to turn over his power to those protesting his rule. "We know where power is going to go. It is going to al-Qaeda, which is directly and completely linked to the Muslim Brotherhood."[71]

Osama bin Laden's death was supposed to bring closure, and something of the same was said about the death of Anwar al-Awlaki as the elimination of al Qaeda's most dangerous, most charismatic recruiter. But Saleh's question captured the mood better. Now there was a mechanism for continuing operations with proven results—unlike all that had happened before or since 9/11. And that mechanism seemed to be the Office of Legal Counsel's newly acquired ability to amend the U.S. Constitution to suit the current occupant of the White House's interpretation of national security needs.

7

A BETTER WAR?

As we end today's wars and reshape our Armed Forces, we will ensure that our military is agile, flexible, and ready for the full range of contingencies. In particular, we will continue to invest in the capabilities critical to future success, including intelligence, surveillance, and reconnaissance; counterterrorism; countering weapons of mass destruction; operating in anti-access environments; and prevailing in all domains, including cyber.
— President Barack Obama, January 3, 2012

If there had been any remaining questions about it, the death of Anwar al-Awlaki settled the matter: the drone had replaced counterinsurgency. The Department of Defense's 2012 strategic guidance document, *Sustaining U.S. Global Leadership*, flatly asserted midway through the document, "U.S. forces will no longer be sized to conduct large-scale, prolonged stability operations."[1]

"Stability ops" was a relatively new Pentagon phrase to describe counterinsurgency objectives in Afghanistan, a somewhat scaled-down ambition from the nation-building dreams of the "new world order" era. What strikes one going through the 2012 Defense Department document besides a repudiation of even those lowered sights, however, is how many points read like an elaboration on Richard Nixon's 1969 "Guam Doctrine," introduced during an ad hoc press conference on that tiny outpost of American power in the Pacific. It was called "Vietnamization," and Nixon offered it as the way out of the tiger trap that had consumed the nation's energies. The situations were not exactly parallel, of course, but there were some significant (and surprising) similarities in the answers called forth by America's two "longest wars."

In 2012 the nation was still suffering the aftereffects of the worst economic crisis since the Great Depression. The Afghan War's costs on top of what Iraq had cost were estimated at over $3 trillion and counting, reaching higher than the Hindu Kush. The original aspirations for ensuring a government in Afghanistan that would pass muster as an evolving democracy were cast aside as Washington looked at the balance sheets. The parallel with Vietnam was obvious: by 1968 the Vietnam War had caused a serious gold drain that eventually forced the United States to stop selling its gold reserves for dollars and led policy makers to reconsider their options—and their nation-building goals. Former secretary of state Dean Acheson, the gray eminence of Cold War statesmen, had warned Lyndon Johnson about the growing economic threat to American global leadership, and insisted the president not do anything to make matters worse, such as sending hundreds of thousands more soldiers into Southeast Asia, as the nation couldn't afford it. On top of that, its European allies had become dismayed and too independent-minded—all because of Vietnam. The military had led the president down a primrose path, said Acheson, one that ended in rain-soaked jungles and rice paddies.[2]

The 1968 election was not simply a referendum on the costly way the Vietnam War had been fought, of course, but while a variety of social issues loomed in the background, bringing that kind of war to an end was a top priority. So long as it appeared Nixon was seeking a "decent interval" during which U.S. troops could be withdrawn gradually while responsibility for combat operations was transferred to the Vietnamese, the nation fretted but its patience held out. What Nixon promised at Guam was a steady reduction in American forces combined with heavier support for creating a large, modern army and air force for the Saigon regime, aka the Republic of Vietnam. He assured Washington's doubting Vietnamese allies (really dependencies) that they would have all they needed, backed up by American airpower on an even higher scale of destructiveness than ever before in the war. He promised he would force Hanoi to cry uncle if it sought to overthrow the Saigon government.

Then on July 25, 1969, Nixon was asked at the Guam press conference about the future of counterinsurgency, and answered, as Obama could have in explicating the 2012 strategic guidance document, "Well, there is a future for American counterinsurgency tactics only in the sense that where one of our friends in Asia asks for advice or assistance, under proper circumstances, we will provide it. But where we must draw the line is in becoming involved heavily with our own personnel, doing the job for them, rather than helping them do the job for themselves."[3]

So the war ended for America in 1973, not with a bang but with a peace agreement that speeded the return of American prisoners of war but was so porous that North Vietnam could pour troops and tanks through it. Saigon fell two years later. But the debate over how Vietnam had been lost had only begun. Long after the war ended, a new spin was put on the Vietnam experience by authors who claimed that Washington had found a leader, General Creighton Abrams, who fought a better war that incorporated tried-and-true counterinsurgency tactics pioneered by the French and British in Algeria and Malaya. Had Americans only been a little more patient, the argument went, they would have seen the light at the end of the tunnel become a bright new day.[4]

These were the opening gambits in the effort to change the American style of war according to a different template of counterinsurgency than the one Nixon described in the Guam Doctrine. And it required a legend that held out General Abrams as the model for future leadership if the U.S. Army was to meet the challenge. When the key moment arrived in Iraq, according to the legend, a great new general did arrive to lead the counterinsurgency-inspired surge in Iraq: David Petraeus, the principal author of Field Manual 3-24, the guide for success in post–Cold War encounters in what used to be called the "Third World." The legend continues that the Iraq "surge" actually worked because of Petraeus's shrewd leadership, but once again there looms the danger of a lost victory because of America's undue haste to leave.

Come forward to our time and to new claims that the military "rolled" President Obama along a primrose path by convincing him against the judgment of some "old hands," including Vice President Joe Biden, to send thirty thousand more troops into Afghanistan in December 2009. When former senator Chuck Hagel, a Vietnam vet, was nominated by Obama after his reelection to succeed Leon Panetta at Defense, the debate over the "lessons" of Vietnam and America's wars in Iraq and Afghanistan came back to the front pages as Senator John McCain, a former prisoner of war in Vietnam and Republican presidential candidate, grilled the nominee about his opposition to the surge. McCain tore into Hagel at confirmation hearings about a January 2007 statement declaring that President George W. Bush's troop surge in Iraq was "the most dangerous foreign policy blunder . . . since Vietnam." McCain now asked Hagel, "Were you correct in your assessment? . . . Were you right or wrong? . . . Yes or no?"

Hagel refused to answer in one word, saying, "I think it's far more complicated than that." As to whether he was right or wrong, he said, "I'll defer that judgment to history." McCain thundered, "I think history has already made a judgment about the surge, sir, and you are on the wrong side of it."[5]

The obvious personalization of the issue between two Vietnam vets forecasts a struggle to control the history of the Iraq and Afghan Wars in years yet to come. Neocon convictions about counterinsurgency as a successful American policy to avoid defeat in the new longest wars have been badly shaken, as they face the reality of perpetual war for perpetual peace. Whenever the question comes up of accelerating American troop withdrawals, their pundits warn that such haste would endanger the "progress" being made. But they no longer command the attention they once did when General Petraeus was being hailed in the *Wall Street Journal* as deserving of the first five-star general rank since World War II.

> The U.S. war against terrorism is now the longest war in U.S. history, and Gen. Petraeus has clearly distinguished himself as a leader worthy of the rank held by Gens. MacArthur, Marshall and Nimitz. A promotion would properly honor his service—and

it would also honor the troops he leads and has led. Today's soldiers have fought as valiantly as any in American history, and they deserve recognition of their leaders. Congressional approval of a fifth star would demonstrate the nation's commitment to their mission.[6]

Depending on one's point of view, the surge either completely altered the outcome of the Iraq War or offered a "decent interval" to glue in a government in Baghdad that had a chance of survival—if everything fell into place. Lawrence Wilkerson, former secretary of state Colin Powell's trusted adviser, commented in 2011 as the last American troops were leaving that experts in and out of government had believed it really did not matter how long the United States stayed in Iraq, whether it was one year or twenty years—the outlook was for a civil war before everything was settled.[7]

The surge built Petraeus's reputation to outsize proportions but did nothing to save Bush's. The most interesting line in the *Wall Street Journal* article quoted above was "Congressional approval of a fifth star would demonstrate the nation's commitment to their mission." In fact, Obama was already backing away from the "mission" as defined in the article and rushing toward drones. Barack Obama won the 2008 election promising to end the Iraq War and had pledged to seek closure to the trauma of 9/11 by bringing Osama bin Laden to justice. Along the way, however, counterinsurgency became devalued, and drones were elevated to the weapon of choice. What Bush's administration had called the "global war on terror" became truly global in Obama's first administration.

The Secrecy of Presidents

The Vietnam War and Watergate had brought about a congressional rebellion against the imperial presidency. Nixon's claims to extralegal powers in wartime were summed up famously in one quotation he gave during an interview with David Frost in 1977.

FROST: Would you say that there are certain situations—and the Huston Plan was one of them—where the president can decide that it's in the best interests of the nation, and do something illegal?

NIXON: Well, when the president does it, that means it is not illegal.

FROST: By definition.

NIXON: Exactly, exactly. If the president, for example, approves something because of the national security, or in this case because of a threat to internal peace and order of significant magnitude, then the president's decision in that instance is one that enables those who carry it out, to carry it out without violating a law. Otherwise they're in an impossible position.[8]

Among the articles of impeachment that were being prepared at the time of his resignation, the House Judiciary Committee rejected a proposed Article V:

In his conduct of the office of President of the United States, Richard M. Nixon, in violation of his constitutional oath faithfully to execute the office of President of the United States and, to the best of his ability, preserve, protect, and defend the Constitution of the United States, and in disregard of his constitutional duty to take care that the laws be faithfully executed, on and subsequent to March 17, 1969, authorized, ordered, and ratified the concealment from the Congress of false and misleading statements concerning the existence, scope and nature of American bombing operations in Cambodia in derogation of the power of the Congress to declare war, to make appropriations and to raise and support armies, and by such conduct warrants impeachment and trial and removal from office.

Instead, the committee settled on obstruction of justice, from the Watergate cover-up. In a tentative foray into the war-making provisions of the Constitution, Congress fought shy of taking on the matter of whether the president's imprimatur protected both himself and his "agencies" (military and civilian) from prosecution for actions later deemed illegal. It could be argued that if the congressional committee had retained that count in its indictment, future presidents could not extend legislation such as the 2001 AUMF to encompass a broad theater of war Congress never intended to create when it approved President Bush's authority to chase down the perpetrators of the 9/11 attacks. One could well understand the White House's reluctance to undertake a time-consuming, emotional enterprise to punish the guilty, who had acted in the belief that they had sufficient authority for their actions—a presidential imprimatur. There is always the argument, too, that such actions would put the presidency on trial in ways that would weaken national security forevermore. Had Congress followed its original intent in the articles of impeachment, however, there might very well have been a different order of priorities facing the new administration.

At the time of the Nixon/Frost interview the imperial presidency had a very bad name. It denoted secrecy, illegal wire taps, illegal bombings, et cetera. But 9/11 turned things around again, and a strong-willed George W. Bush had no difficulty getting through Congress the kind of authorization for wiretaps Nixon would have envied, a blanket authorization to use force against the attackers, and a series of Justice Department authorizations to go outside the Geneva Conventions when dealing with terrorists taken captive. Only when the Iraq War threatened to become a dismal replay of Vietnam did attention return to the issue of presidential usurpations of power in the name of national security.[9]

Obama's initial efforts to achieve greater transparency in government speeded up Freedom of Information Act requests for documents and caused the Office of Legal Counsel "torture memos" to be made public in April, three months after his inauguration. At the time Obama issued the following statement:

While I believe strongly in transparency and accountability, I also believe that in a dangerous world, the United States must sometimes carry out intelligence operations and protect information that is classified for purposes of national security. I have already fought for that principle in court and will do so again in the future. However, after consulting with the Attorney General, the Director of National Intelligence, and others, I believe that exceptional circumstances surround these memos and require their release.[10]

It was a carefully measured statement, calling the memos an "exceptional circumstance" and leaving open nearly any other question. Soon enough the question of what to do about individuals who had acted under Bush's direct or implied instructions arose. In fact, Obama had spoken to that point in postelection interviews, saying he was unlikely to open a broad-gauged inquiry into Bush administration programs such as eavesdropping or treatment of terrorism suspects. Prosecution would proceed only if the Justice Department found that "somebody has blatantly broken the law."[11]

Some commentators approved of, for reasons of pragmatism, Obama's reluctance to get out all the dirty linen and wash it in public. A Harvard classmate of Obama's who had represented Bush administration figures said, "The last thing a new administration wants to do is spend its time and energy rehashing the perceived sins of the old one." But former CIA official Mark Lowenthal approved Obama's stance for another reason: "If agents were criminally investigated for doing something that top Bush administration officials asked them to do and they were assured was legal, intelligence officers would be less willing to take risks to protect the country."[12]

"We're still evaluating how we're going to approach the whole issue of interrogations, detentions, and so forth," Obama told the ABC News program *This Week*, "and obviously we're going to be looking at past practices and I don't believe that anybody is above the law. On the other hand I also have a belief that we need to look forward as opposed to looking backwards. And part of my job is to make sure that for example at the CIA, you've got extraordinarily talented people who are working very hard to keep Americans safe. I don't want them to suddenly feel like they've got to spend all their time looking over their shoulders and lawyering."[13]

There is not a lot of space here between Obama's statement on taking office and Richard Nixon's postpresidential comment to David Frost that presidential approval of an action in the interest of national security enables subordinates who carry out that action to do so without violating any laws. Nixon's resignation, which allowed him to avoid impeachment and trial in the Senate, prevented an open discussion of that contention. But if that view prevails, as it has, then no president can ever be held accountable for anything done in the name of national security. And each president gets a blank slate on the day he or she takes the oath to defend the Constitution of the United States, allowing the new chief executive to design plans without fear of interference from the other branches of government. By not challenging fundamentals of the Bush heritage, wrote critic Tom Engelhardt, Obama accepted the premise of Bush's "global war on terror": "a 'wartime' with no possible end that would leave a commander-in-chief president in the White House till hell froze over."[14] In other words, as presidents continued to refuse to confront the past, the name of the occupant of the White House did not matter: there would always be a commander in chief exercising special war powers in perpetuity.

Obama's embrace of the drone and his reliance on longtime CIA Middle East specialist John Brennan for advice in developing a targeting strategy nevertheless mystified many supporters. The bond between Obama and Brennan was formed during the same weeks when Obama decided against any broad investigation of Bush administration practices. Brennan led Obama's intelligence transition team, and he wanted the job as CIA director—a job Obama was inclined to give him. Leaks to the press about his role in the Bush enhanced interrogation policies produced a furor, however, and Brennan withdrew his name from consideration. He wrote a bitter letter to Obama in which he stoutly denied any role in decision making about waterboarding or "many" of the other enhanced interrogation activities. His critics had ignored his record of honorable service in the CIA, he insisted, including his opposition to the "preemptive war" in Iraq. When he withdrew his name, it appeared for a moment that Obama wanted to make a clean break with the

Bush administration. The moment passed, and the president appointed Brennan to be his special adviser on counterterrorism—with an office in the White House basement.[15]

The Doctrine of Silence

From his White House office Brennan wielded immense powers over drone decisions. He was called the czar of drone warfare—even as the government denied it was waging drone warfare. The American public learned most of what it knew about drone strikes from foreign governments' reactions. Seven weeks after Awlaki was killed, an American-Afghan bombing attack killed twenty-five Pakistani troops at two military outposts. In response Pakistan ordered the CIA to end drone strikes from a base in western Pakistan—putting the United States in a position of having to offer an apology. Pakistan held up shipments of military supplies into Afghanistan as well, but it was the shutdown of drone strikes that caused the most concern.

General Martin Dempsey, chair of the Joint Chiefs, telephoned his counterpart in Islamabad to express regrets, and President Obama was said to be looking into the "tragedy." But Dempsey refused to say there was anything to apologize for. He did agree that "from the outside," it looked like the relationship with Pakistan was "the worst it's ever been." The issue was not simply the Raymond Davis case, nor even the raid that killed Osama bin Laden without Pakistan's knowledge, but the American posture of secrecy and self-justification. It infused Obama's foreign policy about drones and everything else. The Pakistani prime minister, Yousuf Raza Gilani, said his country was reevaluating its relationship with the United States. Asked by a CNN reporter if there was mutual respect, Gilani said, "At the moment not . . . If I can't protect the sovereignty of my country, how can we say that this is mutual respect and mutual interest?"[16]

A United States investigation determined that the NATO attack had been accidental and expressed condolences to the soldiers' families. Ambassador Cameron Munter urged White House officials to produce a video statement and express remorse for the deaths, as anger in Pakistan had reached a fever pitch and the United States needed to move quickly. Defense officials and political advisers both advised the president against the idea, however—a stance that conveyed not a little stubbornness and pique at Pakistan's maneuvering, and worry about the 2012 election and Republican criticism. Obama did not call the Pakistani president for eight days after the incident, as the White House wanted to make sure that it separated regrets from accepting blame. The American attitude made matters worse. It seemed one more instance of Washington unilaterally setting the rules and making self-serving decisions. "Past investigations of similar attacks," said Pakistani military officials, "have not been to our satisfaction and no one was punished." According to those officials, the attacks were not accidental but "blatant aggression."[17]

From later accounts, including those from Pakistan, the argument that it was a case of "blatant aggression" was hard to make. The incident triggered a debate inside the administration, however, about the value of the "signature strikes." The most recent of these had occurred around the time of the air attack on Pakistani soldiers and were aimed at the Haqqani network, which both Washington and Kabul blamed for an attack on the American embassy in Afghanistan. State Department officials and some in the National Security Council said such attacks were counterproductive. Rank-and-file militants, the dissidents said, were easy to replace, and whether Pakistani claims of civilian casualties were exaggerated or not, they were destabilizing the government of a U.S. ally. One former intelligence official told a reporter for the *Los Angeles Times* that the CIA kept a list of its top twenty targets. "There have been times where they've struggled a little bit coming up with names to fill that list."[18]

In an almost comic series of events a week later, an American RQ-170 surveillance drone came down, because of unknown causes, in eastern Iran near the city of Kashmar and was put on display. The Iranians boasted that they had brought the UAV to earth by one of their cyberwar units—thus trumping U.S. pride in one of its technological specialties. The Pentagon responded that it had been shot down, but the condition of the drone as shown on films indicated no visible damage from rocket fire. Indeed, it looked almost pristine and ready to go again when refueled. Just as in 1960 when the first U-2 story was put out that a "weather" plane had strayed over the Soviet Union by accident, the first official response had been that American forces in Afghanistan had lost control of a UAV, and what had turned up in Iran looked like it might be the one. That story, like the U-2 story, crashed within days. In the earlier instance, Soviet officials put the pilot, Francis Gary Powers, on display in an ill-fitting suit that made him look almost clownish. U-2 pilots were supposed to commit suicide in the event of imminent capture, but Powers opted to disobey and spend a few years in Russian prisons instead. Eisenhower then revealed that Powers was part of an ongoing series of secret U-2 missions he defended as necessary because Russia's "closed skies" prevented America from knowing about the Soviet missile program.

In the RQ-170 case, Pentagon officials quickly changed their story to turn an embarrassment into political advantage at a time when administration critics at home, and the conservative Israeli government, led by Benjamin Netanyahu, were clamoring for real action to stop Iran from getting a nuclear weapon. Iran responded by lodging a formal complaint with the UN Security Council over violations of its airspace. But there was no question of an Obama apology in this instance. At a news conference with President Nouri al-Maliki of Iraq, he gave this response to a question: "We've asked for [the drone] back. We'll see how the Iranians respond." An Iranian general retorted, "No nation welcomes other countries' spy drones in its territory, and no one sends back the spying equipment and its information back to the country of origin."[19]

Tehran then announced that it had decoded the information the RQ-170 had obtained on its flight, bringing an outburst from former vice president Dick Cheney that once the aircraft went down, the president should have responded with an air strike to destroy it before the Iranians could have learned anything more, in the same way SEAL Team Six had destroyed a damaged helicopter during the Osama bin Laden raid. "You can do that from the air . . . and in effect, make it impossible for them to benefit from having captured that drone." But instead, Cheney said, Obama "asked nicely for them to return it, and they aren't going to." An Iranian toy company said it planned to send a toy version to President Obama via the Swiss embassy, to fulfill the U.S. wish to have the drone returned.[20]

The comic aspects of the RQ-170 affair soon vanished. Officials acknowledged the dead seriousness of American determination to stay on top of the Iranian nuclear program, the overriding issue in Iranian-American relations since the 2002 "axis of evil" speech George W. Bush delivered to Congress during the run-up to Gulf War II. And in recent months the pressure to do more than employ sanctions against Iran had grown steadily, with more talk about all options on the table and lines that the Iranians must not cross. In March 2009, at the outset of his administration, Obama had attempted to engage the Iranian leadership.

> The United States wants the Islamic Republic of Iran to take its rightful place in the community of nations. You have that right, but it comes with real responsibilities. And that place cannot be reached through terror or arms, but rather through peaceful actions that demonstrate the true greatness of the Iranian people and civilization. . . . We have serious differences that have grown over time. My administration is now committed to diplomacy that addresses the full range of issues before us, and to pursuing constructive ties among the United States, Iran and the international community. This process will not be advanced by threats. We seek, instead, engagement that is honest and grounded in mutual respect.

Obama referred to the "Islamic Republic of Iran" in an effort to brush away his predecessor's refusal to use that term—a supposed irritant in relations. But Secretary of State Hillary Clinton threatened crippling sanctions against Iran if talks failed and it did not end its nuclear program. "We are also laying the groundwork for the kind of very tough . . . crippling sanctions that might be necessary in the event that our offers are either rejected or the process is inconclusive or unsuccessful," Clinton told the House Foreign Affairs Committee.[21]

At various times during the first year of the Obama presidency, the president and secretary of state would refer to steps that might be taken should the Iranians refuse to talk about its nuclear enrichment program. There were new reports also that Iran was close to being able to produce a bomb warhead for its missiles. But American policy makers still believed that there would be ample time to take whatever action was needed. Secretary Clinton commented at one point that it would not make Iran any safer to possess nuclear arms, because the United States would extend a "defense umbrella" over friendly Middle Eastern states in addition to Israel, and increase weapons sales to those countries. Defense Secretary Panetta also spoke about a "wide range of military options" to be used if necessary to prevent Iran from developing nuclear weapons. These included increased arms sales to Iran's potential "rivals" (a very interesting formulation) as well as bellicose statements by U.S. officials. And there was a hint about "other covert efforts targeting Iran's nuclear program."[22] This referred to the use of cyberweaponry—a practice begun during the Bush administration—to target Iranian computers at the Natanz nuclear plant. When computer experts picked up that attack, which they labeled the Stuxnet worm, after it escaped from Iranian computers and sped around the world, the president asked, "Should we shut this thing down?" The answer he got from CIA director Panetta was no, it was still causing havoc with Iran's program, and so Obama authorized the continuation of the cyberattacks.[23]

The president was "acutely aware that with every attack [using cyberweapons] he was pushing the United States into new territory, much as his predecessors had with the first use of atomic weapons in the 1940s, of intercontinental missiles in the 1950s and of drones in the past decade." Moreover, Obama was also acutely aware that any American acknowledgment that it was using cyberweapons, no matter how well justified that use was, "could enable other countries, terrorists or hackers to justify their own attacks."[24]

The comparison with "first use of atomic weapons" is particularly revealing, as well as sobering, because the initiation of atomic warfare was at the heart of Cold War fears that justified so many CIA activities. When the stakes were a nuclear holocaust, there was no question of not accepting the lesser evil of destabilizing a regime or removing a leader. In the current situation, the president told aides that if the cyberattacks failed and Iran developed a nuclear weapon, "there would be no time for sanctions and diplomacy with Iran to work. Israel could carry out a conventional attack, prompting a conflict that could spread throughout the region."[25]

American "control" of the Iranian situation—and its entire Middle Eastern policy—depended upon preempting an Israeli attack, then enlarging the area of secrecy. *New York Times* columnist Roger Cohen agreed that was the case but noted that it made him decidedly uneasy. Referring to a series of actions that began with the killing of an American citizen, Anwar al-Awlaki, Cohen said, "President Obama has gone undercover." The president had remained silent about "a big explosion at a military base near Tehran" that killed a central figure in Iran's nuclear program, nuclear scientists who had perished in the streets of the capital, and the Stuxnet computer worm. One day, Cohen worried, there might be payback. "There has seldom been so big a change in approach to U.S. strategic policy with so little explanation. . . . So why do I approve of all this? Because the alternative—the immense cost in blood and treasure and reputation of the Bush administration's war on terror—was so appalling. In just the same way, the results of a conventional bombing war against Iran would be appalling, whether undertaken by Israel, the United States or a combination of the two."[26]

Cohen's assumption that the wars in Iraq and Afghanistan were the only alternatives to the silence was a measure of how far the country had traveled toward accepting the "lethal presidency" in less than four years. Cohen believed that the president did owe the nation "a speech that sets out why America will not embark again on this kind of inconclusive war [Iraq and Afghanistan] and has instead adopted a new doctrine that has replaced fighting terror with killing terrorists." He could also use that speech, Cohen ended, to explain why Guantánamo was still open.

Offshore Balancing

Peter Beinart, a thoughtful observer, put a name to Obama's pivot toward drones: "offshore balancing." Obama had come into office determined to eschew Bush unilateralism and to reinvigorate diplomacy. The drone policy made sense when one realized that the Obama administration had largely given up on trying to remake Pakistan and Afghanistan.[27]

"Instead of directly occupying Islamic lands," Beinart wrote, "we're trying to secure our interests from the sea, the air, and by equipping our allies." It was also a policy for dealing with American interests in East Asia. "The strategy has deep roots in America, a nation rich in technology and naval power but highly sensitive to casualties." Even in World War II, Franklin Roosevelt had hoped "to limit America's participation in the European theater to air and naval support while the Russians and Brits fought Germany on land." In this reading, Harry Truman's Korean War (which led to Vietnam) and George W. Bush's wars were the exception. Obama's policy resembled Nixon's "Vietnamization." Some might call it a bit amoral, as it involved shirking the missionary call to remake societies and spread democracy, "but it offers a way for the U.S. to maintain influence at reduced cost, which is likely to be the central foreign policy challenge of the next few years."[28]

In the future wars might resemble old-fashioned military campaigns at least in one respect, because they would not be about changing hearts and minds but instead would involve a technologically driven "realist" appraisal of the outside world. As Admiral James "Sandy" Winnefeld told a Strategic Command Cyber Space Conference, "We are not likely to have as our next fight a counterinsurgency." While America had been teaching its troops Arabic and other regional languages to influence people at the village level, the world had changed, and competitors were coming up with new asymmetric advantages. "They've been studying us closely." There were no such things as borders anymore—at least so far as war was concerned. The border between public and private was fading, as countries were using individuals as "proxies."[29]

A perfect example of the kind of war Beinart and Winnefeld imagined was the administration's support for NATO forces as the struggle to depose Colonel Gaddafi, the longtime Libyan dictator, developed in the summer of 2011. Gaddafi's opponents were on the ropes and outside observers feared a mass slaughter at the hands of his hired army when the United Nations authorized NATO to undertake the provision of humanitarian aid and the establishment of no-fly zones to protect the population. At first Obama was reluctant to become involved, even though he was criticized by both Republicans and Democrats for a failure to do more to remove Gaddafi. He would not pursue a regime change policy, he said. But as the NATO mission moved swiftly in that direction, its forces received significant aid. The American military destroyed Gaddafi's air defense capabilities, then turned over day-to-day control to NATO, which would carry out further air strikes.

As the Libyan campaign extended from weeks to months, a somewhat surprising coalition in Congress of Republicans and anti-war Democrats challenged Obama on the grounds that he had violated the 1973 War Powers Resolution Congress had passed to keep Richard Nixon—and future presidents—from waging war without legislative sanctions. House Speaker John A. Boehner wrote the president that a divisive debate had originated in Obama's "lack of genuine consultation . . . and by the lack of visibility and leadership from you and your administration." White House press secretary Jay Carney noted how Boehner and some of his colleagues were expressing views "inconsistent" with past comments "about the constitutionality of the War Powers Resolution."[30]

Tweaking the Republicans did not answer the direct question about whether the administration was in violation of the War Powers Resolution. For that, White House lawyers drafted a thirty-two-page response that centered on the point that there were no

American soldiers fighting in Libya, so the resolution did not apply. It was hard not to feel that something more was at stake here than simply an argument about the kind of intervention Libya represented, something that Boehner alluded to with his comment about "the lack of visibility." During the summer of 2011, while the argument about aiding NATO forces engaged in Libya continued in Congress, there were seemingly conflicting desires expressed for the United States to become more engaged in Syria by helping the rebel cause as it attempted to overthrow another longtime dictator, Bashar al-Assad. There were complaints that the president had let the UN dictate policy and that it was America's duty to intervene by supplying arms, at the very least. In August Obama declared that Assad must resign in favor of a democratic transition, but he shied away from any hint that the United States would put boots on the ground in the country. "The Syrian people have had forty years of induced political coma," said an anonymous official. "People are getting confident, they're engaged politically and they're not afraid anymore. The United States will support their movement but will respect their desire to chart a new course for themselves but without international interference."[31]

The principal reason for not extending military aid to the rebels over the next eighteen months was the fear that al Qaeda had penetrated their ranks and, if they did triumph, it would open up yet another front in the war on terror—one where it would not be easy to eliminate the leaders using drones. But there was absolutely no inclination to try applying counterinsurgency lessons there over the course of many years, either. John Nagl, author of *Learning to Eat Soup with a Knife* (2005) and one of the godfathers of Field Manual 3-24 from his Fort Leavenworth days with David Petraeus, had left the army to become president of the Center for a New American Security, a rendezvous spot for counterinsurgency-oriented researchers and advocates. In a National Public Radio interview at the end of 2011, he was asked what changes he had seen in the decade since 9/11.

Trying to blend the old with the new, Nagl said, the nation now had a military that could confront "non-state actors, terrorists and insurgents, on the ground in Iraq and Afghanistan, and inside a half a dozen or a dozen other countries around the globe, where terrorists are plotting, continuing to work their nefarious deeds." Nagl was close to going off message here, because the official narrative fashioned by John Brennan in his September 2011 speech was that drones were the proper weapons *only* to take out terrorists whose activities posed an imminent threat to American lives or interests. The debate was over how one defined *imminent.* Fighting insurgencies was supposedly a different matter altogether, and there was the rub. But Nagl continued with his discussion of how the military special ops forces had come together with the CIA, and how the goal of the air force in using drones was to establish absolute superiority around the globe. "So that we're seeing big, big changes, I think, in how we think about war, the advance of robots, not just in the air but on the sea, under the sea and on the ground, is going to be, I think, one of the big stories of the next decade."[32]

Already at the time of the interview more than half of those polled thought the United States should not be at war in Afghanistan; less than four months later, that number had grown to nearly 70 percent of respondents. Perhaps more tellingly, almost the same percentage believed the fighting was going "somewhat" or "very" badly.[33] As these facts were soaking into the political landscape surrounding the election year playing fields, however, much worse was to come.

A previously unheralded lieutenant colonel named Daniel L. Davis had been sent to Afghanistan to patrol with American troops, covering nine thousand miles in all. Davis wrote a report for his superiors in the Pentagon on the "true" situation he found there, a report that disputed nearly every detail of the upbeat handouts that had been stuffed into media outlets since the march on Marja. After talking with his minister at the McLean Bible Church, Colonel Davis caused a stir by going public with his views in an article in the *Armed Forces Journal* titled "Truth, Lies and Afghanistan: How Military Leaders Have Let Us Down." His experience, he told reporters, had caused him to doubt reports of progress from everyone, including the new head of the CIA, David H. Petraeus.[34]

The eighty-four-page report he gave to his superiors began, "Senior ranking US military leaders have so distorted the truth when communicating with the US Congress and American people in regards to conditions on the ground in Afghanistan that the truth has become unrecognizable." Within a week *Rolling Stone* had obtained a copy of the unclassified version, and the article Davis wrote for the *Armed Forces Journal* was viewed more than 800,000 times, making it one of the periodical's most widely read articles in a decade. Davis won the Ridenhour Prize for Truth-Telling, awarded by the progressive Nation Institute and the Fertel Foundation. It also made him a pariah in the Pentagon; he told an interviewer he did not know if he could hold on for the two more years needed to qualify for a military pension.[35]

Newsweek's veteran correspondent Leslie Gelb asked Vice President Biden straight out: "What are our vital interests in continuing to fight a major war in Afghanistan?" Al Qaeda had been decimated, Biden began, and was not likely to stage a comeback. So, interrupted Gelb, the United States no longer needed to fight there? Wrong, replied Biden; Americans still had to fight to make sure Pakistan, a country that was home to tens of millions of people and was the possessor of nuclear weapons, did not somehow begin to disintegrate or fall apart. Making Kabul strong enough to negotiate reconciliation would allow the emergence of a government that could resist an al Qaeda resurgence and that would not harbor "any other organization" intending "to do damage to us and our allies."[36]

Getting a firm grasp on such circular arguments was difficult. At the center of the American problem was, as former policy makers saw it, "war fatigue." "Yes," said former defense secretary William Cohen, "the American people are suffering from a tremendous recession in this country, a jobless recovery—if there is such a thing as a recovery taking place—and knowing that we have invested over a trillion and a half dollars in Iraq and Afghanistan, they see no end in sight." Former national security adviser Brent Scowcroft concurred: the Afghan War was "so long, it's so expensive in terms of fatalities and dollars. Yes—we're exhausted."[37]

Real offshore balancing could not come soon enough. The former policy makers agreed that somehow the administration would have to make a better case for sticking it out—whatever the strategy. "The U.S.," said Cohen, "is not going to do it on a scale that we have done in the past."

Exiting the Labyrinth

The early months of 2012 brought a series of events that only increased the demands for lifting the boots out of Afghanistan. On January 30 in an "online town hall" sponsored by Google, Obama took a question from Evan in Brooklyn, who said that the president had "ordered more drone attacks in your first year than your predecessor did in his entire term." Given the persistent reports of civilian casualties, Evan was "curious to know how you feel they help the nation and whether you think they are worth it."

"I want to make sure that people understand that drones have not caused a huge number of civilian casualties," Obama replied. "For the most part, they have been very precise, precision strikes against al-Qaeda and their affiliates." The United States was not just sending in a "whole bunch of strikes willy-nilly." The drone strikes were a "focused effort at people who are on a list of active terrorists, who are trying to go in and harm Americans, hit American facilities, American bases and so on. . . . I think we have to be judicious in how we use drones," he added.[38]

The next day White House press secretary Jay Carney was asked if the president really meant to break the doctrine of silence about drone warfare. Were his statements to Evan purposeful or something of a slip? The dialogue with reporters went this way:

Q: Jay, in the President's Google+ video chat he acknowledged for the first time the classified drone program. Why did he do that?
CARNEY: I'm sorry, can you be more specific?
Q: He acknowledged the drone program for the first time.
CARNEY: Well, I'll tell you, since his first day in office, President Obama has directed that we use all tools of national power in

an aggressive campaign to thwart the terrorist threat posed by al Qaeda and to degrade and ultimately destroy that organization. While al Qaeda has been significantly degraded as a result of our counterterrorism operations, the group continues to pose a serious threat to U.S. interests, including to the homeland. That is why we remain relentless in taking the fight to al Qaeda wherever they seek safe haven and support. And I will also note that a hallmark of our counterterrorism efforts has been our ability to be exceptionally precise, exceptionally surgical and exceptionally targeted in the implementation of our counterterrorism operations. That was the point the President was making. This is something that President Obama has demanded. And all of our efforts, counterterrorism efforts, are designed with precision as an essential component.

Q: Was it purposeful, what he said?

CARNEY: Look, I would just refer you to what the President said and to note that the point he was making is that our counterterrorism efforts, by his order, include very concerted efforts to be targeted and surgical.

Q: He doesn't address whether it was purposeful or not. I mean, that's what I'm asking, if he made a mistake.

CARNEY: He's the Commander-in-Chief of the armed forces of the United States. He's the President of the United States. I would point you to his comments. I'm not going to discuss broadly or specifically supposed covert programs. I would just point you to what he said.[39]

In the weeks after Obama's "revelation," there was a cascade of news about the American ground role in Afghanistan. First Panetta, now secretary of defense, announced that NATO hoped to end its combat mission by the middle of 2013. Then he amended that to say that there might be some troops in active combat roles later. "It's still a pretty robust role that we'll be engaged in," he went on; it wouldn't be a formal combat role, but the troops there would always be combat ready. "We will be because we always have to be in order to defend ourselves." Did this mean that it had been decided to stop seeking out Taliban strongholds inside Afghanistan after mid- to late 2013? No, that was apparently not what he meant. Panetta clarified, "We're committed to an enduring presence there."[40] Yet the "commitment" was as lacking in specifics as the administration's revelations about drone lists and justifications had been.

The news from Afghanistan, on the other hand, was both specific and unwelcome. First there was the accidental burning of Korans by American troops at Bagram Air Base that set off protests and riots. Members of the Afghan parliament called on their countrymen to take up arms and fight. "Americans are invaders, and jihad against Americans is an obligation," said one member of the parliament who represented the district where four demonstrators were killed. President Karzai used the situation to demand that the prison at Bagram, which housed three thousand suspected insurgents, be turned over to his government. Protesters filled the streets around parliament. One man who joined the crowds said the protests were not just about burning Korans but also were about an episode in Helmand where American Marines urinated on dead bodies of insurgents, and a recent air strike in another province that killed eight young Afghans. "They always admit their mistakes," he said. "They burn our Koran and then they apologize. You can't just disrespect our holy book and kill our innocent children and make a small apology."[41]

A few days later a spate of "green on blue" attacks—attacks by Afghan soldiers on American soldiers—apparently provided a warning signal that the Taliban had infiltrated the new defense force the United States was building to take over the combat role in less than two years. At first Secretary Panetta insisted that the "brutal attacks . . . will not alter our commitment to get this job done." The strategy of working closely with Afghan forces would not change, he asserted. Later in the year, as the attacks continued, Panetta claimed they were signs of Taliban desperation. "The reality is, the Taliban has not been able to regain any territory lost. So they're resorting to these kinds of attacks to create havoc." Havoc was a real threat to the American mission, but by the Pentagon's own estimate, only about 10 percent of green-on-blue attacks in-volve Taliban infiltration.[42]

The green-on-blue threat continued, but it was in fact greater than the danger of Taliban infiltration. It was really the same as what the French had feared when they hesitated to build up a Viet-namese army: that at some stage the weapons the Western power supplied would be turned against them, or used in a postoccupation civil war by "unfriendlies." In the midst of the green-on-blue crisis came an incident that may well be remembered as Afghanistan's My Lai. An American soldier left his base in southern Afghanistan in the middle of the night and walked to a nearby village, where he shot and killed sixteen civilians. Everything was working against the idea of continuing a land war (or occupation) in Afghanistan—and pushing American policy makers not only toward a speedier withdrawal but also toward more drone flights and attacks.

It was becoming clear, however, that the president's off-the-cuff comments to an online town hall questioner had left him in an untenable position. Even while 77 percent of Democrats supported the drone policy in polls—without really knowing what it entailed—Obama found himself in danger of losing control of the momentum of drone warfare.

The Loyal Opposition

A few conservatives who had opposed George W. Bush's methods of rationalizing dubious acts as powers accruing to the "unitary presidency"—a theory that claimed the Constitution's authors meant the opposite of what they said—had begun to speak out. First there was Jack Goldsmith, who left the OLC in 2004 after protesting the torture memos and turned to the public arena to voice his con-cerns. He published a memoir, *The Terror President* (2007), and said of the new use being made of the Office of Legal Counsel that its "power to interpret the law is the power to bestow on government officials what is effectively an advance pardon for actions taken at the edges of vague criminal statutes."

Even before Obama's imperfect acknowledgment of drone warfare, Goldsmith had written that "technical covertness" was wrong.

> It is wrong . . . for the government to maintain technical covertness but then engage in continuous leaks, attributed to government officials, of many (self-serving) details about the covert operations and their legal justifications. It is wrong because it is illegal. It is wrong because it damages (though perhaps not destroys) the diplomatic and related goals of covertness. And it is wrong because the Executive branch seems to be trying to have its cake (not talking about the program openly in order to serve diplomatic interests and perhaps deflect scrutiny) and eat it too (leaking promiscuously to get credit for the operation and to portray as lawful).[43]

Goldsmith was far from an absolutist about whether or not international law supported drone strikes in general, saying that John Brennan and Harold Koh had elaborated on those questions and that there was not much more that could be said "to change the mind of critics who believe the strikes violate international law." But there had been practically nothing said officially about whether the executive branch possesses the power to kill an American citizen. The president had had widespread support on the Awlaki strike but wanted to be assured that the action was done legally "and with care." "The government could easily reveal this more detailed legal basis for a strike on as U.S. citizen," Goldsmith argued, "without reference to particular operations, or targets, or means of fire, or countries."

Former CIA director Michael Hayden from the Bush years put a sharper edge on Goldsmith's main point: "This program rests on the personal legitimacy of the president, and that's not sustainable. I have lived the life of someone taking action on the basis of secret O.L.C. memos, and it ain't a good life. Democracies do not make war on the basis of legal memos locked in a D.O.J. safe."[44]

The president's statements in the online town hall on January 30 and Jay Carney's follow-up the next day did not meet Goldsmith's various criteria and did not come close to answering Hayden's charge, as Amy Davidson, a senior editor at the *New Yorker,* later wrote in her blog.

> Brennan and other officials interviewed by the *Times* and *Newsweek* said that Obama had enormous faith in himself. It would be more responsible, though, if he had less—if he thought that he was no better than any other President we've had or ever will. The point isn't just the task, or burden, he takes on, but the machine he has built for his successors to use. . . . In the end we are not really being asked to trust Obama, or his niceness, but the office of the Presidency. Do we?[45]

Attorney general Eric Holder went to Northwestern University in early March 2012 to address the question of whether it was legal under U.S. laws to kill citizens without giving them full Fifth Amendment rights to a court trial. He began by invoking John F. Kennedy's assertion that only a few generations were asked to defend "freedom in its hour of maximum danger." Against that background, Holder claimed that in 2012 "it is clear that, once again, we have reached an 'hour of danger.'" Each day, he said, he received a briefing on the "most urgent threats" of the past twenty-four hours. "I go to sleep each night thinking of how best to keep our people safe." Despite recent national security successes, always topped by the killing of Osama bin Laden, "there are people plotting to murder Americans, who reside in distant countries as well as within our own borders."[46]

In other words, Americans lived under a permanent cloud of imminence. But just as surely as the nation was at war, we were also a nation of laws and values. This was not just his view. "My judgment is shared by senior national security officials across the government," Holder said, then went into a long discussion of how the courts had successfully tried terrorists and given them long sentences. In addition, military commissions had been "reformed" in order to encourage countries that had refused to cooperate on certain antiterrorist efforts "in providing evidence or extraditing suspects" to change their minds.

Then he reached the heart of the matter, as he saw it. "It is preferable to capture suspected terrorists where feasible—among other reasons, so that we can gather valuable intelligence from them—but we must also recognize that there are instances where our government has the clear authority—and, I would argue, the responsibility—to defend the United States through the appropriate and lawful use of lethal force." After that came the layers of reasoning behind his assertion. First, Congress had authorized the president to use all necessary and appropriate force against al Qaeda, the Taliban, and associated forces. Second, because we were in an armed conflict, the United States was authorized under international law to use lethal force against "enemy belligerents." And third, the Constitution empowered the president to protect the nation "from any imminent threat of violent attack." Each of these justifications had been challenged, of course, beginning with the interpretation Holder offered of the Authorization to Use Military Force (AUMF) that Congress passed on September 17, 2011, the vague definition of "enemy belligerents," and, as Brennan himself had said the previous September, how one defined the meaning of *imminent*.

George W. Bush, of course, expanded the 2001 AUMF (for Afghanistan) and the 2002 AUMF (regarding) Iraq to make himself commander in chief of a global war on terrorism. The Pentagon's chief counsel, Jeh Johnson—a former student of Harold Koh, he was proud to say—had recently performed something of a sleight of hand about this transformation.

The AUMF, the statutory authorization from 2001, is not open-ended. It does not authorize military force against anyone the Executive labels a "terrorist." Rather, it encompasses only those groups or people with a link to the terrorist attacks on 9/11, or associated forces.

On the other hand, he told students at Yale University's law school:

There is nothing in the wording of the 2001 AUMF or its legislative history that restricts this statutory authority to the "hot" battlefields of Afghanistan. Afghanistan was plainly the focus when the authorization was enacted in September 2001, but the AUMF authorized the use of necessary and appropriate force against the organizations and persons connected to the September 11 attacks—al Qaeda and the Taliban—without a geographic limitation.[47]

Holder repeated Johnson's assertion: "Our legal authority is not limited to the battlefields in Afghanistan." Furthermore, it was legal to attack senior members of the al Qaeda leadership "and associated forces." This was not a novel concept, he said. It went back to World War II, the most frequently cited antecedent being the tracking and destruction of the plane carrying Admiral Isoroku Yamamoto, the commander of the forces that attacked Pearl Harbor. Now the issue seemed to be "assassination" versus "lawful targeting." As we have seen, presidential executive orders from the time of Gerald Ford and Ronald Reagan had outlawed assassination. Yamamoto was certainly an "enemy belligerent," and targeting him was no different, really, from shooting the commander of a machine-gun nest as he was on his way to the mess hall. Yet in the Yamamoto case there had been a formal declaration of war against Japan. Since 9/11 any distinctions between "assassination" and "lawful targeting" had all but vanished, with congressional and judicial acquiescence, and the cited authorization for lethal action had been extended, as Jeh Johnson said it should not be, "against anyone the Executive labels a 'terrorist.'"

Holder objected to the use of the loaded term *assassination* and insisted that it was misplaced. These were not unlawful killings, but the legitimate use of force against an imminent threat of violence. It was true that the Fifth Amendment came into play when the target was a U.S. citizen. But the courts had recognized that due process under that amendment had to take into account "national security operations" and the "realities of combat." "The evaluation of whether an individual presents an 'imminent threat' incorporates consideration of the relevant window of opportunity to act, the possible harm that missing the window would cause to civilians, and the likelihood of heading off future disastrous attacks against the United States."

All these considerations—and there were many more listed in the speech Holder gave—left the president free to act: "Some have argued that the President is required to get permission from a federal court before taking action against a United States citizen who is a senior operational leader of al Qaeda or associated forces. This is simply not accurate. 'Due process' and 'judicial process' are not one and the same, particularly when it comes to national security. The Constitution guarantees due process, not judicial process."

So now "due process" and "judicial process" were joined to "imminent" and "associated forces" in the lexicon one had to know in order to understand drone warfare. Holder had precise definitions for them all. In reporting on the speech, Charlie Savage in the *New York Times* said it was "notable" for its assertion that it was legal to kill a U.S. citizen without a judicial review under certain circumstances. It was also notable for the absence of specific legal citations, added Savage, and fell far short of the detail contained in the OLC memo that was the basis for the attack on Awlaki, the one the *Times* had filed a lawsuit to obtain under the Freedom of Information Act.[48]

Next up to the podium was John Brennan for his second round, the cleanup batter on the Obama team. Some months later Obama's chief counterterrorism adviser would tell a congressional committee considering his nomination to head the CIA that Holder might be wrong, and that the idea of a court to determine when it was right to kill a U.S. citizen had actually been under consideration during the administration's deliberations. Again the reporter was sharp-eyed Charlie Savage: "Mr. Brennan was noncommittal, noting that lethal operations are generally the sole responsibility of the executive branch. But he said the administration had 'wrestled with' the concept of such a court and called the idea 'certainly worthy of discussion.'"[49]

But back in April, Brennan had gone to the Woodrow Wilson International Center for Scholars, where, as he emphasized, Barack Obama had delivered his first big speech on foreign policy as he began his race for the White House five years earlier. For the most part Brennan's speech, which he billed as a direct response to the call for more transparency, simply rehearsed arguments Holder had made. He announced that al Qaeda was but a shadow of itself, but that shadow now fell across a wider area than ever, extending well into Africa as far as Nigeria. There had been few "unilateral captures" outside of Afghanistan since 9/11 because, first, our "partners have been able to kill or capture dangerous individuals themselves," and second, these terrorists were "skilled at seeking remote, inhospitable terrain—places where the United States and our partners simply do not have the ability to arrest or capture them." He asserted that the United States respected state sovereignty and international law.

What was also new was his introduction of the notion of "significant threat" as a qualification for the "kill list."

> We do not engage in lethal action in order to eliminate every single member of al-Qa'ida in the world. Most times, and as we have done for more than a decade, we rely on cooperation with the other countries that are also interested in removing these terrorists with their own capabilities and within their own laws. Nor is lethal action about punishing terrorists for past crimes; we are not seeking vengeance.

By "significant threat," he said, he meant not the mere possibility that an individual might attack us at some point in the future; rather, the individual would have to be actively engaged as an operational leader of al Qaeda or one of its "associated forces," adding, "Or perhaps the individual possesses unique operational skills that are being leveraged in a planned attack."[50]

Thus Brennan left open several side avenues leading out from the main line of his thinking. Vengeance was not a motive, but previous acts counted when considering the imminence question. And imminence could increase if the individual was deemed to possess "unique operational skills" or presumed political leadership qualities. In effect, drone war death warrants were like "John Doe" warrants police used in chasing down suspects. Perhaps without quite meaning to do so, Brennan actually confirmed what many thought about drone warfare: that the United States could well be fighting in other countries' civil wars and that the term "unique operational skills" covered myriad attributes, but in the signature case of Awlaki it meant being inspirational. During the speech a woman rose "to speak out on behalf of innocent victims" killed by drone strikes in Pakistan, Yemen, and Somalia. A burly guard lifted her and carried her out as she shouted out the names of alleged drone victims and declared she was speaking out "on behalf of the Constitution—on behalf of the rule of law."

With Brennan's speech the administration rested its case. Then on Sunday, May 29, 2012, the *New York Times* pulled aside the curtain that had hung over White House deliberations and decisions. Jo Becker and Scott Shane titled the long article—really a mini-history of the administration's reimagining of the war on terror— "Secret 'Kill List' Proves a Test of Obama's Principles and Will." Two statements framed the article: first, Obama was "a realist who, unlike some of his fervent supporters, was never carried away by his own rhetoric"; second, his national security team had advised him in 2008 that the bywords of his campaign and presidency should be "Pragmatism over ideology."

In a sense, the authors were telling the American public that Barack Obama had never been what they thought he was: "A few sharp-eyed observers inside and outside the government understood what the public did not. Without showing his hand, Mr. Obama had preserved three major policies—rendition, military commissions and indefinite detention—that have been targets of human rights groups since the 2001 terrorist attacks."

That was pretty plain. But the article was even more specific about "Terror Tuesdays," the weekly White House meetings at which, at his insistence, Barack Obama presided and was presented with "what one official calls the macabre 'baseball cards' of an un-conventional war." His aides told the reporters that he had several reasons for being so personally involved in the fateful decisions. He was a student of writings on war by Augustine and Thomas Aquinas

and believed he should "take moral responsibility for such actions."
The control he exercised "also appears to reflect Mr. Obama's striking self-confidence: he believes, according to several people who
have worked closely with him, that his own judgment should be
brought to bear on strikes."

The article described how shocked the president had been at
some of the errors in the drone strikes that caused civilian deaths,
and how he and his drone adviser John Brennan worked hard to
bring better discipline. Protection of innocent life, said Michael
Hayden, a former CIA director, "was always a critical consideration."
But then pragmatism took over again and Obama "embraced" signature strikes as an accepted method for getting at terrorist planning
meetings. "It in effect counts all military-age males in a strike zone
as combatants . . . unless there is explicit intelligence posthumously
proving them innocent."

It is at this point that we begin to understand why the administration had refused to release the memo from the OLC that justified
the killing of Anwar al-Awlaki. Any attempt to cover all the policies "embraced" by President Obama in one memo or a series of
memos would cause the whole rationale to collapse in a heap of
legal jargon that would convince no one. It was much better to talk
about precision and lives saved as opposed to airplane bombings
and ending the war in Afghanistan sooner than the Pentagon
wanted. Only "crazy leftists," as one Obama spokesperson put it,
would continue to complain that the president was not perfect.

But within days—hours, even—the *Times* article was reverberat-
ing across the Web and then solidifying into hard copy in magazines
and newspapers. For some it came as an unpleasant surprise that
there actually had been debates inside the administration about
how far down the "Qaeda totem pole" one could go—"how much
killing will be enough." Others commented on statements about
the president's chief political adviser, David Axelrod, sitting in on
the "Terror Tuesday" meetings, "his unspeaking presence a visible
reminder of what everyone understood: a successful attack [in the
United States by al Qaeda] would overwhelm the president's other
aspirations and achievements." Still others would concentrate on

the blowback of drone attacks on foreign policy efforts, as illustrated in this quote: "His focus on strikes has made it impossible to forge, for now, the new relationship with the Muslim world that he had envisioned. Both Pakistan and Yemen are arguably less stable and more hostile to the United States than when Mr. Obama became president."

Soon after the article was published, said one of its authors, Scott Shane, the administration began to write a rule book for targeted killings. Revelations about the president's central role "in the shifting procedures for compiling 'kill lists'" provided the impetus. The president was afraid to leave an "amorphous" program to his successor: "There was concern that the levers might no longer be in our hands."[51]

Once Obama defeated Mitt Romney, the urgency seemed not so great—the administration could relax a bit and make sure such a rule book did not hamper important targeting goals for places where signature strikes had been used most often, Pakistan. The assertion that this new form of a "better war" could not be entrusted to a future president without safeguards in place revived the "trust us" standard and placed it higher than ever. But more than that, it skipped right past the question of whether the Oval Office could act by itself in writing such a rule book, to say nothing of how easy such an action would make it for any future president to take out rules that proved difficult to manage or just plain irksome.

Obama's reelection set the stage for a fundamental debate on American military strategy when the president nominated John Brennan to head the Central Intelligence Agency.

8

AMERICAN HUBRIS

*Do the United States and its people really want to tell those of us who
live in the rest of the world that our lives are not of the same value as
yours? That President Obama can sign off on a decision to kill us with
less worry about judicial scrutiny than if the target is an American?
Would your Supreme Court really want to tell humankind that we,
like the slave Dred Scott in the 19th century, are not as human as you
are? I cannot believe it.*

—Bishop Desmond M. Tutu, letter to the *New York Times*,
February 11, 2013

A letter written by Bishop Desmond M. Tutu to the editors of the
New York Times in February 2013 referred to an article that had
appeared in that paper about an idea floating around the hearings
on John Brennan's nomination to head the Central Intelligence
Agency—the idea of a special court to vet the killing of American
citizens. Even the most ardent drone supporters had become ner-
vous about setting a precedent when it came to targeting citizens.
But Tutu's letter challenged *all* drone warfare. The Nobel Peace
Prize winner tied the deadly use of drones to the 1857 *Dred Scott*
decision in order to place claims of moral outrage at the top of the
agenda. He did not concern himself with arguments about the precision of drone attacks or that fewer people died as a result than
would have been the case in bombing raids. He argued instead that
drones were a weapon used exclusively for death-dealing strikes
within countries the West sometimes called "failed states," popu-
lated by non-Western peoples.

The failure to understand Tutu's point offers evidence of just how
far American policy makers have sealed themselves into their

Hazmat suits. But a few have not, such as Hank Crumpton, a former CIA Counterterrorist Center officer who told Mark Mazzetti there should be a huge debate about when and where we apply lethal force. In a place like Yemen or Somalia or Pakistan, he said, "it seems like just another part of war."

> But, he asked, what if a suspected terrorist is in a place like Paris, or Hamburg, or somewhere else drones can't fly, "and you use a CIA or [military] operative on the ground to shoot him in the back of the head?
>
> "Then," he said, "it's viewed as an assassination."[1]

From the opposite end of the spectrum came a warning that Tutu's argument could not be ignored, for it reflected a general shifting of the sands of ethical warfare away from the old just-war theories, like those advanced by Tutu's fellow Nobel Peace Prize laureate President Barack Obama. Western society, with its growing concerns about torture and the universal nature of human rights, had moved toward "an increasingly empathetic culture," wrote James Jay Carafano, a foreign and defense policy specialist with the *Heritage Foundation*. Carafano was hardly happy about the implication, as he saw it, that "feelings rather than reason" would come to rule international affairs. The just-war tradition that Obama had invoked from the time of his Nobel speech was falling before the onslaught of the "lawfarers," whose efforts to blur the line between law and political advocacy threatened to "undermine America's legitimate efforts to exercise its sovereignty and act in its own interests as it sees fit."

All the same, he conceded, President Obama's passion for drones had speeded up the undoing of just-war doctrine: "The president may have to ponder if he accelerated that change by pursuing a strategy fixated on playing global whack-a-mole with terrorist leaders. An overreliance on technological 'fixes,' after all, always strikes a nerve among people who prize the heart far beyond the head."[2]

Others might argue that technological fixes in warfare such as the atomic bomb had ruled both the head and the heart of many

Western policy makers, especially in confrontations with "backward" societies. From the beginning, the whole idea of the "American way" of war preferred using machines to avoid losing men. Metropolitan armies rode tanks, flew airplanes, and dropped bombs from the skies. But the point to consider here is that President Obama's second term opened with perhaps the most significant debate—or at least the potential for a debate—about the nation's direction in both foreign and domestic policy since the end of the Cold War. George H.W. Bush had pursued a "new world order" by driving Noriega out of Panama and chasing Saddam Hussein out of Kuwait. Clinton used airpower in Kosovo. After 9/11 George W. Bush focused on Iraq's imaginary weapons of mass destruction, and so could not find Osama bin Laden; President Obama had accomplished closure on that era by bringing its author to "justice."

But the Game of Drones continued, with the stakes getting ever higher, or lower, depending upon one's viewpoint. The idea of a special court—one that would meet in secret to oversee death sentences—was in the air at the time of the Senate hearings on Brennan's nomination. But also before the public eye was a sixteen-page Department of Justice white paper leaked to NBC News, a document that derived from still-secret memos from the Office of Legal Counsel used to justify the killing of Anwar al-Awlaki.

Various members of Congress had requested access to those memos on fourteen different occasions since February 2011, continuing right up to the Brennan hearings two years later—without success. During lawsuits to see the memos brought by the American Civil Liberties Union and the *New York Times*, government lawyers argued that the plaintiffs had not defined what was meant by calling for documents about a "targeted killing program," as if such a program did not exist. The Senate Judiciary Committee under Democratic control supported the administration's noncompliance in the requests. But Iowa Republican Charles Grassley complained that on January 20, 2009, the newly inaugurated President Barack Obama promised his would be the most transparent administration in U.S. history. "So we've got a license to kill Americans, and we don't know the legal basis for the license to kill Americans. And we

oughta know that. And we're not going to find out if we don't legis-
late it because our letters haven't been answered."[3]

Arizona Republican Jon Cornyn, a staunch conservative, added:

> We're not mere supplicants of the Executive Branch. We are a
> coequal branch of government with the Constitutional responsi-
> bility to conduct oversight. . . . So it is insufficient to say, "[P]retty
> please, Mr. President, pretty please, Mr. Attorney General, will
> you please tell us the legal authority by which you claim the au-
> thority to kill American citizens abroad?" It may be that I would
> agree with their legal argument, but I simply don't know what it
> is, and it hasn't been provided.[4]

The Department of Justice memorandum would be the closest
thing to an official response that Congress would get—and it shocked
readers out of their post–inaugural parade daydreaming about the
next four years.

Revelations

Although the administration was careful to say that nothing "classified" had been revealed in the memo NBC News obtained, the
language of the memo certainly suggested it was an amalgam of the
still secret justifications locked away in Attorney General Holder's
safe. By leaking the document and not calling it "classified," the
administration apparently hoped to satisfy demands for more information and clarification without breaking with its stolid insistence
that "national security" issues were at stake should the actual memos
be released.

If one was not disturbed reading the early sections of the white
paper, on page fourteen there was this sentence: "A lethal operation
against an enemy leader undertaken in national self-defense or during an armed conflict that is authorized by an informed, high-level
official and carried out in a manner that accords with applicable
law of war principles would fall within a well established variant of
the public authority justification and therefore would not be murder."

Who would qualify as an informed, high-level official? A new CIA director, John Brennan, who for four years had been known as the "czar of drones"? The chair of the Joint Chiefs of Staff? A drone pilot who spotted a target of opportunity from the kill list?

When the white paper appeared, the "informed" public had not yet absorbed all the revelations about presidentially decreed death sentences from six months earlier, or the follow-up story about the White House concern to write a rule book lest someone less trustworthy win a presidential election and gain entrance to the Oval Office. But John Bellinger, a legal adviser in the State Department during the Bush years (the post now held by drone defender Harold Koh), had already expressed concern about the legal risks of heavy reliance on drone warfare. He feared it could become Obama's "Guantánamo." The problem was that the legality of drone warfare (as it was practiced by the United States) had not been accepted by other nations, including America's allies, and human rights groups. For a time Bellinger had thought that there was only a 25 percent chance these criticisms would malign the administration, given the overwhelming support Obama had when he became president. "But over the last eighteen months," he wrote in January 2013, "I have seen a crescendo in international criticism, resulting in lawsuits in the U.S., Britain, and Pakistan, and a potential decrease in intelligence cooperation . . . I would not be surprised if, in the next year, war crimes charges are brought against senior Obama officials in a European country with a universal jurisdiction law. The Administration is increasingly on the back foot internationally in explaining and defending the legal aspects of the drone program. It needs to step up its efforts."[5]

The white paper's talk about an informed, high-level official's authority to act in place of the president—or even without his knowledge—raised a host of new questions not only about the memo's argumentation but also about the events surrounding its construction. The afternoon the first *Times* article appeared, May 29, Jake Tapper of ABC News questioned White House press secretary Jay Carney on the air, asking how the president squared the "guilty until proven innocent" standard used in "signature strikes" with his past language on human rights and avoiding civilian casualties. This administration had tools, Carney said, "that allow for the kind of precision that in the past was not available."

> TAPPER: It's fact that he has tools to avoid civilian casualties.
>
> CARNEY: Mmm, hmm.
>
> TAPPER: So you are disputing the *New York Times* story or the Dan Klaidman excerpt in the *Daily Beast* today that there have been civilian casualties?
>
> CARNEY: I'm not—I don't have the assessments of civilian casualties. I'm certainly not saying that we live in a world where the effort to fight against al-Qaida, against people who would, without compunction, murder tens of thousands if not millions of innocents—
>
> TAPPER: I'm not talking about them. I'm talking about the innocent people that the United States kills.
>
> CARNEY: No, no, no. No, but . . . we don't live in a world where it is possible to achieve, you know, no civilian casualties.[6]

In the days and weeks before and after the *Times* article, the United States carried out a series of drone strikes in Pakistan. The strikes had little—in fact, nothing—to do with saving Americans in the homeland, but reeked of retaliation for Pakistan's continued refusal to reopen supply lines into Afghanistan after the clash the previous winter that had left twenty-four Pakistani soldiers dead, and its sentencing of Dr. Shakeel Afridi to thirty-three years in prison for his aid to Americans in planning the attack at Abbottabad that killed Osama bin Laden. Bill Roggio, the editor of *Long War Journal*, reported that nearly twenty strikes had been carried out in recent months, including two in recent days: "No senior leaders from al Qaeda, the Taliban, or other allied terror groups have been reported killed in either strike. A US intelligence official involved in the drone program in the country told *The Long War Journal* that the strikes would continue now that Pakistan has refused to reopen NATO's supply lines for the International Security Assistance Force in Afghanistan."[7]

A week or so later, American officials claimed that they did hit an important target, senior al Qaeda leader Abu Yahya al-Libi. He was so important, it was said, that they would be hard pressed to find any one person to step into his shoes. Libi fit the Awlaki mold and was much better suited to leadership roles than Ayman al-Zawahiri, al Qaeda's current number one. He had "gravitas" as a long-standing leader in the movement, and "his religious credentials meant he had the authority to issue fatwas and provide guidance to the Pakistan-based operation." It was no longer required, evidently, to demonstrate imminence—membership in al Qaeda was enough. There were two strikes that day. The first killed Libi, and a second killed "12 more militants who had arrived at the scene." These follow-up strikes that killed people who came to the scene were an especially sore spot with the Pakistani government. Islamabad called anew for an end to the drone strikes, issuing a statement that they represented "a clear red line for Pakistan." "Many observers believe that the attacks have been a means of applying pressure on Islamabad," reported the BBC, "after a deal to reopen NATO supply routes fell through."[8]

More interesting than what many observers believed, however, was the BBC's comment that the United States did not normally talk about individual drone operations, but this one came after the *New York Times* revealed the president "personally approves or vetoes each drone strike." In other words, the official statements were a follow-up to Jay Carney's assertion that Americans had the tools to take out the really bad guys with precision. That did not answer the question, however, about signature strikes against anyone who shows up at the scene within a given period of time.

Strikes in the tribal areas continued at a high rate throughout the summer, each drawing a protest from Islamabad, until the question of national sovereignty seemed but a quaint reference to long-ago days. "A volley of C.I.A. drone strikes in Pakistan's tribal belt early Friday," reported the *New York Times*, "killed at least 18 people . . . capping a week of missile attacks that have renewed tensions between Pakistan and the United States, but may have killed a major militant leader." In Vietnam body counts, the magic kill ratio to defeat an insurgency was ten to one; do that and you win the war. Now it seemed that you could kill eighteen without losing one—but the war continued anyway.[9]

The article also noted that American officials were eager to confirm another big kill, Badruddin Haqqani, whose family's crime syndicate had long bedeviled U.S. efforts in Afghanistan through high-profile kidnappings, smuggling, and day-to-day militant operations. Furthermore, Pakistani officials, who had reopened the supply lines (maybe drone pressure worked), had proposed that they carry out future strikes using their fleet of American-built F-16s. "The Obama administration has rejected those demands, saying the covert campaign offers the most effective tool against militants in an area where the Pakistani state has largely lost control."[10] Covert, in this sense, meant secret from Islamabad, because of fears that the ISI and the Haqqanis sometimes worked together.

Thus the summer of 2012 saw a more audacious use of drones by the CIA—presumably working not under an expanded version of either of the Authorizations for Use of Military Force of 2001 and 2002 but Article II of the Constitution, which named the president commander in chief of the armed forces and pledged him to defend the Constitution. These legal niceties had everything to do with the question of whether such attacks could be called acts of war or acts of self-defense. Using the latter rationale, the CIA had truly become the president's private army with rules all its own outside any current international obligations under laws of warfare between sovereign states. The killings of Libi and Haqqani blurred the distinctions somewhat, as American officials wanted to claim the former death under Article II (a global terrorist eliminated) and the latter under the Authorization to Use Military Force (an enemy combatant killed in pursuit of the Afghan War). But the CIA had planned and executed the attacks in both instances. The solution would be to name the Haqqanis "a terrorist entity"—that would take care of it.

Also in the summer of 2012, the Obama administration reaffirmed commitments to the authoritarian regimes in Kazakhstan and Turkmenistan as rewards for their "assistance in Afghanistan and the fight against terrorism." Washington, wrote Walter Pincus, "seems to be seeking long-term footholds in these two countries, which are adjacent to Russia, China and Iran." There was much talk in the summer about a pivot to Asia as the Afghan War (or, at least, American participation in the Afghan War) dwindled. The sums of aid proposed were tiny compared with the cost of one or two drones, but it allowed the regimes to claim "to their people that they have the Obama administration's endorsement." Next up there might well be requests, under the rubric of fighting terrorism, for drone bases.[11]

The spread of new drone bases went on apace, some of them closely guarded secrets—for example, one in Saudi Arabia. It was constructed after two failed strikes in Yemen—the first aimed at Awlaki—killed dozens of civilians and a popular deputy governor, "inciting angry demonstrations and an attack that shut down a critical oil pipeline." The Obama administration had asked the *Times* and the *Washington Post* to keep the existence of the base secret, on the usual grounds of "national security." "The first time the C.I.A. used the Saudi base was to kill Mr. Awlaki in September 2011."[12]

One reason for the continued stonewalling about drone strikes that everyone knew were "made in the USA" was to conceal the existence of this Saudi base. After the Department of Justice white paper emerged, however, the two papers decided they had made a mistake in agreeing to keep silent. If there was to be a full debate, the public had a right to know everything it could about how the drone war was conducted. The Brennan nomination also prompted the break, out of concern that his leading role constituted a fair subject for discussion. The public editor of the *New York Times*, Margaret Sullivan, explained all of this in an editorial.

> I'll be writing more about this, including how The Times is trying in court to obtain an important, classified memo on the killing of an American, Anwar al-Awlaki, in a drone strike. His teenage son, also an American citizen, was also killed by a drone. The lack of due process and government accountability in those deaths are

worthy of the attention The Times is giving it—and more—in articles from Washington, in reporters on the ground in the region of the strikes, and in court.[13]

One would be hard pressed to find a similar challenge to officialdom when the government has declared that it is at "war" with an enemy force. During World War II posters in factories and military bases proclaimed, "Loose Lips Sink Ships." That was enough. Things had changed radically since then, beginning with revelations about the way the government had obtained the Tonkin Gulf Resolution in 1964, which enabled Lyndon Johnson to send half a million American troops to Southeast Asia under false pretenses, and George W. Bush's claims that Iraq had a panoply of weapons of mass destruction ready for use against the "free world."

The rationale for drone warfare, of course, was that normal conditions of warfare did not exist in this case—and likely ones in the future. Counterinsurgency theory had posited wars without front lines; now drone theory and practice simply assumed that national boundaries did not really mean sovereignty. If states were unable or unwilling to chase down "terrorists" in remote areas, the United States would do it, with or without permission. In some cases, for example Yemen, local rulers found that drones offered an advantage in fighting insurgents—who could always be labeled jihadist militants—and no more need be said. But if drone warfare ignored national boundaries, the blowback at home also meant that official statements no longer commanded automatic obedience whenever the magic words "national security" appeared in press briefings or Justice Department court filings.

The argument government officials made in requesting that the base be kept secret warned that publication could set off protests inside Saudi Arabia if it were revealed, potentially destabilizing America's staunch ally. "The Saudis might shut it down because the citizenry would be very upset," Times editors were told.[14]

Concern about the stability of America's chief Middle Eastern oil supplier was not something new. At the end of World War II when the United States sought its first air base in Saudi Arabia,

the negotiations were complicated by the Saudi royal family's fear
of stirring up the population against the idea of such an intrusion.
The main selling point Washington had was that such a base would
increase domestic communications—and control. Leaping forward
to the period before the Second Gulf War, Paul Wolfowitz, a key
planner in the Department of Defense, told an interviewer that removing Saddam Hussein from the scene would enable the United
States to get its ground forces out of Saudi Arabia.

> Their presence there over the last 12 years has been a source of
> enormous difficulty for a friendly government. It's been a huge
> recruiting device for al Qaeda. In fact if you look at bin Laden,
> one of his princip[al] grievances was the presence of so-called
> crusader forces on the holy land, Mecca and Medina. I think just
> lifting that burden from the Saudis is itself going to open the
> door to other positive things.[15]

There is a well-informed argument that the government itself
ceased pressure to keep its secret because it wanted John Brennan
to be seen in a good light in terms of his influence with Saudi Arabia in getting the base built. Brennan had been CIA station chief
in Riyadh in the 1990s, and his views of the jihadist threat in Yemen paralleled Saudi concerns. There may also have been a tripar-
tite understanding that matters were even more delicate in Yemen
owing to popular opposition to American drone strikes, let alone
the installation of a base. Yemeni president Ali Abdullah Saleh had
finally been forced into retirement, but the new president, Abdu
Rabu Mansour Hadi, had not been able to improve his standing at
home. Hadi's "fierce praise for the American drone-strike program,
which is unpopular here," wrote Robert Worth in the New York
Times, "has further eroded his small base of public support. He is
widely said to fear for his life and has appointed many family members and old allies to security positions."[16]
Despite what drones were doing to undermine the governments
in Islamabad and Sana, other states seemed comfortable with the
benefits that came with hosting American drone bases. In late Jan-

uary 2013 Niger joined five other African countries with drone bases on their territory, including Morocco, Senegal, Burkina Faso, Uganda, and Djibouti. "Many people in North Africa rate the risk from al-Qaeda higher," wrote the editor of a defense magazine, "than they did 12 months ago." Some trustworthy countries, such as the United Arab Emirates, were even allowed to buy Predator drones for their own use.[17]

The 2012 Defense Planning Guide promised that U.S. forces would "conduct a sustainable . . . presence abroad" that would include rotational deployments, along with bilateral and multilateral training exercises. "These activities reinforce deterrence, help to build the capacity and competence of U.S., allied, and partner forces for internal and external defense, strengthen alliance cohesion, and increase U.S. influence." But then this caveat appeared in italics: *"However, with reduced resources, thoughtful choices will need to be made regarding the location and frequency of these operations."*[18]

As recently as two years earlier, Defense Department planning guides had repeated the "oath" that the United States would be able to fight two major wars at the same time. Now the military only needed to be able to fight one war, but it would be responsible for "denying the objectives of—or imposing unacceptable costs on—an opportunistic aggressor in a second region."[19] Americans now lived in a world where there was no distinction between near and far, national borders existed only in atlases, and the difference between war and peace could not be defined.

Reactions and Justifications

"The Obama administration has a doctrine," worried veteran Middle East journalist Roger Cohen in the *Times*. "It's called the doctrine of silence." Cohen approved of the drone strategy because it caused less bloodletting than the wars in Iraq and Afghanistan, which also might end up costing at least $3.7 trillion. Yet he was uneasy with its "legally borderline, undercover operations . . . [that] invite repayment in kind, undermine the American commitment to the rule of law, and make allies uneasy." Obama owed the world a speech, said Cohen, about why he would not embark on another "inconclusive" war and had instead "adopted a new doctrine that has replaced fighting terror with killing terrorists."[20]

No speech was going to chase away the feeling that the time had come for a major reassessment of where the United States was heading—and the danger that the deadliest and most successful drone strikes would be on the constitutional foundations of American democracy. Former secretary of state Madeleine Albright took a question on a national television show about the appropriateness of drone warfare and skirted the constitutional issue completely. She called the debate over drones "most complicated and fascinating," because during her time in office and the Kosovo crisis, some in the Clinton administration had called bombing immoral, instead making the argument that "you should have boots on the ground." But she thought, "Why should we get more people killed, why do you have to have boots on the ground when you can take care of the terrible things that are happening from the air?"[21]

But, she admitted, while drone strikes have been very effective in "getting rid of people that are bound and determined to attack us . . . it has become a very complicated issue and I think there should be a public discussion about the appropriateness of them." Albright, of course, was famous for having said during the years before the second Gulf War that the sanctions on Iraq that were causing terrible hardships for that country's children, including deaths, were a terrible choice but worth it in the end to get rid of Saddam Hussein. Ends and means, then, were the proper platform to discuss foreign policy questions.

The white paper sought to do more than just list ends and means—its goal was to put legal supports under the various branches of claimed authority for the drone strikes. The white paper's purpose, its opening statement explained, was to set forth a legal framework "for considering the circumstances in which the U.S. government could use lethal force in a foreign country outside the area of active hostilities against a U.S. citizen who is a senior operational leader of al-Qaeda or an associated force"—that is, someone actively engaged in planning operations to kill Americans.[22]

So we are told at the outset that the legal argument is restricted to providing a justification for killing Anwar al-Awlaki—or an approximate equal who is a U.S. citizen. Later the question of equivalence gets muddled as the white paper's authors seek to find a way out of a predicament caused by "minimum requirements" for addition to the kill list: "This paper does not attempt to determine the minimum requirements necessary to render such an operation lawful, nor does it assess what might be required to render a lethal operation against a U.S. citizen lawful in other circumstances. It concludes only that the stated conditions would be sufficient to make lawful a lethal operation in a foreign country directed against a U.S. citizen with the characteristics described above." To provide specific examples instead of such generalities would, of course, limit the scope of drone warfare at a time when bases were being built in almost spree-like fashion to handle hundreds if not thousands of cases of "imminent" danger to U.S. citizens.

Even as the white paper sought to seal over gaps between the claims for the Authorization to Use Military Force and Article II of the Constitution, it unwittingly called attention to some jagged edges that stuck out from the less than perfect paste job that had put together the white paper from an assortment of still-secret memos. The president appeared taken aback, for example, when on one of the outlets he had used so successfully to get his message across, Google+ Hangouts, he was asked this question by a video blogger named Lee Doren: "A lot of people are very concerned that your administration now believes it's legal to have drone strikes on American citizens, and whether or not that's specifically allowed with citizens within the United States. And if that's not true, what will you do to create a legal framework to make American citizens within the U.S. know that drone strikes cannot be used against American citizens?"[23]

Obama dodged a categorical answer: "Well first of all, there has never been a drone used on an American citizen on American soil." Then he added, "We respect and have a whole bunch of safeguards in terms of how we conduct counterterrorism operations outside of the United States. The rules outside of the United States are going to be different than the rules inside the United States, in part because our capacity to capture a terrorist in the United States are very different than in the foothills or mountains of Afghanistan or Pakistan."[24]

This answer deserves a somewhat extended comment because it goes to the heart of the drone rationale. To begin with, it assumes that tracking down a terrorist is completely different from a stand-off with a killer holed up in a shack somewhere, a situation in which local authorities most often use lethal force. But the white paper talked about the problem of a narrow "window of opportunity" as a key factor in eliminating "imminent" threats, and it attempted to turn the White House definition of "imminent" into a sliding scale, not a particular point. "Certain aspects of this legal framework require additional explication," the white paper's authors said. "First, the condition that an operational leader present an 'imminent' threat of violent attack against the United States does not require the United States to have clear evidence that a specific attack on U.S. persons and interests will take place in the immediate future." The authors used the example of 9/11 for proof, to demonstrate that such a restriction would not allow the nation time to prepare a defense.

Why wouldn't that also be a factor inside the United States? Obama said the rules inside the United States and for foreign countries were "different," but he did not specifically refer to American citizens—suggesting both that foreign terrorists loose in the United States could be subject to drone strikes and that constitutional rights did apply to American citizens engaged in ongoing terrorism planning in other countries. Finally, the president talked about yet unwritten "rules" as if there were something in the offing and as if the executive office would simply seek something like the Gulf of Tonkin Resolution or the September 2001 Authorization to Use Military Force. Conspicuously, he did not mention the possibility of a court overview for drone strikes, an idea being bruited about in the Brennan hearings.

Even more to the point, 9/11 really had nothing to do with Awlaki—the principal subject of the white paper. Obama did say, "I am not somebody who believes that the president has the authority to do whatever he wants or whatever she wants whenever they want just under the guise of counterterrorism. There have to be legal checks and balances on it." Apparently, however, he also believed that with the white paper the OLC had provided him with the necessary guidance on what was and was not legal. Whatever other checks and balances were needed had already been explained by Holder in his speech at Northwestern as being satisfied by poststrike consultations with designated members of Congress.

Taken as a whole, the white paper was an almost perfect example of the shopworn but nonetheless valuable legal adage "Hard cases make bad law." Or, in this instance, hard cases make for poor legal opinions from the Office of Legal Counsel. The *New York Times* put it another way: "It was disturbing to see the twisted logic of the administration's lawyers laid out in black and white." It had the air of an ex post facto rationalization for a policy already carried out and brought back unwelcome memories of OLC memos for George W. Bush justifying torture, indefinite detention, and kidnapping. The document coyly referred to another memo specifically providing the legal reasoning for killing Awlaki even as the administration still refused to show that document to Congress, let alone the public. It had failed to back up its claim that he was an active terrorist, and the administration "has vigorously fought any court hearing over the killing of Mr. Awlaki or his 16-year-old son, who was killed in a subsequent attack." So much for checks and balances.[25]

Going forward, said the editorial, a court should be created to render verdicts before such death sentences were carried out. The likelihood of that happening so long as the CIA and the Pentagon "shared" authorizations, the former under covert action rationales and the latter under Article II, was very low. For one thing, what would happen to signature strikes, or poststrike follow-ups? Of course, the real problem was that the white paper's deliberate emphasis on "resolving" the Awlaki "case" was intended to clear away obstacles to the widespread use of drones. If a court was created to protect "American citizens" living abroad accused of terrorist plotting from having their constitutional rights infringed upon in the most drastic fashion possible, the judges would have little to do except brush away cobwebs from the bench.

That was why the question to President Obama about the right to kill an American citizen inside the United States proved difficult to answer in straightforward fashion: the white paper had specified in its opening statement that it laid out a legal framework for killing a traitorous U.S. citizen in a "foreign" country—nothing else. But its elaboration, as we have seen, referred to broader issues of drone warfare, such as "window of opportunity" and the meaning of "imminent."[26]

The same day the *Times* editorial appeared, the administration's out-front guy, press secretary Jay Carney, once again took on the burden of responding to questions that, as he put it, raised "understandable questions" about the white paper. Three times Carney was asked about the meaning of "imminent," and how the government could determine such a threat without specific evidence. Three times the press got a variation of this answer: "And I can just say that this President takes his responsibilities very seriously, and first and foremost, that's the responsibility, to protect the United States and American citizens."

In February 2013 Stanley McChrystal, who had been cashiered for intemperate remarks by his staff but whose usefulness had come to an end anyway when Obama shifted to drones, gave an interview that added a very much needed historical perspective to the American struggles in the Afghan-Pakistan region. "If you go back to the British tactics on the North-West Frontier," he said in an interview, "the 'butcher and bolt' tactics, where they would burn an area and punish the people and say, 'Don't do that anymore,' and simultaneously offer a stipend to the leader [to remain friendly]—that approach worked for a fair amount of time. . . . But it certainly didn't solve the problems." Drone strikes were the American counterpart to the old British tactics. "Although to the United States, a drone strike seems to have very little risk and very little pain, at the receiving end, it feels like war. Americans have got to understand that. . . . If you go back in history, I can't find a covert fix that solved a problem long term. There were some necessary covert actions, but there's no 'easy button' for some of these problems."[27]

In a sense McChrystal agreed with Steve Coll's argument from four years earlier: covert actions were largely stopgap measures, not long-term strategies. But they have long-term aftereffects. In midsummer 2012 Coll had warned that Obama had used the death of bin Laden not to close the door on Bush-era tactics (as Coll had hoped would happen) but to throw it wide open.

> Awlaki was certainly a murderous character; his YouTube videos alone would likely convict him at a jury trial. Yet the case of Awlaki's killing by drone strike is to the due-process clause what the proposed march of neo-Nazis through a community that included many Holocaust survivors in Skokie, Illinois, was to the First Amendment when that case arose, in 1977. It is an instance where the most onerous facts imaginable should lead to the durable affirmation of constitutional principle, as Skokie did. Instead, President Obama and his advisers have opened the door to violent action against American citizens by future Presidents when the facts may be much less compelling.[28]

The problem with fastening one's arguments to the Awlaki case, however, was that it left unquestioned much larger issues.

The nomination of John Brennan, some argued, would actually curb the CIA's role in authorizing widespread drone strikes, given Brennan's repeated claims that during the Bush administration he opposed waterboarding, and his strong assurances during congressional hearings on his nomination that he would not have anything to do with it.

> SENATOR CARL LEVIN: Well, you've read opinions as to whether or not waterboarding is torture. And I'm just asking, do you accept those opinions of the attorney general? That's my question.
> BRENNAN: Senator, I've read a lot of legal opinions. I read an Office of Legal Counsel opinion from the previous administration

that said waterboarding could be used. So from the standpoint
of that, I can't point to a single legal document on the issue.
But as far as I'm concerned, waterboarding is something that
never should have been employed, and as far as I'm concerned,
never will be if I have anything to do with it.

LEVIN: Is waterboarding banned by the Geneva Conventions?

BRENNAN: I believe the attorney general also has said it's contrary
and in contravention of the Geneva Convention. Again, I'm
not a lawyer or a legal scholar to make the determination as to
what's in violation of an international convention.

Brennan's touchiness about previous OLC opinions suggests,
however, that he was engaged in a defensive maneuver to protect
the CIA mandate—in its broadest sense, which included signature
strikes—as the key to maintaining its post–9/11 prominence as the
president's private army. Even after his appearance before the Senate committee, the White House engaged in an effort to ensure
that his nomination succeeded (without revealing the contents
of the secret OLC memos) by buying Republican votes with promises that the legislators would receive the e-mails that provided the
controversial talking points used by the intelligence agencies after
the attack in Benghazi, Libya, that resulted in the death of the
American ambassador there, J. Christopher Stevens, and three other
Americans—an issue that Republicans had tried to use against
Obama in the failed effort to elect Mitt Romney. "Such a conces-
sion would probably win at least some Republican votes for Mr.
Brennan," wrote two reporters who learned of the maneuver from
congressional staff members.[29]

That President Obama would continue to hold out on the OLC
memos, and even release data that seemed on the surface to be confirming that a less than fully honest response had been given to
charges about how the Benghazi event was manipulated to keep
the real story quiet during the election campaign, does not encourage confidence in the president's 2013 pledge in the State of
the Union speech that "in the months ahead, I will continue to
engage with Congress to ensure not only that our targeting,

detention and prosecution of terrorists remains consistent with our laws and system of checks and balances, but that our efforts are even more transparent to the American people and to the world."[30]

Thirty days after John F. Kennedy was assassinated in 1963, former president Harry S. Truman wrote an op-ed piece for the *Washington Post* that began, "I think it has become necessary to take another look at the purpose and operations of our Central Intelligence Agency—CIA." Truman had set up the agency as an arm of the president, he said, because the chief executive needed to have at hand the most accurate and up-to-date information possible from all corners of the world; too many times intelligence reports from various places had resulted in conflicting conclusions and were of little use in enabling the president to reach right decisions. But "for some time," Truman wrote, "I have been disturbed by the way CIA has been diverted from its original assignment. It has become an operational and at times a policy-making arm of the Government. This has led to trouble and may have compounded our difficulties in several explosive areas."

There were searching questions that needed to be answered.

I, therefore, would like to see the CIA be restored to its original assignment as an intelligence arm of the President, and that whatever else it can properly perform in that special field—and that its operational duties be terminated or properly used elsewhere. We have grown up as a nation, respected for our free institutions and for our ability to maintain a free and open society. There is something about the way the CIA has been functioning that is casting a shadow over our historic position and I feel that we need to correct it.[31]

The issue Truman raised had to do with the growth of an agency that had begun to act as a "policy-making" organization. In 2013, that issue remained unaddressed.

The sudden advent of full-scale drone warfare has been a shocking development. In speaking of the need for a "rule book," Obama's aides commented that the United States is in a position not unlike that it encountered at the dawn of the atomic age, when there was a pressing need for new rules of warfare. Connected to the drone phenomenon has been the spread of transnational movements that interact with one another constantly, pushing hard against traditional ideas of national sovereignty until those concepts are near collapse. On one side, of course, there are what we call (with some lack of precision) "terrorist" organizations, some acting out belief systems as murderous commands, others simply frustrated with the way the world doesn't work for them. At the same time, from another direction arises a growing transnational force that conservatives (and others) have called "lawfare," which seeks to establish global standards for human rights, building upon such things as the Geneva Conventions but going well beyond them, as in nascent United Nations efforts to play a leading part in setting rules for drone warfare.

American policy makers feel challenged by both sets of pressures, and so far they have been unable to reconcile national interests with a strategy that will satisfy demands for changes in the world order. Drones are an exciting prospect for holding down American casualties and killing fewer civilians than in old-style wars. But the "lesser evil" argument really doesn't work when in the long run the strikes create new enemies and force the construction of new kill lists. Another argument, that there isn't anything one can do about the march of technology, is at base a teleological assertion, for there is no inevitability that drone warfare must increase. Truman dropped the first atomic bombs in Japan, and then considered but rejected the use of atomic bombs in Korea; Eisenhower considered and rejected their use in Indochina. Those appear to be the last times really serious consideration was given to the use of nuclear weapons—except as intimidating tests on remote Pacific islands, tests that eventually had to be stopped because they were polluting the earth's atmosphere. What seems clear from the atomic experience is that military actions have both material and moral repercussions—and that they engender reactions from other actors on the world stage.

Not only do drones threaten the nation's future by creating and sustaining an endless, seemingly mystical war against terrorism, but defending drones requires the abandonment of the Constitution. And that will mean the perpetrators of 9/11 have won.[32]

AFTERWORD
THE NEW NORMAL?

When technology at the service of expediency dictates our policies, we are no longer the nation we were created to be and that we continue to tell ourselves we are, a constitutional democracy.

Gary Hart, "A Plague of Drones," March 9, 2013

It was an astounding moment. For thirteen hours Kentucky senator Rand Paul and one or two others filibustered the nomination of John Brennan as CIA director, demanding the White House provide a definitive statement ruling out drone strikes against American citizens on American soil. "I will speak until I can no longer speak," he said. "I will speak as long as it takes, until the alarm is sounded from coast to coast that our Constitution is important, that your rights to trial by jury are precious, that no American should be killed by a drone on American soil without first being charged with a crime, without first being found to be guilty by a court."[1]

Rand is a Tea Party favorite and the son of Ron Paul, the former House member who made a run for the 2012 Republican Party nomination espousing "unorthodox" foreign policy views. Unlike his father, Rand Paul does not want to be seen as a Libertarian absolutist or isolationist. But his demand for absolute clarity on the administration's drone policy drew attention to the whole question of the "rules"—or lack thereof—about drone warfare. Indeed, it is not too much to say that this speech and his follow-ups have suddenly made him a serious contender for the Republican presidential nomination in 2016. Clearly he has struck a chord that continues to vibrate, pushing him higher in the Republican pecking order.

"In March, his 13-hour filibuster to protest the Obama administration's drone warfare tactics electrified the blogosphere on both the left and right," Karen Tumulty reported in the *Washington Post*, "with Twitter registering 450,000 tweets using the hashtag #stand-withrand."[2] Then, in the wake of the filibuster came a bigger news story that was directly related to the drone questions raised by Rand Paul. A former contract worker for the National Security Administration (NSA), Edward Snowden, made headlines by revealing the existence of a top secret government program, PRISM, that scooped up information about telephone calls, e-mails, Internet usage, etc., of American citizens in an effort to thwart new terrorist attacks. The ensuing debate saw the so-called government-surveillance scandals taking a real toll on Obama's popularity, according to public opinion polls. Support for the president among younger voters, for example, plummeted by 17 percent. An article in the *Daily Beast* noted, "These results might give Chris Christie and Rand Paul hope about their 2016 prospects presenting themselves as the balance to eight years of Obama."[3]

Before the surveillance question seized hold of the nation's imagination, Obama believed he had regained the initiative in the debate over drones. In his 2013 State of the Union message, he had promised to be more transparent about his counterterrorism policy, saying, "I recognize that in our democracy, no one should just take my word for it that we're doing things the right way." A sharp-eyed reader of the State of the Union speech would note that the president never actually used the word *drones* in the text. So what did engaging Congress actually mean? Democratic regulars, of course, wanted nothing to do with the views of the Pauls, father or son. A few Republicans joined in to relieve Paul, including Tea Party types. Their opposition was put down to simple politics—anything to embarrass President Obama on any issue.

There was a lone Democrat, Ron Wyden, who got up to speak—but only after making it clear that he was not opposed to all drone warfare, just that there had not been a proper public debate about it. The Oregon senator was careful not to make too many ripples and said he would vote for John Brennan's nomination, but also said he believed his colleague from Kentucky had raised some important points. "The executive branch should not be allowed to conduct such a serious and far-reaching program by themselves without any scrutiny," said Wyden, "because that's not how American democracy works. That's not what our system is about."[4]

Wyden even hastened to tell his home state newspaper *The Oregonian* that he did not really believe he had "joined" the filibuster, because his remarks did not extend it to any degree. And he said he accepted attorney general Eric Holder's statement that the administration had "no intention" of carrying out drone strikes on citizens suspected of being terrorists on American soil, except in "an extraordinary circumstance" such as a major terrorist attack. But what satisfied Wyden still seemed "more than frightening" to Rand Paul. As his speech continued, he began to talk about long-contested events of the Vietnam War. Many college campuses in the 1960s were full of people, he said, who might have been considered enemies of the state.

"Are you going to drop . . . a Hellfire missile on Jane Fonda?" Paul asked.[5]

Now there was a question sure to rouse the sleepy-eyed in the Senate chamber! When the Kentucky senator went down this road he touched a nerve—in fact, several nerves—that broadened the debate into something much more consequential in its implications than a delay in Brennan's nomination. Vietnam was somehow always hovering somewhere over the politics of the present, and bringing up movie star Jane Fonda's supposed role in giving aid and comfort to the enemy by visiting Hanoi drew attention to the killing of U.S. citizen Anwar al-Awlaki by a drone strike in 2011.

Holder saw danger ahead if he did not add some clarification. He sent Rand Paul a short letter emphasizing that the president did not have the authority to use drones against Americans not "engaged in combat" on U.S. soil. So Jane Fonda would have been spared, if that was what worried Paul. But both men were trailing ambiguities in their wake. "Engaged in combat," for example, could have several meanings. Imploring a crowd to go occupy a ROTC building? Had there been drones back then, would such speeches be called "engaging in combat"? Fanciful, yes, at least in that era—but a lot had changed in terms of what the government could or could not do besides read e-mails since 9/11. Also, there were many more citizens around with big stakes in the fate of seldom-discussed places (such as, say, Chechnya) and who were angry about American policies and determined to strike a blow for some cause. Yet Paul claimed a victory for the Constitution. "In the end," he said, "I think it was a good healthy debate for the country to finally get an answer that the Fifth Amendment applies to all Americans."[6]

Holder and Paul appeared to be talking about two different situations. But there was at least a symbolic connection, for what did the term *combatant* really mean, on or off U.S. soil? The charges against Awlaki surfaced again when the surviving 2013 Boston Marathon bomber, Dzohokar Tsarnaev, said he and his dead brother had "viewed the Internet sermons of Anwar al-Awlaki" and had been inspired in part by the Muslim preacher.[7] We do not have a transcript of the initial bedside interrogation, and it was conducted without Miranda warnings under post–9/11 rulings regarding public safety exceptions, but there is no reason to doubt that Dzohokar did say he and his brother were influenced by Awlaki's sermons. He denied, however, having had any contact with the preacher. More to the point, Dzohokar also said that he was motivated by the wars in Iraq and Afghanistan, which he saw as anti-Muslim crusades. But, not surprisingly, news organizations leapt upon the name Awlaki. A CNN report headlined "From the Grave, the Cleric Inspiring a New Generation of Terrorists" stated, "That's as of now, that's what Dzhokhar is saying. And we should say we've seen this before, this is one of the reasons why the cleric, Anwar al-Awlaki put up videos online. He's now—he's now been killed by a drone strike. But that's why he did it, to radicalize individuals in different parts of the world."[8]

It appeared that, for CNN, the strike against Awlaki was perfectly justified to eliminate such a menace. But the claim that he radicalized individuals in different parts of the world from beyond the grave suggests something else: that the killing of Awlaki by an American drone had made him a martyr. Far from proving the worth of drone assassinations, the evidence would indicate killing him did the opposite.

Whatever one thinks about the debates over the Awlaki role in the Boston Marathon bombings, the Rand Paul filibuster had an immediate effect in lessening public support for drone warfare, at least in terms of attacks on American citizens. Polls suggested that support for attacks on Americans abroad declined by 13 percent among Republicans and 17 percent among Democrats.[9]

Effectiveness, meanwhile, had become one of the most contested questions regarding drones. The administration pointed to the declining number of drone strikes in Pakistan as proof that they were effective in eliminating terrorists. But if martyrs were created by such strikes, did that indicate success over the long run? By the end of Obama's first term, more than 92 percent of Pakistanis disapproved of his leadership; and, perhaps more important, more than half of those polled, 55 percent, believed that closer contact between the West and the Muslim world was more of a threat than a benefit for the latter.[10]

It was not Rand Paul's filibuster alone that forced a serious debate on drone warfare's implications, of course; it was the administration's carefully phrased responses about drone warfare over the four years plus since Obama had entered the White House. Even when trying to prevent the door from opening wider, Attorney General Holder had considerable trouble finding the right words. And that was in large part because Congress had abandoned its duty to guard against White House "mission creep" after 9/11, with the executive branch assuming it had sole responsibility for formulating national security policy. So Rand Paul's impact can be exaggerated, but he did pull a lever that threw open a huge truckload of unanswered questions that tumbled noisily onto the steps of the Capitol.

He received enough attention, moreover, to make others take a look at that pile and realize you couldn't keep walking around it to get into the building. Illinois senator Richard Durbin, a steadfast Obama loyalist throughout the rocky days of the president's first term, wasted little time in suggesting that Congress was uneasy with the drone policy (or lack thereof) and that he was in touch with people in the White House about the need for a full accounting of the situation and what could be done about it. In a wide-ranging interview with the *Wall Street Journal*, Durbin delivered a critique not about specific military policies but about the entire framework of national security policy since 9/11, beginning with how the original Authorization for Use of Military Force (AUMF) had been stretched to cover a map of the world.

> From a constitutional viewpoint, it goes to this authorization for the use of military force. I don't believe many, if any, of us believed when we voted for that—and I did vote for it—that we were voting for the longest war in the history of the United States and putting a stamp of approval on a war policy against terrorism that, 10 years plus later, we're still using. So there are unanswered questions about that authorization, the use of military force, which we're going to get into, and then complex questions, such as where can we use drones as a lethal weapon, against whom? What are the checks and balances of the system? Is this a wide open opportunity for any president to use lethal force anywhere against anyone?
>
> Now, the good news is the president, this president, has invited us to establish what he calls a legal architecture on the use of drones, and I think we should. I've been in contact with folks at the national security level in the White House to talk about this hearing, and I hope we start to answer or at least address some of the key policy questions that flow from this at this hearing.[11]

The hearings Durbin held in late April opened with a telling announcement that these were, in fact, the first ever on drone warfare. As the chair of the Subcommittee on the Constitution, Civil Rights and Human Rights of the U.S. Senate Committee on the Judiciary, he opened the session by saying, "More transparency is needed to maintain the support of the American people and the international community" in regard to drone strikes. Then he added, "I am disappointed that the administration declined to provide witnesses to testify at today's hearing," a statement that drew support from other senators of both parties. Clearly, Durbin was not willing to play along any longer with the "trust us" mantra the White House had thrown over the drones since 2009.

The president, said Durbin, had a "unique responsibility" to protect and defend the country. His authority to do so, however, was based upon the rule of law, "which has been abused during times of war." This was, wrote a reporter for the *Miami Herald*, an apparent reference to George W. Bush and torture. But Durbin insisted it also referred to drone strikes. "There are long-term consequences, especially when these airstrikes kill innocent civilians. . . . That's why many in the national security community are concerned that we may undermine our counterterrorism efforts if we do not carefully measure the benefits and costs of targeted killing."[12]

Durbin's hearings were notable for the dramatic testimony from a Yemeni witness who had seen the aftermath of drone strikes—another big first in congressional responses to the White House's continued insistence upon the precision of military weapons. Farea al-Muslimi, a Yemeni activist and journalist who had studied in the United States, told the senators about a village that was bombed the week before the hearings. He testified that while the attack killed five suspected members of al Qaeda, the raid also "terrified the region's poor farmers." The purported central target, the well-known figure Hamid al-Radmi, could have been apprehended instead of assassinated. "The Yemeni government could easily have found and arrested him," the witness testified. "Even the local government could have captured him if the U.S. had told them to do so."[13]

Here was a direct challenge to Washington's persistent claim that targets were selected because it was impossible to get at them in any other way, because of either unfriendly terrain or high risk of casualties for American soldiers. Aside from the psychological collateral damage done to the village, and the resulting hatred for the United States it caused in wider regions of Yemen, Muslimi had exploded the contention that capture was always chosen over using lethal force when possible. Micah Zenko, a fellow of the Council on Foreign Relations and a commentator on drone warfare, followed up the hearing by wryly noting that new CIA head "John Brennan tells policymakers to read earlier comments by John Brennan for any clarification" on how the program works. He left it at that, since it said all that need be said about the administration's ring-'round-the-mulberry-bush attitudes.[14]

Even before the hearings Durbin had raised his questions about the original AUMF and what it had become: blanket approval for almost any military or clandestine action the administration wished to use anywhere. Here was another break with post–9/11 orthodoxy. Indeed, even as the Democratic senator was raising questions about the AUMF, other voices were calling for a new law to expand its scope to include still more contingencies. The original law was vague enough, giving the Bush and Obama White Houses the supposed authority to carry out attacks on "associates" of those guilty of per-petrating the 9/11 attacks. "The farther we get away from 9/11 and what this legislation was initially focused upon," a senior Obama official said, "we can see from both a theoretical but also a practical standpoint that groups that have arisen or morphed become more difficult to fit in."[15]

Courts had already expanded the original AUMF whenever the White House requested authority to include associates of al Qaeda, even though that word *associates* was not used in the original legis-lation. Now intelligence agencies in the administration were trying to see if it could be enlarged still further to include "associates of associates." Some in the administration were trying to halt the pro-cess, with one anonymous source saying, "You can't end the war if you keep adding people to the enemy who are not actually part of the original enemy."[16]

A related issue was raised at the hearings by Rosa Brooks, a Georgetown University law professor who had been a Pentagon consultant and was a frequent commentator on international af-fairs. Most of the debate on drones, she noted, focused on the ad-ministration's Orwellian interpretation of the term "imminence," but Obama had espoused an equally elastic theory of sovereignty: "In a nutshell, the U.S. legal theory of sovereignty is this: 'We have it; you don't.'" But to blame only conservatives for the assumption that the United States enjoyed the right to intervene with drones wherever it wished ignored the entire reordering of the international system after World War II. The famous white paper on the legality of drone strikes posited that the United States could strike a target where a state was "unwilling or unable to" suppress an imminent threat. Her point, however, was not that President George W. Bush had come along and used 9/11 to wage two wars on the flimsy excuse of Saddam Hussein's supposed weapons of mass destruction but the larger question of how "human rights norms have done as much to erode traditional ideas of sovereignty as have more U.S.-centric theories of counterterrorism." In essence, she said, both the human rights community and the U.S. counterterrorism community increasingly shared a similar view of sovereignty as a privilege states can earn or lose, rather than an inherent right of statehood.[17]

The point was that humanitarian intervention, good intentions, and the like were cousins of liberal imperialism. Her authority for such a statement was former UN secretary-general Kofi Annan, who asserted in 1999, "When we read the [UN] Charter today, we are more than ever conscious that its aim is to protect individual human beings, not to protect those who abuse them." She then tied this to the International Commission on Intervention and State Sovereignty's report on the fundamental duty of sovereign states to protect their populations, which was published after 9/11 but begun well before then. Sovereignty required states to protect their peoples against repression; insurgency; internal war; and, where the "state is unwilling or unable to halt or avert it, the principle of non-intervention yields to the international responsibility to protect," according to the report. The commission was an ad hoc body formed under the auspices of the United Nations that was working on its report at the time of the 9/11 attacks. Its major focus was on the terrible events in Rwanda and Kosovo.

But even so the commission did not give carte blanche for drone warfare. Instead it addressed the rights and obligations of states under attack from terrorists, as in the terrible events of 9/11, in a way that imposed limits.

In particular, the precautionary principles outlined in our report do seem to be relevant to military operations, both multilateral and unilateral, against the scourge of terrorism. We have no difficulty in principle with focused military action being taken against international terrorists and those who harbour them. But military power should always be exercised in a principled way, and the principles of right intention, last resort, proportional means and reasonable prospects outlined in our report are, on the face of it, all applicable to such action.[18]

As Brooks said, her argument did not necessarily legitimize drone strikes, but she feared that there were troubling parallels between the rationales for UAVs and for humanitarian intervention. It was certainly true that administration officials had defended drone warfare as the most "humanitarian" way of protecting the American population against terrorist attacks, because it saved the lives of soldiers and avoided large-scale assaults on foreign countries. And that made for a connecting line liberals could grab hold of and explain why Bush had been wrong and Obama right—even if the latter used drones as a weapon of choice. But hers were cautionary words about the need to look deep inside the American rationale for continuing to expand the campaign. There were other troubling issues about stressing "humanitarian" arguments, which tended to provide rationalizations the public could accept all too easily.

In her testimony Rosa Brooks reemphasized the question of whether drones "worked' in getting rid of enemies or—invoking Donald Rumsfeld of all people—defeated the purpose of eliminating the underlying causes of the threat.

As the Obama administration increases its reliance on drone strikes as the counterterrorism tool of choice, it is hard not to wonder whether we have begun to trade tactical gains for strategic losses. What impact will U.S. drone strikes ultimately have on the stability of Pakistan, Yemen, or Somalia? To what degree—especially as we reach further and further down the terrorist food chain, killing small fish who may be motivated less by ideology than economic desperation—are we actually creating new grievances within the local population—or even within diaspora populations here in the United States? As Defense Secretary Donald Rumsfeld asked during the Iraq war, are we creating terrorists faster than we kill them?

She also commented,

This flexible interpretation of the AUMF creates few constraints, and has lowered the threshold for using force. Repealing the AUMF would not deprive the president of the ability to use force if necessary to prevent or respond to a serious armed attack: the president would retain his existing discretionary power, as chief executive and commander in chief, to protect the nation in emergencies. Repealing the 2001 AUMF would, however, likely reduce the frequency with which the president resorts to targeted killings.[19]

Brooks was no "extremist" and did not rule out drones if a rule of law could be found to govern their use, and she had sagely noted that much of the support for drones stemmed, at least in an indirect way, from assaults on previously sacrosanct definitions of national sovereignty by human rights advocates. But she worried that, the way things were developing, the United States was actually handing a playbook for murder over to less scrupulous states instead of providing moral leadership in this "new normal" world.

Exactly one month later, on May 23, 2013, President Obama delivered his long-promised speech on national security. America was at a crossroads, he said. "We must either define the nature and scope of the struggle, or else it will define us." The speech then went on to describe how the al Qaeda threat had diminished in Pakistan and Afghanistan, with those enemies spending most of their time worrying about survival than plotting new attacks on the United States or nearby places. He promised an end to direct involvement in Afghanistan by the end of 2014. But then the speech hit a pivot point as he described how al Qaeda affiliates had grown up in Yemen, Somalia, and the Arabian Peninsula and were still not eliminated entirely in Iraq. He said, "Beyond Afghanistan, we must define our effort not as a boundless global war on terror but rather as a series of persistent, targeted efforts to dismantle specific networks of violent extremists that threaten America." In many cases, this will involve partnerships with other countries, he explained. "In Yemen," he continued, "we are supporting security forces that have reclaimed territory from AQAP."

Obama went on much in the same vein as his 2007 speech at the Wilson Center that launched his presidential campaign.

> Despite our strong preference for the detention and prosecution of terrorists, sometimes this approach is foreclosed. Al-Qaida and its affiliates try to gain a foothold in some of the most distant and unforgiving places on Earth. They take refuge in remote tribal regions. They hide in caves and walled compounds. They train in empty deserts and rugged mountains. In some of these places, such as parts of Somalia and Yemen, the state has only the most tenuous reach into the territory. In other cases, the state lacks the capacity or will to take action.

While some hearers nodded solemnly at this point, others closed their eyes and saw these remarks rising from the pages of Joseph Conrad's *Heart of Darkness*, the famous novel about the imperial "mission" in Africa.

The president then added an interesting justification for the drone strikes against signature targets, stating that it was impossible to expect to repeat the success of going into Pakistan to get Osama bin Laden. The cost of that venture, he now said, had caused such a backlash that only now, in 2013, were relations with Pakistan being rebuilt into a solid partnership. It was a very skillful use of one of his greatest "successes," one that counted heavily in the 2012 election, to turn the tables on drone critics by calling the operation a one-off.

Commentators of all stripes soon took turns interpreting the speech. Nearly all agreed that it had resulted from Obama's deep sense of unease about the way drone warfare had developed, but was equally born of frustration about the obstacles to change, whether closing "Gitmo" or taking the CIA out of the operational phases of carrying out attacks on suspected terrorists, both of which he had hoped to do. Some pointed out that he was unlikely to get Congress to respond to other means of fighting the war on terror, such as using foreign aid to attack the causes of unrest in Muslim countries or supporting moves to alleviate the Arab-Israeli impasse that would challenge the United States' all-out backing of Israel. For some, therefore, it was just a speech about presidential angst and not really different from previous speeches, despite its warning about the peril to democracy. One commentary featured a significant difference from the text (at least as delivered). Peter Baker said the president and his team tightened standards for striking targets from "a significant threat to U.S. interests" to a "continuing, imminent threat to U.S. persons." That wording would have marked a significant change, largely eliminating a significant ambiguity in the new policy. But the president's actual wording restored much of the ambiguity: "We act against terrorists who pose a continuing and imminent threat to the American people and when there are no other governments capable of effectively addressing the threat."[20]

Less than a week after the speech, a drone strike in Pakistan killed Hakimullah Mehsud, the purported deputy commander of the Taliban in Pakistan, in the tribal area of North Waziristan. Reuters reported the death with the double-edged comment that, while his death was a blow for the militants, "it could also be viewed as a setback for incoming Prime Minister Nawaz Sharif's efforts to end violence." Sharif had called the drone strikes a "challenge" to Pakistan's sovereignty. And the foreign ministry denounced drone strikes in general as "counter-productive" acts that "entail loss of innocent civilian lives, have human rights and humanitarian implications and violate the principles of national sovereignty, territorial integrity and international law."[21]

Six others were killed in the attack, which occurred less than a week after Obama's big speech announcing new constraints. White House press secretary Jay Carney did not mention these anonymous others, only Mehsud, who, he said, "has participated in cross-border attacks in Afghanistan against U.S. and NATO personnel and horrific attacks against Pakistani civilians and soldiers." The new standard of "continuing imminent" had been met. It was not so hard, after all.[22]

Of all the early responses to Obama's speech and to the signature strike in North Waziristan, Akbar Ahmed's was perhaps the most informed about the continuing damage to American interests. Ahmed is a former official of the Pakistani government and now the chair of Islamic studies at American University. In his *New York Times* op-ed, he argued that the drone war, when carried on in places like Waziristan, only deepened the problems of governance in remote areas. The only way to rebuild any semblance of the rule of law was to work with elders of the tribes, who served to maintain stability through structures of authority that were the best way to eliminate Taliban intruders in Pakistan, al Qaeda in the Arabian Peninsula, and Somalia's Al Shabab. He wrote, "America has deployed drones into these power vacuums, causing ferocious backlashes against central governments while destroying any positive image of the United States that may have once existed."[23]

With Ahmed's commentary in mind, now read again President Obama's justification of drone strikes over all other methods.

> Al-Qaida and its affiliates try to gain a foothold in some of the most distant and unforgiving places on Earth. They take refuge in remote tribal regions. They hide in caves and walled compounds. They train in empty deserts and rugged mountains. In some of these places, such as parts of Somalia and Yemen, the state has only the most tenuous reach into the territory. In other cases, the state lacks the capacity or will to take action.

Ahmed had some advice for the president. "American policy makers would do well to heed a Pashto proverb: 'The Pashtun who took revenge after a hundred years said, I took it quickly.' "

Perhaps the most eloquent words in Obama's May 23 address—the longest speech except the State of the Union he's given thus far—was his reference to James Madison on the dangers of perpetual war to a democracy: "We have to be mindful of James Madison's warning that no nation could preserve its freedom in the midst of continual warfare." It was an important warning to himself and all future occupants of the White House—that the war as it had developed since 9/11 carried a poison that was as dangerous to the public as the ricin-laced letters sent to the president and intercepted by the FBI. The lesson was, as Obama said, "Neither I nor any president can promise the total defeat of terror. We will never erase the evil that lies in the hearts of some human beings nor stamp out every danger to our open society."[24]

NOTES

Introduction

1. Katie Glueck, "Robert Gibbs: I Was Told Not to 'Acknowledge' Drones," *Politico*, February 25, 2013, www.politico.com/story/2013/02/gibbs-i-was-told-dont-admit-drones -88025.html.

2. "Rumor: Obama Waives Sanctions on Countries Using Child Soldiers," MSN News, February 5, 2013.

3. Peter Beinart, "Follow the Leader," *Daily Beast*, February 25, 2013, www.thedai lybeast.com/newsweek/2013/02/25/peter.beinart.

4. Richard Cohen, "Barron's Law," *Washington Post*, October 11, 2011.

5. Richard Clarke, "Give Drones a Medal," New York *Daily News*, December 2, 2012. (Italics added.)

6. John Glaser, "Did Lindsey Graham Accidentally Divulge Secret Drone Casualty Estimates?" February 20, 2013, *Antiwar.blog*, antiwar.com/blog/2013/02/20/did-lindsey -graham-accidentally-divulge-secret-drone-casualty-estimates.

1. The Dream Candidate

1. Barack Obama, "Against Going to War with Iraq," October 2, 2002, en.wikisource .org/wiki/Barack_Obama.

2. Seymour M. Hersh, "Torture at Abu Ghraib," *New Yorker*, May 10, 2004.

3. Rich Lowry, "Oh Bama! 'The Belief in Things Not Seen,'" *National Review Online*, July 28, 2004, old.nationalreview.com/lowry200407281612.asp.

4. Evidently the idea that a new Great Emancipator led the United States in the twenty-first century was thought too good to pass up. But it backfired. In the first place, it did not go unnoticed that he spoke from the safety of a huge ship hovering off the shore of California. And his arrival in a fighter jet became a point of mockery. Origi-nally the White House had claimed that the carrier was too far off the California coast for a helicopter landing and a jet would be needed to reach it. On the day of the speech, however, the *Lincoln* was only thirty miles from shore. White House spokesman Ari Fleischer later admitted that Bush "could have helicoptered, but the plan was already in place." "2003 Mission Accomplished Speech," *Wikipedia*, accessed May 15, 2013, en.wikipedia.org/wiki/2003_Mission_Accomplished_speech.

5. Ruy Teixeira, "Public Opinion Snapshot: The Verdict on the Surge," Center for American Progress, June 29, 2007, www.americanprogress.org/issues/2007/06/snapshot _surge.html.

6. Ibid.

7. Barack Obama, "The War We Need to Win," speech at the Woodrow Wilson Center, August 1, 2007, www.wilsoncenter.org/sites/default/files/obamasp0807.pdf.

8. "Transcript of President Bush's Speech at the Veterans of Foreign Wars Convention," *New York Times*, August 22, 2007.

9. Josh Rogers, "Obama: Iraq Troop Surge Isn't Working," New Hampshire Public Radio, July 20, 2007.

10. Obama, "War We Need to Win."

11. "President Discusses Global War on Terror," September 5, 2006, georgewbush -whitehouse.archives.gov/news/releases/2006/09/20060905-4.html.

12. Obama, "War We Need to Win."

13. The authorship of the Woodrow Wilson Center speech's ideas seems to have come from Bruce Riedel, at least on the sections dealing with Pakistan and the Afghan War. See James Mann, *The Obamians: The Struggle Inside the White House to Redefine American Power* (New York: Viking, 2012), 86–87.

14. Ibid.

15. Ibid.

16. Jake Tapper, "MoveOn.org Ad Takes Aim at Petraeus," ABC News, September 10, 2007, abcnews.go.com/Politics/Decision2008/story?id=3581727.

17. Ibid.

18. On the Anbar Awakening, as it was called, see Steve Coll, "The General's Dilemma," *New Yorker*, September 8, 2008.

19. Ibid.

20. Quotes from the January 31, 2008, Democratic candidates debate taken from a transcript of the debate, which is available online from various sources. McCain's comments are from John M. Broder and Elisabeth Bumiller, "McCain and Obama Trade Jabs on Iraq," *New York Times*, February 27, 2008.

21. Andrew Malcolm, "Obama Website's Opposition to Successful Surge Gets Deleted," *Los Angeles Times*, July 16, 2008.

22. Barack Obama, "My Plan for Iraq," *New York Times*, July 14, 2008.

23. Ibid.

24. "Obama's Remarks on Iraq and Afghanistan," *New York Times*, July 15, 2008.

25. "Obama Calls Situation in Afghanistan 'Urgent,'" CNN, July 21, 2008, www .cnn.com/2008/POLITICS/07/20/obama.afghanistan/.

26. Joe Klein, "Can Obama and Petraeus Work Together," *Time*, June 24, 2010.

27. Joe Klein, "Why Barack Obama Is Winning," *Time*, October 22, 2008.

28. Sara Just, "Obama: Surge Succeeded But Too Costly," *Political Radar* blog, ABC News, September 8, 2008, abcnews.go.com/blogs/politics/2008/09/obama-surge-suc/.

29. Ibid.

30. Obama's remarks and the scene in Grant Park are detailed in Jonathan Alter's *The Promise: President Obama, Year One* (New York: Simon & Schuster, 2010), 38–39.

31. John Nagl, foreword to *The U.S. Army/Marine Corps Counterinsurgency Field Manual* (Chicago: University of Chicago Press, 2007), xix.

32. Elisabeth Bumiller, "Gates Vows Active Role in Staying On at Pentagon," *New York Times*, December 3, 2008.

33. Transcript of news conference, December 1, 2008, available from several online sources.

34. All quotations taken from Gates's speech, "Landon Lecture (Kansas State University)," November 26, 2007, www.defense.gov/Speeches.aspx?SpeechID=1199.

35. Condoleezza Rice, "Rethinking the National Interest: American Realism for a New World," *Foreign Affairs*, July/August 2008, 2–25.

36. Ibid.

37. Ibid.

2. Afghanistan Shortchanged

1. Peter Finn and Anne E. Kornblut, "Guantanamo Bay: Why Obama Hasn't Fulfilled His Promise to Close the Facility," *Washington Post*, April 23, 2011.

2. Ann Scott Tyson, "Gates Backs Buildup of U.S. Troops in Afghanistan." *Washington Post*, November 22, 2008.

3. Meredith Buei, "Gates: Terror Groups in Pakistan Greatest Threat to Afghanistan, US," Voice of America, September 23, 2008.

4. Ann Scott Tyson, "Gates Predicts 'Slog' in Afghanistan: U.S. Military Can Achieve Limited Goals in Conflict," *Washington Post*, January 28, 2009.

5. Henry A. Kissinger, "A Strategy for Afghanistan," *Washington Post*, February 26, 2009.

6. Ibid.

7. The reference was to Justice Potter Stewart's quip that he would know what pornography was when he saw it. Spencer Ackerman, "Holbrooke on Afghanistan: 'We'll Know It When We See It,'" *Washington Independent*, August 12, 2009.

8. Mark Landler and Thom Shanker, "U.S. May Label Pakistan Militants as Terrorists," *New York Times*, July 14, 2010.

9. Bruce Riedel, *The Search for Al Qaeda: Its Leadership, Ideology and Future* (Washington, DC: Brookings Institution Press, 2010), 154.

10. "Afghan Expert Riedel Weighs Obama's Strategic Options," transcript, *PBS NewsHour*, October 16, 2009, www.pbs.org/newshour/bb/asia/july-dec09/afghanistan3_10-16.html.

11. Bruce Riedel, "A Plan B in Afghanistan," Brookings Institution, August 2, 2010, www.brookings.edu/opinions/2010/0802_afghanistan_riedel.aspx.

12. "White Paper of the Interagency Policy Group's Report on U.S. Policy Toward Afghanistan and Pakistan," *New York Times*, March 27, 2009.

13. Daniel Klaidman, *Kill or Capture: The War on Terror and the Soul of the Obama Presidency* (New York: Houghton Mifflin Harcourt, 2012), 21–23.

14. Ibid.

15. David Kilcullen and Andrew McDonald Exum, "Death from Above, Outrage Down Below," *New York Times*, May 17, 2009.

16. Ibid.

17. Karen DeYoung and Joby Warrick, "Drone Attacks Inside Pakistan Will Continue, CIA Chief Says," *Washington Post*, February 26, 2009.

18. Josh Gerstein, "Leon Panetta Wars Against Politicization of CIA," *Politico*, May 18, 2009, www.politico.com/news/stories/0509/22676.html.

19. "Obama's Strategy for Afghanistan and Pakistan, March 2009," Council on Foreign Relations primary sources, March 27, 2009, www.cfr.org/pakistan/obamas-strategy-afghanistan-pakistan-march-2009/p18952.

20. Interestingly, David Sanger reports that the threat of a "particularly virulent" strain of Pakistani Taliban gaining access to a nuclear weapon was the stuff of Naval War College crisis games until early in 2009, when there appeared intelligence reports on the possibility as a real danger. These came along, it should be noted, as a precursor to a second surge decision. David E. Sanger, *Confront and Conceal: Obama's Secret Wars and Surprising Use of American Power* (New York: Crown 2012), 58–59.

21. Ibid.

22. "Transcript: Secretary Gates on 'FNS,'" *FOX News Sunday*, Fox News, March 29, 2009, www.foxnews.com/story/0,2933,511368,00.html.

23. Trudy Rubin, "Gen. Petraeus Makes the Case for Obama's War," *Philadelphia Inquirer*, April 12, 2009.

24. "Secretary Robert Gates Interview with CNN," April 29, 2009, www.defenselink.mil/transcripts/transcript.aspx?trandscriptid=4411.

25. Bob Woodward, *Obama's Wars* (New York: Simon & Schuster, 2010), 85–86.

26. Ellen Knickmeyer and Jonathan Finer, "Insurgent Leader Al-Zarqawi Killed in Iraq," *Washington Post*, June 8, 2006.

27. Kelley B. Vlahos, "The Dark Legacy of Gen. McChrystal," Antiwar.com, July 23, 2010, original.antiwar.com/vlahos/2010/07/12/the-dark-legacy-of-gen-mcchrystal/.

28. Mary Tillman with Narda Zacchino, *Boots on the Ground by Dusk: My Tribute to Pat Tillman* (New York: Modern Times Books, 2008), 289–97. The Tillman family sent President Obama an e-mail when the appointment was made and before the congressional hearing on his nomination. In a foreword to the paperback edition, she wrote: "McChrystal's actions should have been grounds for firing. That is why it was so disturbing to us when President Obama instead promoted McChrystal to the position of top commander in Afghanistan last year. I had sent the president an email and a letter reminding him of McChrystal's involvement in Pat's cover-up. I suggested McChrystal should be 'scrutinized very carefully' by the Senate Armed Services Committee. I also contacted the staffs of Senator Patrick Leahy and Senator James Webb and expressed my concerns."

29. Mark Thompson, "Why the Pentagon Axed Its Afghanistan Warlord," *Time*, May 12, 2009; Fred Kaplan, "It's Obama's War Now," *Slate*, May 11, 2009, www.slate.com/articles/news_and_politics/war_stories/2009/05/its_obamas_war_now.html.

30. Julian E. Barnes, "Americans Won't Accept 'Long Slog' in Afghanistan War, Gates Says," *Los Angeles Times*, July 19, 2009.

31. Sanger, *Confront and Conceal*, 25.

32. The document can be found at articles.washingtonpost.com/2009-09-21/news/36848328_1_international-security-assistance-force-civilian-casualties-review-plans.

33. These last two quotes are from Bob Woodward's analysis of the report, "McChrystal: More Forces or 'Mission Failure,'" *Washington Post*, September 21, 2009. The *Post's* position on the ensuing debate was pretty clear.

34. George Packer, "Reading the McChrystal Report," *Interesting Times* blog, *New Yorker*, September 23, 2009, www.newyorker.com/online/blogs/georgepacker/2009/09/reading-the-mcchrystal-report.html.

35. Ewen MacAskill, "Barack Obama 'Risks Suez-like Disaster' in Afghanistan, Says Key Adviser," *The Guardian*, November 12, 2009.

36. Peter Baker and Elisabeth Bumiller, "Obama Is Considering Strategy Shift in Afghan War," *New York Times*, September 23, 2009.

37. Sanger, *Confront and Conceal*, 29.

38. "Text of the Secret Eikenberry Cables Advising Against the Surge in Afghanistan," America at War, January 27, 2010, afpakwar.com/blog/archives/3727.

39. Baker and Bumiller, "Obama Is Considering Strategy Shift."

40. Thom Shanker and Eric Schmitt, "General Denies Rift with Obama over Afghan Strategy," *New York Times*, September 24, 2009.

41. Nancy A. Youssef, "Gates to Army: We'll Follow Obama's Orders on Afghanistan," McClatchy Newspapers, October 5, 2009.

42. Frederick W. Kagan and Kimberly Kagan, "In Afghanistan, Real Leverage Starts with More Troops," *Washington Post*, November 27, 2009.

43. Peter Baker, "How Obama Came to Plan for 'Surge' in Afghanistan," *New York Times*, December 6, 2009.

44. Jonathan Alter, *The Promise: President Obama, Year One* (New York: Simon & Schuster, 2010), 383–85.

45. Ibid., 374ff.

46. Walter Alarkon, "Petraeus Says Obama Told Him Iraq Surge Was a Success," *The Hill*, December 6, 2009, thehill.com/homenews/administration/70787-petraeus-says-obama-told-him-iraq-surge-was-a-success; Dana Milbank, "Obama's Afghan Deadline All But Missed," *Washington Post*, December 3, 2009.

47. Rajiv Chandrasekaran and Greg Jaffe, "McChrystal's Afghanistan Plan Stays Mainly Intact," *Washington Post*, December 7, 2009.

48. Kilcullen quoted in Trudy Rubin, "Worldview: Obama's Detrimental Deadline," Philly.com, July 25, 2010, articles.philly.com/2010-07-25/news/24969811_1_afghan-government-taliban-factions-afghan-people.

49. Mark Landler and Jeff Zeleny, "Among Obama Aides, Debate Intensifies on Troop Levels," *New York Times*, November 12, 2009.

3. A Tale of Two Speeches

1. "Remarks of President Barack Obama—As Prepared for Delivery: Responsibly Ending the War in Iraq," speech at Camp Lejeune, North Carolina, February 27, 2009,

www.whitehouse.gov/the_press_office/Remarks-of-President-Barack-Obama-Responsi
bly-Ending-the-War-in-Iraq.

2. Anders Fogh Rasmussen, "A New Momentum for Afghanistan from NATO; a Transition but Not an Exit Strategy," *Washington Post*, December 4, 2009.

3. Quoted in Oliver Stone and Peter Kuznick, *The Untold History of the United States* (New York: Gallery Books, 2012), 592.

4. Quoted in Arianna Huffington, "Sartre Meets Afghanistan: Obama's 'No Exit' Strategy," *Huffington Post*, December 7, 2009, www.huffingtonpost.com/arianna
-huffington/sartre-meets-afghanistan_b_383529.html (emphasis added).

5. Eric Schmitt, "Obama Issues Order for More Troops in Afghanistan," *New York Times*, December 1, 2009.

6. Ibid.

7. George Will, "This Will Not End Well," *Washington Post*, December 3, 2009.

8. George McGovern, "A Sharp Turn Toward Another Vietnam," *Washington Post*, December 13, 2009.

9. Eliot Cohen, "Obama's COIN Toss," *Washington Post*, December 6, 2009.

10. Niall Ferguson, "An Empire at Risk," *Newsweek*, November 28, 2009.

11. David E. Sanger, *Confront and Conceal: Obama's Secret Wars and Surprising Use of American Power* (New York: Crown, 2012), 63–64.

12. Scott Wilson and Jon Cohen, "Poll Finds Broad Support for Obama's Counter-Terrorism Policies," *Washington Post*, February 8, 2012.

13. Eric Schmitt, "Two Top Aides Show Unity on Afghan Strategy," *New York Times*, December 9, 2009.

14. Associated Press, "Petraeus Warns New Surge Progress Will Be Slow," NBC News, December 9, 2009, www.nbcnews.com/id/34345847/.

15. Scott Shane, "The War in Pashtunistan," *New York Times*, December 5, 2009.

16. Ibid.

17. Associated Press, "Petraeus Warns New Surge Progress Will Be Slow."

18. Mark Landler, "Petraeus Warns of a Long and Expensive Mission in Afghanistan," *New York Times*, December 10, 2009.

19. Maureen Dowd, "A Game That's Not So Great," *New York Times*, December 13, 2009.

20. Ibid.

21. Peter Walker and Elana Schor, "Crowds Gather in Berlin to Hear Obama's Foreign Policy Speech," *The Guardian*, July 24, 2008.

22. "Full Script of Obama's Speech," July 24, 2008, CNN Politics, edition.cnn
.com/2008/POLITICS/07/24/obama.words/.

23. "Brooks, Marcus Discuss Potential Peace Prize Backfire, Rangel Controversy," *PBS NewsHour*, October 9, 2009, www.pbs.org/newshour/bb/politics/july-dec09/brooks
marcus_10-09.html.

24. Thorbjørn Jagland, quoted in James Fallows, "Obama's Nobel Speech," *The Atlantic*, www.theatlantic.com/technology/archive/2009/12/obamas-nobel-speech
/31598/."

25. James Mann, *The Obamians: The Struggle Inside the White House to Redefine American Power* (New York: Viking Press, 2012), 89. Many of the details of the Power-Obama relationship are from this source.

26. Ibid., 152–53.

27. Samantha Power, "Our War on Terror," *New York Times Book Review*, July 27, 2007. All quotes in this section are taken from this source.

28. Stanley Kurtz, "Samantha Power's Power: On the Ideology of an Obama Adviser," *National Review*, April 5, 2011.

29. David Brooks, "Obama's Christian Realism," *New York Times*, December 15, 2009.

30. Ted Widmer, "Obama's Nobel Speech: Sophisticated and Brave," *New York Times*, December 12, 2009.

31. Ibid.

32. Martin Luther King Jr., "Beyond Vietnam: A Time to Break Silence," speech at Riverside Church, New York, April 4, 1967, www.informationclearinghouse.info/article 2564.html.

33. "Toast Remarks by the President at the 2009 Nobel Banquet," December 10, 2009, www.whitehouse.gov/the-press-office/toast-remarks-president-2009-nobel-banquet.

34. Mann, *Obamians*, 334; Sanger, *Confront and Conceal*, xix–xx.

35. Jo Becker and Scott Shane, "Secret 'Kill List' Proves a Test of Obama's Principles and Will," *New York Times*, May 29, 2012.

36. Ibid.

37. Kristina Wong, "President Obama's Joke About Predator Drones Draws Fire," *Political Punch* blog, ABC News, May 3, 2010, abcnews.go.com/blogs/politics/2010/05 /president-obamas-joke-about-predator-drones-draws-fire/.

4. On to Marja!

1. "Afghan President's Brother, Ahmad Wali Karzai, Killed," BBC News, South Asia, July 12, 2011; Karen DeYoung and Craig Whitlock, "U.S. Forces Set Sights on Taliban Bastion of Kandahar," *Washington Post*, March 31, 2010.

2. Mark Mazzetti, *The Way of the Knife: The CIA, a Secret Army, and a War at the Ends of the Earth* (New York: Penguin, 2013), 205–6.

3. Jane Perlez, "Rebuffing U.S., Pakistan Balks at Crackdown," *New York Times*, December 14, 2009.

4. Quoted in Jonathan Steele, *Ghosts of Afghanistan: Hard Truths and Foreign Myths* (Berkeley, CA: Counterpoint Press, 2011), 361.

5. Ibid., 334.

6. Julian Borger and Simon Tisdall, "Talk to Taliban for Peace, Says Afghan Envoy," *The Guardian*, January 2, 2010; Mark Landler and Helene Cooper, "U.S. Wrestling with Olive Branch for Taliban," *New York Times*, January 27, 2010.

7. Dexter Filkins and Mark Landler, "Afghan Leader Is Seen to Flout Influence of U.S.," *New York Times*, March 30, 2010.

8. The most recent confirmation of this important aspect of the reasons for the coup against Diem comes from Lien-Hang T. Nguyen's *Hanoi's War: An International History of the War for Peace in Vietnam* (Chapel Hill: University of North Carolina Press, 2012), 62: "When the Ngo brothers, particularly Diem's brother Nhu, expressed interest in this scheme [French president Charles de Gaulle's proposal for neutralizing Vietnam] and initiated talks with the NLF as a means to corner the Americans, who had grown more critical of their administration, they not only signed their own death warrants, but they may have increased" anxiety among North Vietnamese warhawks like Le Duan, who were anxious to settle affairs quickly and reunite Vietnam under their leadership.

9. Mark Thompson, "U.S. Troops Prepare to Test Obama's Afghan War Plan," *Time*, February 9, 2010.

10. Greg Jaffe and Craig Whitlock, "Battle for Marja Not Only Militarily Significant," *Washington Post*, February 22, 2010.

11. Michael Hastings, *The Operators: The Wild and Terrifying Inside Story of America's War in Afghanistan* (New York: Blue Rider Press, 2012), 226–31.

12. Rajiv Chandrasekaran, *Little America: The War Within the War for Afghanistan* (New York: Knopf, 2012), 140.

13. "Army Sees Marjah Offensive as a Model for Afghan Military Strategy," *PBS NewsHour*, February 26, 2010, www.pbs.org/newshour/bb/military/jan-june10/afghanistan2_02-26.html; Thompson, "U.S. Troops Prepare to Test Obama's Afghan War Plan."

14. Thompson, "U.S. Troops Prepare to Test Obama's Afghan War Plan."

15. John Kruzel, "Mullen Discusses Marja, Personnel Policy Issues," *Defense Video and Imagery Distribution System*, February 26, 2010, www.dvidshub.net/news/printable/45904.

16. John J. Kruzel, "After Marja, 'Kandahar Will Be Next,' Mullen Says," Armed Forces Press Service, March 4, 2010, www.defense.gov/news/newsarticle.aspx?id=58187.

17. Ibid.

18. C.J. Chivers, "Afghans Voice Their Fears Amid Marja Campaign," *New York Times*, February 22, 2010.

19. C.J. Chivers and Rod Nordland, "Marines in Afghan Assault Grapple with Civilian Deaths," *New York Times*, February 17, 2010.

20. "Army Sees Marjah Offensive as a Model."

21. Chandrasekaran, *Little America*, 143–44.

22. Sangar Rahimi and Richard A. Oppel Jr., "Afghanistan's President Receives a Mixed Reception in a Visit to Newly Won Marja," *New York Times*, March 8, 2010.

23. Richard A. Oppel Jr., "Tighter Rules Fail to Stem Deaths of Innocent Afghans at Checkpoints," *New York Times*, March 26, 2010.

24. Joshua Partlow and Scott Wilson, "Obama Presses Karzai for Cooperation," *Washington Post*, March 29, 2010.

25. Ibid.; Jennifer Lowen, "Obama to Karzai: Progress Needed in Afghanistan," *Army Times*, March 29, 2010.

26. Matthew Rosenberg, "Karzai Says He Was Assured CIA Would Continue Delivering Bags of Cash," *New York Times*, May 4, 2013.

27. Joshua Partlow and Scott Wilson, "Karzai Rails Against Foreign Presence, Accuses West of Engineering Voter Fraud," *Washington Post*, April 2, 2010.

28. Bob Woodward, *Obama's Wars* (New York: Simon & Schuster: 2010), 348–49.

29. Julian E. Barnes, "Afghan Taliban Getting Stronger, Pentagon Says," *Los Angeles Times*, April 29, 2010.

30. "Remarks by President Obama and President Karzai of Afghanistan in Joint Press Availability," May 12, 2010, www.whitehouse.gov/the-press-office/remarks-presi dent-obama-and-president-karzai-afghanistan-joint-press-availability.

31. Hastings, *The Operators*, 288–89.

32. Karen DeYoung and Greg Jaffe, "U.S. 'Secret War' Expands Globally as Special Operations Forces Take Larger Role," *Washington Post*, June 4, 2010.

33. For the struggle over Rumsfeld's plan, see Lloyd C. Gardner, *The Long Road to Baghdad: A History of U.S. Foreign Policy from the 1970s to the Present* (New York: The New Press, 2009).

34. DeYoung and Jaffe, "U.S. 'Secret War.'"

35. Ibid.

36. Sebastian Rotella, "Times Square Bombing Investigation Focuses on Suspected Role of Pakistani Army Major," *ProPublica*, May 21, 2010, www.propublica.org/article /times-square-bombing-investigation-focuses-on-pakistani-major.

37. Dion Nissenbaum, "McChrystal Calls Marjah a 'Bleeding Ulcer' in Afghan Campaign," McClatchy Newspapers, May 26, 2010.

38. Ibid. Succeeding quotations about the frontline conference are from this source.

39. Gareth Porter, "McChrystal Strategy Shifts to Raids—and Wali Karzai," May 24, 2010, Inter Press Service.

40. Ibid.

41. Rod Nordland, "Afghan Strategy Focuses on Civilian Effort," *New York Times*, June 8, 2010.

42. Karen DeYoung, "Results of Kandahar Offensive May Affect Future U.S. Moves," *Washington Post*, May 23, 2010.

43. Rajiv Chandrasekaran, "In Afghan Region, U.S. Spreads the Cash to Fight the Taliban," *Washington Post*, May 31, 2010

44. Ernesti Londono, "Karzai Removes Afghan Interior Minister and Spy Chief," *Washington Post*, June 7, 2010; Dexter Filkins, "Karzai Is Said to Doubt West Can Defeat Taliban," *New York Times*, June 11, 2010.

45. Filkins, "Karzai Is Said to Doubt West Can Defeat Taliban."

46. James Risen, "U.S. Identifies Vast Mineral Riches in Afghanistan," *New York Times*, June 13, 2010.

47. Ibid.

48. Jim Lobe, "Timing of Leak of Afghan Mineral Wealth Evokes Scepticism," Inter Press Service, June 14, 2010.

49. "Press Availability with Secretary Gates from the NATO Ministerial at NATO Headquarters, Brussels, Belgium," U.S. Department of Defense news transcript, June 11, 2010, www.defense.gov/transcripts/transcript.aspx?transcriptid=4642; Gareth Porter,

"McChrystal Faces 'Iraq 2006 Moment' in Coming Months," Inter Press Service, June 16, 2010.

50. Dexter Filkins, "Convoy Guards in Afghanistan Face an Inquiry," *New York Times*, June 6, 2010.

51. Bob Herbert, "The Courage to Leave," *New York Times*, June 15, 2010.

52. Michael J. Carden, "Defense Officials Cite Progress, Challenges in Afghanistan," Armed Forces Press Service, June 15, 2010, www.defense.gov/News/NewsArticle.aspx?ID=59645.

53. Adam Entous, "Questions on Afghan Strategy Touch Nerve in Pentagon," Reuters, June 15, 2010.

54. Ibid.

55. Thom Shanker and Elisabeth Bumiller, "Military and Pentagon Leaders Urge Patience for Afghan Mission," *New York Times*, June 16, 2010.

56. Michael Hastings, "The Runaway General," *Rolling Stone*, June 22, 2010. Quotations that follow are taken from this article.

57. Chandrasekaran, *Little America*, 217–19.

58. Hastings, *The Operators*, 292–93.

59. Ibid., 319–21.

60. Thomas E. Ricks, "In Afghanistan, Petraeus Will Have Difficulty Replicating His Iraq Success," *Washington Post*, June 27, 2010.

61. Karen DeYoung, "Obama Says He Is 'Confident' in War Leadership," *Washington Post*, June 26, 2010.

62. Leslie Gelb, "Petraeus Locked Obama In," *Daily Beast*, June 29, 2010.

63. Elisabeth Bumiller, "Petraeus Pledges Look at Strikes in Afghanistan," *New York Times*, June 29, 2010.

5. The War of the Drones

1. Spencer Ackerman, "How I Was Drawn into the Cult of David Petraeus," *Danger Room* blog, *Wired*, November 11, 2012, www.wired.com/dangerrooom/2012/11/petraeus-cult-2/.

2. Greg Miller and Julie Tate, "CIA Shifts Focus to Killing Targets," *Washington Post*, September 1, 2011.

3. Jane Mayer, "The Predator War," *New Yorker*, October 26, 2009.

4. Ibid.

5. James Bennet, "U.S. Cruise Missiles Strike Sudan and Afghan Targets Tied to Terrorist Network," *New York Times*, August 21, 1998.

6. Richard Clarke, "Give Drones a Medal," New York *Daily News*, December 2, 2012.

7. Karen DeYoung, "Secrecy Defines Obama's Drone War," *Washington Post*, December 19, 2011.

8. "Spying on the Home Front," interview with John Yoo, *Frontline*, January 10, 2007, www.pbs.org/wgbh/pages/frontline/homefront/interviews/yoo.html.

9. Clarke, "Give Drones a Medal."

10. This subject is fully explored in Louis Fisher, *Presidential War Power*, 2nd ed. (Lawrence: University of Kansas Press, 2004), chap. 8. Quotation is from page 200.

11. Conor Friedersdorf, "The Bizarre Story of How Drones Helped Get Us into the Iraq War," *The Atlantic*, October 2012.

12. Mayer, "Predator War."

13. David Ignatius, "Charting a Post-Petraeus Era," *Washington Post*, November 14, 2012.

14. Daniel Klaidman, *Kill or Capture: The War on Terror and the Soul of the Obama Presidency* (Boston: Houghton Mifflin Harcourt, 2012), 121–22.

15. David Kilcullen and Andrew McDonald Exum, "Death from Above, Outrage Down Below," *New York Times*, May 16, 2009.

16. "U.S. Airstrikes in Pakistan Called 'Very Effective,'" CNN, May 18, 2009.

17. "Voters Are Gung-Ho for Use of Drones but Not Over the United States," Rasmussen Poll, February 13, 2012.

18. Steve Coll, "More on the Drone War," *Think Tank* blog, *New Yorker*, May 18, 2009, www.newyorker.com/online/blogs/stevecoll/2009/05/more-on-the-drone-war.html.

19. Ibid.

20. Scott Shane, "C.I.A. to Expand Use of Drones in Pakistan," *New York Times*, December 3, 2009.

21. Quoted in ibid.

22. Interview of Micah Zenko by Greg Bruno, "Raising the Curtain on U.S. Drone Strikes," Council on Foreign Relations, June 2, 2010, www.cfr.org/pakistan/raising-curtain-us-drone-strikes/p22290.

23. David E. Sanger, *Confront and Conceal: Obama's Secret Wars and Surprising Use of American Power* (New York: Crown, 2012), 255.

24. Ibid.

25. DeYoung, "Secrecy Defines Obama's Drone War."

26. Adam Entous, "Special Report: How the White House Learned to Love the Drone," Reuters, May 18, 2010.

27. Klaidman, *Kill or Capture*, 215–16.

28. Ibid.

29. Ibid.; Marcy Wheeler, "Five Questions for John Brennan," *Empty Wheel*, February 7, 2013, www.emptywheel.net/2013/02/07/five-questions-for-john.

30. Harold Hongju Koh, "The Obama Administration and International Law," speech at Annual Meeting of the American Society of International Law, Washington, DC, March 25, 2010, www.state.gov/s/l/releases/remarks/139119.html.

31. See Thom Hartmann and Sam Sacks, "Obama Breaks the Golden Rule on Drones," *Daily Take*, December 1, 2012, truth-out.org/news/item/13085-obama-breaks-the-golden-rule-on-drones.

32. Koh, "Obama Administration and International Law" (emphasis in original).

33. John Yoo, "Obama, Drones and Thomas Aquinas," *Wall Street Journal*, June 7, 2012.

34. Tara McKelvey, "Interview with Harold Koh, Obama's Defender of Drone Strikes," *Daily Beast*, April 8, 2012.

35. James Risen and David Johnston, "Threats and Responses: Hunt for Al Qaeda; Bush Has Widened Authority of C.I.A. to Kill Terrorists," *New York Times*, December 15, 2002.

36. "Statement of Harold Hongju Koh Before the Senate Judiciary Committee, Subcommittee on the Constitution on Restoring the Rule of Law," September 16, 2008, www.law.yale.edu/documents/pdf/News_&_Events/Kohtestimony091608RuleofLaw.pdf.

37. Entous, "Special Report: How the White House Learned to Love the Drone."

38. Ibid.

39. Joby Warrick and Peter Finn, "Amid Outrage over Civilian Deaths in Pakistan, CIA Turns to Smaller Missiles," *Washington Post*, April 26, 2010.

6. The Meaning of Two Deaths

1. "Press Briefing by Press Secretary Jay Carney and Assistant to the President for Homeland Security and Counterterrorism John Brennan," May 2, 2011, www.white house.gov/the-press-office/2011/05/02/press-briefing-press-secretary-jay-carney-and -assistant-president-homela.

2. Ibid.

3. "Press Briefing by Press Secretary Jay Carney," May 3, 2011, www.whitehouse .gov/the-press-office/2011/05/03/press-briefing-press-secretary-jay-carney-532011.

4. Ibid.

5. Ibid.; Robert Booth, "The Killing of Osama bin Laden: How the White House Changed Its Story," *The Guardian*, May 4, 2011; Mark Owen and Kevin Maurer, *No Easy Day: The Firsthand Account of the Mission That Killed Osama bin Laden: The Autobiography of a Navy SEAL* (New York: Dutton, 2012), 235–36. When a member of the assault team—the pseudonymous "Mark Owen," whose real name is Matt Bissonnette— finally told the inside story, it turned out that two women were standing over the fallen bin Laden weeping and wailing, and one rushed in anger at an assaulter when he entered the room. Owen does not mention the woman being shot—another variation in the story.

6. In addition to Owen and Maurer, *No Easy Day*, another source is by the respected Osama bin Laden researcher Peter L. Bergen's *Manhunt: The Ten-Year Search for bin Laden from 9/11 to Abbottabad* (New York: Crown, 2012). It would take too much space to detail the discrepancies in these books (and other accounts as well), but readers will find that the authors do not agree on important questions about how many shots were fired, whether those present in the compound had loaded weapons close at hand, and how bin Laden died.

7. David E. Sanger, *Confront and Conceal: Obama's Secret Wars and Surprising Use of American Power* (New York: Crown, 2012), 107.

8. Nicholas Schmidle, "Getting bin Laden: What Happened That Night in Abbottabad," *New Yorker*, August 8, 2011.

9. "Press Briefing by Press Secretary Jay Carney and Assistant to the President for Homeland Security and Counterterrorism John Brennan," May 2, 2011.

10. Adam Entous, Julian E. Barnes, and Matthew Rosenberg, "Signs Point to Pakistan Link," *Wall Street Journal*, May 4, 2011.

11. Sanger, *Confront and Conceal*, 62.

12. Ibid., 66.

13. Spencer Ackerman, "'Unprecedented' Drone Assault: 58 Strikes in 102 Days," *Danger Room* blog, *Wired*, December 17, 2010, www.wired.com/dangerroom/2010/12/unprecedented-drone-strikes-hit-pakistan-in-late-2010/.

14. Scott Shane, "C.I.A. Is Disputed on Civilian Toll in Drone Strikes," *New York Times*, August 11, 2011.

15. Ernesto Londono and Karin Brulliard, "Mullen: Eliminating Pakistani Safe Havens Is Key," *Washington Post*, December 17, 2010.

16. Ibid.; Chris Allbritton, "U.S. Wants Pakistan Trial Invasion, but Will Wait," Reuters, December 17, 2010.

17. Greg Miller and Karin Brulliard, "Top CIA Spy in Pakistan Pulled amid Threats After Public Accusation over Attack," *Washington Post*, December 18, 2010.

18. Ibid.

19. Chalmers Johnson, *Dismantling the Empire: America's Last Best Hope* (New York: Metropolitan Books, 2010), 129–30.

20. Miller and Brulliard, "Top CIA Spy in Pakistan."

21. Entous, Barnes, and Rosenberg, "Signs Point to Pakistan Link."

22. By far the best account of the Davis case is Mark Mazzetti, *The Way of the Knife: The CIA, a Secret Army, and a War at the Ends of the Earth* (New York: Penguin, 2013), 1–4, 257–59, 261–65, et al. The quotation is from p. 264.

23. David Zucchino, "Drone Strikes in Pakistan Have Killed Many Civilians, Study Says," *Los Angeles Times*, September 24, 2012.

24. Matthew Green and Anna Fifield, "Pakistan Arrests Five 'CIA Informants,'" *Financial Times*, June 15, 2011.

25. Ibid.

26. Scott Baldauf, "Pakistan Jails Doctor Who Helped Find bin Laden: Why the US May Not Intervene," *Christian Science Monitor*, May 23, 2012.

27. "Press Briefing by Press Secretary Jay Carney and Assistant to the President for Homeland Security and Counterterrorism John Brennan," May 2, 2011.

28. "Lawrence Wright: Bin Laden's Death 'Long in Coming,'" interview by Terry Gross, *Fresh Air*, National Public Radio, May 2, 2011, www.npr.org/2011/05/02/135917389/lawrence-wright-bin-ladens-death-long-in-coming.

29. Jim Garamone, "Bin Laden's Death May Impact Afghanistan, Gates Says," Armed Forces Press Service, May 6, 2011.

30. See the important article by Karen DeYoung, "U.S. Speeds Up Direct Talks with Taliban," *Washington Post*, May 16, 2011.

31. Karen DeYoung and Scott Wilson, "With bin Laden Dead, Some Escalate Push for New Afghan Strategy," *Washington Post*, May 10, 2011.

32. Ibid.

33. DeYoung, "U.S. Speeds Up Direct Talks with Taliban."

34. Greg Miller, "Increased U.S. Drone Strikes in Pakistan Killing Few High-Value Militants," *Washington Post*, February 21, 2011.

35. Julian E. Barnes, "U.S. Expands Drone Flights to Take Aim at East Africa," *Wall Street Journal*, September 21, 2011.

36. Nick Turse and Tom Engelhardt, *Terminator Planet: The First History of Drone Warfare, 2001–2050* (New York: Dispatch Books, 2012), 82–84.

37. Kimberly Dozier, "U.S. Counterterror Chief: Al Qaeda Now on the Ropes," *Washington Times*, September 1, 2011.

38. Elisabeth Bumiller and Jane Perlez, "Pakistan's Spy Agency Is Tied to Attack on U.S. Embassy," *New York Times*, September 22, 2011.

39. Ibid.

40. Niall Ferguson's article "Complexity and Collapse: Empires on the Edge of Chaos," *Foreign Affairs*, March–April 2010 (a bone-chilling title far more scary than Paul Kennedy's weighty 1987 study, *The Rise and Fall of the Great Powers*), argued that "defeat in the mountains of the Hindu Kush or on the plains of Mesopotamia has long been a harbinger of imperial fall." What happened to the Soviet Union twenty years ago in Afghanistan, he contends, demonstrates that empires do not have a predictable life cycle as historians like to claim, with imperial dissolution a slow-acting phenomenon with multiple overdetermining causes: "Rather, empires behave like all complex adaptive systems. They function in apparent equilibrium for some unknowable period. And then, quite abruptly, they collapse." Drones were something new under the sun that might prolong an empire's life span—indefinitely!

41. Dozier, "U.S. Counterterror Chief."

42. Seth Hettena, "The Anwar Awlaki Timeline," n.d., accessed January 23, 2013, awlaki.sethhettena.com. Many details of his life are taken from this invaluable source.

43. Susan Schmidt, "Imam from Va. Mosque Now Thought to Have Aided Al-Qaeda," *Washington Post*, February 27, 2008.

44. Ibid.

45. Larry Shaughnessy, "Hasan's E-mail Exchange with al-Awlaki; Islam, Money and Matchmaking," *Security Clearance* blog, CNN, July 20, 2012, security.blogs.cnn.com/2012/07/20/hasans-e-mail-exchange-with-al-awlaki-islam-money-and-matchmaking/.

46. Megan Chuchmach and Brian Ross, "Al Qaeda Recruiter New Focus in Fort Hood Killings Investigation," *The Blotter* blog, ABC News, November 10, 2009, abcnews.go.com/Blotter/al-qaeda-recruiter-focus-fort-hood-killings-investigation/story?id=9045492.

47. Steven Stalinsky, "On Al-Jazeera.net—First Interview with U.S.-Born Yemen-Based Imam Anwar Al-'Awlaki on Major Nidal Hasan and the Fort Hood Shooting: Nidal [Hasan] Contacted Me a Year Ago," Special Dispatch No. 2713, Middle East Media Research Institute, December 23, 2009, www.memri.org/report/en/0/0/0/0/0/0/3859.htm.

48. Jo Becker and Scott Shane, "Secret 'Kill List' Proves a Test of Obama's Principles and Will," *New York Times*, May 29, 2012. This article proved controversial itself, as it became a subject of inquiries about leaks of classified information, as well as a foun-

dation piece for drone warfare critics citing Fifth Amendment requirements for due judicial process.

49. Kaitlin Furnaro, "Abdulmutallab's Bomb Didn't Explode Because of Dirty Underwear," *Global Post*, September 28, 2012.

50. Eric Schmitt and Thom Shanker, *Counterstrike: The Untold Story of America's Secret Campaign Against Al Qaeda* (New York: Times Books, 2011), 231.

51. Mark Mazzetti, Charlie Savage, and Scott Shane, "How a U.S. Citizen Came to Be in America's Cross Hairs," *New York Times*, March 9, 2013.

52. "Abdulmutallab: Cleric Told Me to Bomb Jet," CBS News, March 18, 2010, www.cbsnews.com/2100-201_162-6174780.html; Peter Finn, "Awlaki Directed Christmas 'Underwear Bomber' Plot, Justice Department Memo Says," *Washington Post*, February 10, 2012; Josh Meyer, "U.S. Cleric Linked to Airline Bombing Plot," *Los Angeles Times*, December 31, 2009.

53. "Abdulmutallab: Cleric Told Me to Bomb Jet"; Schmidt, "Imam from Va. Mosque."

54. Schmidt, "Imam from Va. Mosque."

55. Sudarsan Raghavan and Michael D. Shear, "Yemen Strikes at al-Qaeda Meeting," *Washington Post*, December 25, 2009.

56. "General Petraeus Meeting with Saleh on Security Assistance, AQAP Strikes," January 4, 2010, WikiLeaks 10SANAA4, www.cablegatesearch.net/cable .php?id=10SANAA4.

57. Matthew Cole, Richard Esposito, and Brian Ross, "U.S. Mulls Legality of Killing American al Qaeda 'Turncoat,'" *The Blotter* blog, ABC News, January 25, 2010, abcnews.go.com/Blotter/anwar-awlaki-us-mulls-legality-killing-american-al-qaeda -turncoat/story?id=9651830.

58. Peter Finn, "Secret U.S. Memo Sanctioned Killing of Aulaqi," *Washington Post*, September 30, 2011; Michael Hastings, "The Rise of the Killer Drones: How America Goes to War in Secret," *Rolling Stone*, April 16, 2012.

59. Finn, "Secret U.S. Memo."

60. Daniel Klaidman, *Kill or Capture: The War on Terror and the Soul of the Obama Presidency* (New York: Houghton Mifflin Harcourt, 2012), 255–56.

61. Ibid., 261.

62. Finn, "Secret U.S. Memo."

63. The president's statements are included in Stephanie Condon, "Obama: Anwar al-Awlaki's Death a 'Major Blow' to al Qaeda and Affiliates," CBS News, September 30, 2011, www.cbsnews.com/8301-503544_162-201139.

64. Richard Cohen, "Who Signed Anwar al-Awlaki's Death Warrant?" *Washington Post*, October 10, 2011.

65. Joby Warrick, "Cheney: After Yemen Strike, Obama Owes Apology to Bush," *Washington Post*, October 2, 2011.

66. Carrie Budoff Brown, "Harman: Release Legal Memo on Alwaki Strike," *Politico Live* blog, October 2, 2011, www.politico.com/blogs/politicolive/1011/Harman _Release_legal_memo_on_drone_strike.html.

67. Hastings, "Rise of the Killer Drones."

68. "Remarks of John O. Brennan, 'Strengthening Our Security by Adhering to Our Values and Laws,'" September 16, 2011, www.whitehouse.gov/the-press-office/2011/09/16/remarks-john-o-brennan-strengthening-our-security-adhering-our-values-an.

69. Tom Junod, "The Lethal Presidency of Barack Obama," *Esquire*, August, 2012. Sensitive to Obama's significance as the first black president, and his dilemmas in determining national security policies, Junod's writing is the most moving effort yet to question the direction he has taken by becoming the first self-acknowledged "lethal" president.

70. Ryan Grim, "Robert Gibbs Says Anwar al-Awlaki's Son, Killed by Drone Strike, Needs 'Far More Responsible Father,'" *Huffington Post*, October 24, 2012, www.huffingtonpost.com/2012/10/24/robert-gibbs-anwar-al-awlaki_n_2012438.html.

71. "Anwar al-Awlaki Killed in Yemen—As It Happened," *The Guardian*, September 30, 2011.

7. A Better War?

1. Department of Defense, *Sustaining U.S. Global Leadership: Priorities for 21st Century Defense*, January 3, 2012, 6, www.defense.gov/news/defense_strategic_guidance.pdf.

2. Lloyd C. Gardner, *Pay Any Price: Lyndon Johnson and the Wars for Vietnam* (Chicago: Ivan R. Dee, 1995), 444–46.

3. Richard Nixon, "Informal Remarks in Guam with Newspapers," July 25, 1969, American Presidency Project, www.presidency.ucsb.edu/ws/?pid=2140.

4. The "better war" theme of Creighton Abrams is pursued by Lewis Sorley, *A Better War: The Unexamined Victories and Final Tragedy of America's Last Years in Vietnam* (New York: Harcourt Brace, 1999).

5. Fred Kaplan, "Inquisitor McCain," *Slate*, February 1, 2013, www.slate.com/articles/news_and_politics/war_stories/2013/02/chuck_hagel_confirmation_hearing_john_mccain_grilled_the_former_nebraska.html.

6. Pete Hegseth and Wade Zirkle, "A Fifth Star for David Petraeus," *Wall Street Journal*, January 13, 2011.

7. Jeffrey Steinberg, "US Needs an 'Alert and Knowledgeable Citizenry' to Avoid Imperial Wars," *Salem-News.com*, December 29, 2011, www.salem-news.com/print/21497.

8. James Reston Jr., *The Conviction of Richard Nixon: The Untold Story of the Frost/Nixon Interviews* (New York: Three Rivers Press, 2007), 103–4; "I Have Impeached Myself," edited transcript of the Frost/Nixon interviews broadcast in May 1977, *The Guardian*, September 7, 2007.

9. Charlie Savage, *The Return of the Imperial Presidency, and the Subversion of American Democracy* (New York: Little, Brown, 2007). Savage had been writing about the question before the war turned south, but his theme gained traction as a result of the news from Iraq.

10. "President Obama's Statement on the Memos," *New York Times*, April 16, 2009.

11. David Johnston and Charlie Savage, "Obama Reluctant to Look into Bush Programs," *New York Times*, January 12, 2009.

12. Ibid.

13. "'This Week' Transcript: Barack Obama," ABC News, January 11, 2009, abc news.go.com/ThisWeek/Economy/story?id=6618199&page=1#.UZtwXUqFlrs.

14. Tom Engelhardt, "How Did Obama Become Our Most Imperial President?" AlterNet, April 29, 2012, www.alternet.org/story/155196/how_did_obama-become_our _most_imperial_president.

15. The letter, dated November 25, 2008, can be found at www.theatlantic.com /daily-dish/archive/2008/11/brennan-withdraws/208166.

16. Rob Crilly et al., "US Refuses to Apologise for Pakistan Air Strike That Killed 24 Soldiers," Daily Telegraph, November 29, 2011; Reza Sayah and Nick Paton Walsh, "Pakistan's Prime Minister Warns United States," CNN, November 28, 2011, www.cnn .com/2011/11/28/world/asia/pakistan-us.

17. Salman Masood, "In Protest over NATO Strike, Pakistan Will Skip Afghan Conference," New York Times, November 29, 2011; Helene Cooper and Mark Mazzetti, "Obama Refrains from a Formal 'I'm Sorry' to Pakistan," New York Times, November 30, 2011.

18. Ken Dilanian, "CIA Has Suspended Drone Attacks in Pakistan, U.S. Officials Say," Los Angeles Times, December 23, 2011.

19. Much of the information about the incident presented here is taken from an excellent summary, "Iran-U.S. RQ-1770 Incident," Wikipedia.

20. Ibid.

21. New Beginnings: Foreign Policy Priorities in the Obama Administration, Hearing Before the Committee on Foreign Affairs, U.S. House of Representatives, 111th Cong., April 22, 2009.

22. Mark Landler and David E. Sanger, "Clinton Speaks of Shielding Mideast from Iran," New York Times, July 22, 2009; Joby Warrick and Greg Miller, "Stealth Drone Highlights Tougher U.S. Strategy on Iran," Washington Post, December 7, 2011.

23. David E. Sanger, "Obama Order Sped Up Wave of Cyberattacks Against Iran," New York Times, June 1, 2012.

24. Ibid.

25. Ibid.

26. Roger Cohen, "Doctrine of Silence," New York Times, November 28, 2011.

27. Peter Beinart, "Obama's Foreign Policy Doctrine Finally Emerges with 'Off-shore Balancing,'" Daily Beast, November 28, 2011, www.thedailybeast.com/articles /2011/11/27/obama-s-fore.

28. Ibid.

29. Colin Clark, "U.S. Military to Scrap Counterinsurgency; Focus on Pacific, Says Vice-Chairman," Breaking Defense, November 27, 2011, breakingdefense.com/2011/11/17/ u-s-military-is-scrapping-coin-focusing-on-pacific-says-vice/.

30. Scott Wilson, "Obama Administration: Libya Action Does Not Require Congressional Approval," Washington Post, June 15, 2011.

31. Joshua Hersh, "Obama, Syrian President Assad Must Step Down," Huffington Post, August 18, 2011, www.huffingtonpost.com/2011/08/18/obama-assad_n_930229.html.

32. "How Iraq, Afghanistan Have Changed the Military," Talk of the Nation, National Public Radio, December 26, 2011.

33. Elizabeth Bumiller and Allison Kopicki, "Support in U.S. for Afghan War Drops Sharply, Poll Finds," *New York Times*, March 26, 2012.

34. Scott Shane, "In Afghan War, Officer Becomes a Whistle-Blower," *New York Times*, February 5, 2012.

35. Tim Mak, "Award for War Whistleblower," *Politico*, April 23, 2012, www.politico.com/news/stories/0412/75516.html#ixzz2KdIf12Cj.

36. "Joe Biden on Iraq, Iran, China and the Taliban," interview by Leslie H. Gelb, *Daily Beast*, December 19, 2011, www.thedailybeast.com/newsweek/2011/12/18/joe-biden-on-iraq-iran-china-and-the-taliban.html.

37. "Former US Officials See War 'Fatigue' from Afghan Conflict," Voice of America, January 31, 2012, www.voanews.com/content/former-us-officials-see-war-fatigue-from-afghan-conflict-138424439/168400.html.

38. Karen DeYoung, "After Obama's Remarks on Drones, White House Rebuffs Security Questions," *Washington Post*, January 31, 2012.

39. "Press Briefing by Jay Carney," January 31, 2012, www.whitehouse.gov/the-press-office/2012/01/31/press-briefing-press-secretary-jay-carney-13112.

40. Craig Whitlock, "Panetta: U.S., NATO Will Seek to End Afghan Combat Mission Next Year," *Washington Post*, February 1. 2012.

41. Alissa J. Rubin, "Afghan Protests Over the Burning of Korans at a U.S. Base Escalate," *New York Times*, February 22, 2012.

42. Mark Thompson, "Green on Blue," *Battleland* blog, *Time*, March 2, 2012, battleland.blogs.time.com/2012/03/02/green-on-blue/.

43. Jack Goldsmith, "More on al-Aulaqi and Transparency," *Lawfare*, October 5, 2011, www.lawfareblog.com/2011/10/more-on-al-aulaqi-and-transparency.

44. Quoted in Amy Davidson, "The President's Kill List," *Daily Comment* blog, *New Yorker*, May 30, 2012, www.newyorker.com/online/blogs/comment/2012/05/the-presidents-kill-list.html.

45. Ibid.

46. "Attorney General Eric Holder Speaks at Northwestern School of Law," *Justice News*, March 5, 2012.

47. Jeh C. Johnson, "National Security Law, Lawyers and Lawyering in the Obama Administration," speech at Yale Law School, New Haven, CT, February 22, 2012.

48. Charlie Savage, "U.S. Law May Allow Killings, Holder Says," *New York Times*, March 6, 2012.

49. Mark Mazzetti and Scott Shane, "Drones Are Focus as C.I.A. Nominee Goes Before Senators," *New York Times*, February 7, 2013.

50. John O. Brennan, "The Ethics and Efficiency of the President's Counterterrorism Strategy," speech at the Wilson Center, Washington, DC, April 30, 2012, transcript and video available at www.wilsoncenter.org/event/the-efficacy-and-ethics-us-counterterrorism-strategy.

51. Scott Shane, "Election Spurred a Move to Codify U.S. Drone Policy," *New York Times*, November 24, 2012.

8. American Hubris

1. Mark Mazzetti, *The Way of the Knife: The CIA, a Secret Army, and a War at the Ends of the Earth* (New York: Penguin, 2013), 125–26.

2. James Jay Carafano, "Drone Strikes and Just War," *National Interest*, February 15, 2013.

3. Marcy Wheeler, "Members of Congress Have Asked for the Targeted Killing Memos 14 Times," *Empty Wheel*, February 8, 2013, www.emptywheel.net/2013/02/08; Marcy Wheeler, "Cornyn Called Targeted Killing a 'Program,' Too," *Empty Wheel*, August 10, 2012, www.emptywheel.net/2012/08/10.

4. Wheeler, "Cornyn Called Targeted Killing a 'Program,' Too."

5. John Bellinger, "New York Times on Noor Khan Lawsuit," *Lawfare*, January 31, 2013, www.lawfareblog.com/2013/01/new-york-times-on-noor.

6. Jake Tapper, "Why Libya and Not Syria, and Drones Killing Innocents—Today's Q's for O's WH—5/29/12," *Political Punch* blog, ABC News, May 29, 2012, abcnews.go.com/blogs/politics/2012/05/why-libya-and-not-syria-and-drones-killing-innocents-todays-qs-for-os-wh-52912/.

7. Bill Roggio, "US Drones Kill 8 in Pair of Strikes in North Waziristan," *Long War Journal*, May 28, 2012, www.longwarjournal.org/archives/2012/05/us_drones_kill_5_in.php#ixzz2LCC5tMEU.

8. "Al-Qaeda Commander Abu Yahya al-Libi Killed—US Officials," BBC News, June 5, 2012, www.bbc.co.uk/news/world-asia-18334377.

9. Declan Walsh and Eric Schmitt, "Militant Leader Believed Dead in Pakistan Drone Strike," *New York Times*, August 24, 2012.

10. Ibid.

11. Walter Pincus, "Doing Business with Despots?" *Washington Post*, August 27, 2012.

12. Robert F. Worth, Mark Mazzetti, and Scott Shane, "Drone Strikes' Dangers to Get Rare Moment in Public Eye," *New York Times*, February 5, 2013.

13. Margaret Sullivan, "The Times Was Right to Report—at Last—on a Secret Drone Base," *New York Times*, February 6, 2013. For more on the controversy, see Karen McVeigh, "US Newspapers Accused of Complicity as Drone Report Reopens Security Debate," *The Guardian*, February 6, 2013.

14. Sullivan, "Times Was Right to Report."

15. Lloyd C. Gardner, *Three Kings: The Rise of an American Empire in the Middle East After World War II* (New York: The New Press, 2009), 32–33; "Excerpts from the News Transcript of Sam Tannenbaus' *Vanity Fair* Interview with Paul Wolfowitz," U.S. Department of Defense, May 9, 2003.

16. Marcy Wheeler, "Is This Why the Press Finally Revealed the Saudi Drone Base?" *Empty Wheel*, February 18, 2013, www.wemptywheel.net/2013/02/18/is-this-why-the-press; Robert F. Worth, "Yemen, Hailed as Model, Struggles for Stability," *New York Times*, February 19, 2013.

17. Wheeler, "Is This Why the Press Finally Revealed the Saudi Drone Base?"; "Niger Agrees to US Drones on Its Territory," *Al Jazeera*, January 30, 2013, www.aljazeera.com/news/africa/2013/01/2013131300246143363.html.

18. Department of Defense, *Sustaining U.S. Global Leadership: Priorities for 21st Century Defense*, January 3, 2012, 5–6, www.defense.gov/news/defense_strategic _guidance.pdf.

19. Elisabeth Bumiller and Thom Shanker, "Obama Puts His Stamp on Strategy for a Leaner Military," *New York Times,* January 5, 2013.

20. Roger Cohen, "Doctrine of Silence," *New York Times*, November 28, 2011.

21. Kevin Robillard, "Madeline Albright: Drones 'Very Effective,' " *Politico*, February 19, 2013, www.politico.com/story/2013/02/madeleine-albright-drones-very-effective -87777.html.

22. All quotations that follow will be taken from the undated "Department of Justice White Paper: Lawfulness of Lethal Operations Directed Against a U.S. Citizen Who Is Senior Operational Leader of Al-Qa'ida or an Associated Force," released to NBC News, January 29, 2013.

23. Quoted in Conor Friedersdorf, "This Stay-at-Home Mom Gave Obama a Tougher Interview Than 60 Minutes," *The Atlantic*, February 15, 2013, www.theatlan tic.com/politics/archive/2013/02/this-stay-at-home-mom-gave-obama-a-tougher-inter view-than-60-minutes/273206.

24. Ibid.

25. "To Kill an American," editorial, *New York Times*, February 5, 2013.

26. One should also note another problem with the administration's position about not revealing the specific memorandum on Awlaki. As Marcy Wheeler has pointed out, Judge Colleen McMahon, in considering the ACLU efforts to secure the document, raised crucial questions about whether either the 2001 AUMF or Article II, separately or together, made the strike legal, since the Constitution placed the question of treason under Article III, and reserved it for court decisions. See Marcy Wheeler, "Colleen McMahon: The Covert Op That Killed Anwar al-Awlaki Was Illegal," *Empty Wheel*, February 17, 2013, www.emptywheel.net/2013/02/17.

27. Dylan Byers, "McChrystal on Drones: A 'Covert Fix for a Complex Problem,' " *Dylan Byers on Media* blog, *Politico*, February 15, 2013, www.politico.com/blogs/media /2013/02/mcchyrstal-on-drones-a-covert-fix-for-a-complex-problem-157126.html.

28. Steve Coll, "Kill or Capture," *Daily Comment* blog, *New Yorker*, August 2, 2012, www.newyorker.com/online/blogs/comment/2012/08/kill-or-capture.html.

29. Scott Shane and Mark Mazzetti, "White House Tactic for C.I.A. Bid Holds Back Drone Memos," *New York Times*, February 21, 2013.

30. "Obama's 2013 State of the Union Address," *New York Times*, February 12, 2013.

31. Harry S. Truman, "Limit CIA Role to Intelligence," *Washington Post*, December 22, 1963.

32. See Jill Lepore, "How Much Military Is Enough," *New Yorker*, January 28, 2013. Lepore quotes Andrew Bacevich on the parallel dangers of the Cold War and the Great War on Terror. "The mystical war against Communism," Bacevich said in congressional testimony, "finds its counterpart in the mystical war on terrorism." Mystification, he said, leads us to exaggerate threats and ignore costs: "It prevents us from seeing things as they are."

Afterword: The New Normal?

1. Ed O'Keefe and Aaron Blake, "Rand Paul Launches Talking Filibuster Against John Brennan," *Washington Post*, March 6, 2013.

2. Karen Tumulty, "Is Rand Paul Going Mainstream, or Vice Versa?," *Washington Post*, June 19, 2013.

3. John Avlon, "In Wake of Surveillance Stories, Barack Obama's Poll Numbers Plummet," *Daily Beast*, June 17, 2013, www.thedailybeast.com/articles/2013/06/17/in-wake-of-surveillance-stories-barack-obama-s-poll-numbers-plummet.html.

4. Jeff Mapes, "Wyden Aids Rand Paul's Senate Filibuster, but Only to a Degree," *The Oregonian*, March 7, 2013.

5. Ibid.

6. David Jackson, "Bush Lawyer Defends Obama on Drones," *USA Today*, March 8, 2013.

7. Eric Schmitt, Mark Mazzetti, Michael B. Schmidt, and Scott Shane, "Boston Plotters Said to Initially Target July 4 for Attack," *New York Times*, May 2, 2013.

8. Paul Cruickshank and Tim Lister, "From the Grave, the Cleric Inspiring a New Generation of Terrorists," CNN, April 24, 2013, www.cnn.com/2013/04/24/us/boston-awlaki-influence.

9. Brett Logiurato, "Since Rand Paul's Historic Filibuster, There Has Been a Dramatic Shift in Public Opinion on Drone Strikes," *Business Insider*, April 11, 2013, www.businessinsider.com/rand-paul-filibuster-drone-polling-polls-2013-4.

10. Andrew Dugan and Mohamed Younis, "Pakistani Disapproval of U.S. Leadership Soars in 2012," *Gallup World*, February 14, 2013, www.gallup.com/poll/160439/2012-pakistani-disapproval-leadership-soars.aspx.

11. "Transcript: Sen. Durbin on the Budget, Social Security, Drones," *Washington Wire* blog, *Wall Street Journal*, March 20, 2013, blogs.wsj.com/washwire/2013/03/20/transcript-sen-durbin-on-the-budget-social-security-drones/.

12. Jonathan S. Landay, "Senate Hearing Blasts Obama's Refusal to Share Details of Drone Program," *Miami Herald*, January 23, 2013.

13. John Knefel, "Yemeni Whose Village Was Bombed Testifies at First Senate Drone Hearing," *Rolling Stone*, April 24, 2013, www.rollingstone.com/politics/news/yemeni-whose-village-was-bombed-testifies-at-first-senate-drone-hearing-20130424.

14. Ibid.

15. Greg Miller and Karen DeYoung, "Administration Debates Stretching 9/11 Law to Go After New al-Qaeda Offshoots," *Washington Post*, March 6, 2013.

16. Ibid.

17. Rosa Brooks, "Hate Obama's Drone War? Blame the Bleeding-Heart Human Rights Crusaders," *Foreign Policy*, February 14, 2013, www.foreignpolicy.com/articles/2013/02/14/hate_obamas_drone_war.

18. International Commission on Intervention and State Sovereignty, *The Responsibility to Protect* (Ottawa, ON: International Development Research Centre, 2001), idl-bnc.idrc.ca/dspace/bitstream/10625/18432/6/116998.pdf.

19. *The Constitutional and Counterterrorism Implications of Targeted Killing: Testimony Before the Senate Judiciary Subcommittee on the Constitution, Civil Rights, and Human Rights*, 113th Cong. (2013) (statement of Rosa Brooks, Professor of Law, Georgetown University Law Center; Bernard L. Schwartz Senior Fellow, New America Foundation).

20. The quotation is from Peter Baker, "In Terror Shift, Obama Took a Long Path," *New York Times*, May 27, 2013. There are obviously many other commentaries, but see also Peter Bergen and Jennifer Rowland, "9 Myths About Drones and Guantanamo," CNN, May 24, 2013, www.cnn.com/2013/05/22/opinion/bergen-nine-myths-drones -gitmo. Bergen and Rowland's commentary actually was first published before the speech was delivered, but it was an appropriate reaction nevertheless.

21. Saud Mehsud, "Pakistani Taliban Pick New Deputy After Drone Strike: Sources," Reuters, May 30, 2013; Jibran Ahmad, "U.S. Drone Kills Pakistan Taliban Number Two: Security Officials," Reuters, May 29, 2013.

22. Mehsud, "Pakistani Taliban Pick New Deputy."

23. Akbar Ahmed, "The Drone War Is Far from Over," *New York Times*, May 31, 2013.

24. "Text of President Obama's May 23 Speech on National Security," *Washington Post*, May 23, 2013.

INDEX

drone warfare (cont.)
  Obama administration pragmatism in,
    176, 209–11
  Obama administration "rule book" for,
    ix, 131, 211, 216, 231–32
  Obama comfort with, 91–92
  OLC and AUMF legal basis for,
    viii–ix, 74, 172–73, 175, 208–9,
    210, 214–17, 219, 224–30, 242, 245
  in Pakistan, 41, 72–73, 134–35, 144,
    151–52, 153, 154–55, 188–89, 217–19
  Panetta backing, 42–43, 133
  Paul, Rand, on rules of, 235, 237–38
  public opinion on, xi, 74, 133, 135, 144,
    155, 188–89, 216, 218–19, 223–24,
    239
  al Qaeda impact from, 136–37, 159–60,
    161–62, 210, 218
  Republicans on legal justifications for,
    140–41, 214–15
  targeted assassination in, 136–37
  terrorist increase from, 41–42, 73,
    135–36, 232, 238, 239, 244–45,
    247–48
  transnational governance and, 232
  Tutu challenging, 212–13
  Vietnam War protests and rules over,
    237–38
  Zenko on, 135–36, 241–42
drones and drone program
  under Bush, George W., administration,
    xii, 72–73, 128–29, 131–32
  CIA directing, 42, 127, 128–29,
    132–33, 153, 171, 173–74, 188, 219,
    229–30
  Clarke on, xii, 128–29
  under Clinton, Bill, 127–28, 129
  defense and budget cuts, xi, 223
  Iran capture of, 189–91
  judicial court for, 212, 214, 226,
    227–28
  media on, 73, 78, 132–34, 171, 175, 194,
    199–200, 210–11, 216–22, 223–24,
    227–28
  9/11 connection to, 128–29, 133, 134,
    140
  for Obama administration, 41–42, 110,
    127, 130–31, 133–34, 151, 160, 176,
    183, 199
  as "offshore balancing," 194, 199
  operating locations, 160–61, 220,
    222–23
  Pentagon involvement in, 128–29, 135

predator, xii
Riedel on, 126
secrecy, vii, 40, 41, 74, 132–33, 135–36,
  171, 188, 199–200, 202–3, 220–24
technology and, 134, 144, 160, 213, 232
  as UAV, vii, 127–31
U.S. leadership love affair with, 143
due process, 163, 172–73, 175, 207, 235
duplicity, ISI, 40, 47
Durbin, Richard, 239–42

economy, Afghan, 116–17
economy, U.S., 180
Eikenberry, Karl, 58–59, 75, 121–22,
  123–24
election fraud, Afghanistan, 52, 77, 105
elections, 2006, 9
Emanuel, Rahm, 132
embassy, U.S., 153–54, 230–31
empathy, 213
employment, Taliban, 49, 79, 97, 100
exceptionalism, American, 66
experience, COIN, 71
Exum, Andrew, 73, 132–33, 134

Fallows, James, 81–82
federal budget, x–xi
Ferguson, Niall, 72
Field Manual 3–24, counterinsurgency
  manual, 29, 75, 124, 196
  coordination key in, 25
  on insurgent ideology, 115
  Kandahar in, 95
  Petraeus role in, 181
Flournoy, Michele, 119
Fonda, Jane, 237
foreign policy
  of Bush, George W., administration,
    15
  CIA in making, 231
  just-war doctrine impact on U.S.,
    213–14
  Obama administration, vii–viii, 30–31,
    41, 84–85, 193–94, 219–22, 223–24
  Obama administration confusion in
    statements on, 41
  Obama administration secrecy over,
    vii–viii, 193–94, 220–22, 223–24
  Obama on war and, x, 12–13, 15–16,
    80–81, 194–95, 207–8
  of transnational governance, 84–85
  U.S. Middle East and South Asia,
    73–74

insurgency linked to, 118
in Kandahar, 114
Marja assault and officials from, 102–3
Obama administration relationship
with, 52–53, 77–79, 100, 105–6,
108–10, 158, 159
peace negotiations for, 98–99, 109,
115–16, 159
troop surge for correcting, 60
Kazakhstan, 219–20
Keane, Jack, 49–50
Kerry, John, 8, 77, 158–59
Khan, Samar, 173–74
Kilcullen, David, 56, 64, 73, 132–33, 134
"kill list," 208, 225, 264n48. *See also*
targeting and targeting list
King, Martin Luther, Jr., 86
Kissinger, Henry, 36, 84
Klaidman, Daniel, 173
Koh, Harold Hongju and Koh speech
drone warfare and international law
in, 138–39
drone warfare legality from, 136–37,
138–39
on Obama administration and regime
change versus continuity, 139
on Obama-Clinton doctrine, 140
on presidential authority for
assassination, 142–43
targeting list legal basis from, 143
Kurtz, Stanley, 84–85

law and legal basis
assassination compared to targeting,
206–7
for assassination of U.S. citizens, 204,
206–7, 225
for al-Awlaki, Anwar, drone attack,
137, 171–73, 209, 210, 214, 225, 227,
229, 270n26
for drone warfare, viii–ix, 136–37,
138–42, 171–73, 175–76, 208–9, 211,
214, 215–17, 219, 224–30, 242, 245
international, 138–39, 203, 216
of 9/11, 140, 142
OLC and AUMF drone warfare,
viii–ix, 74, 172–73, 175, 208–9, 210,
214–17, 219, 224–30, 242, 245
for presidential authority, 143, 204–7,
215
for targeting list, 143, 206, 225
lawfare, 138–39
"lethal presidency," 176, 193–94, 266n69

Levin, Carl, 120, 176, 229–30
liberal imperialism, 243–44
al-Libi, Abu Yahya, 218
Libya, 195–96, 230–31
Lowry, Richard, 6–7
Lugar, Richard, 158

Malik, Rehman, 162
Marcus, Ruth, 81
Marja campaign
COIN in, 101, 109
Kandahar and, 93, 94, 96, 113
Karzai government officials installed
after, 102–3
McChrystal boast of "government in
box" after, 97, 102–3
McChrystal role in, 99–100, 101,
104–5, 112
perception in, 99–100
region of, 99
Taliban in, 99–102, 112
U.S. and local trust in, 101–2, 103–4
U.S. military leadership on, 93, 97
McCain, John, 18–19, 22, 42, 182
McChrystal, Stanley, 49, 65, 124, 254n28
on Afghan defense force training,
74–75, 107
on Afghan War troop withdrawal,
74–75
Afghanistan report from, 52–56, 59,
106–7
background and accomplishments of,
50–51, 104
at Brussels meeting, 117
on drone strikes, 228–29
Eikenberry and, 75, 121–22
Kandahar role of, 109–10
Marja campaign role of, 99–100, 101,
104–5, 112
on Marja "government in box," 97,
102–3
media and, 120–21, 122–23
Obama administration relationship
with, 59–60, 120–23
secrecy surrounding, 50–51
troop surge requested by, 54
McConnell, Mike, 40
McGovern, George, 71
McKelvey, Tara, 141–42
McKiernan, David, 48, 49
media and pundits
Afghan War coverage of, 70–72,
119–23, 197–98

PUBLISHING IN THE PUBLIC INTEREST

Thank you for reading this book published by The New Press. The New Press is a nonprofit, public interest publisher. New Press books and authors play a crucial role in sparking conversations about the key political and social issues of our day.

We hope you enjoyed this book and that you will stay in touch with The New Press. Here are a few ways to stay up to date with our books, events, and the issues we cover:

- Sign up at www.thenewpress.com/subscribe to receive updates on New Press authors and issues and to be notified about local events
- Like us on Facebook: www.facebook.com/newpressbooks
- Follow us on Twitter: www.twitter.com/thenewpress

Please consider buying New Press books for yourself; for friends and family; or to donate to schools, libraries, community centers, prison libraries, and other organizations involved with the issues our authors write about.

The New Press is a 501(c)(3) nonprofit organization. You can also support our work with a tax-deductible gift by visiting www.thenew press.com/donate.